THINKING BLACK

This book was first published in 1912 and contains the impressions and perspectives of a highly individual and some might say "idiosyncratic" pioneer missionary.

As would be expected the writing style, content and views expressed are from a very different era and at times may jar with current, more enlightened thinking. It is important however to understand that in many ways Dan Crawford was ahead of his time in embracing differences in thinking and culture. His over-arching thesis was that to work successfully amongst the native population one had to understand their practices and communicate in ways which at times were not natural to those from a European background.

This is a spiritually challenging book and captures with a sense of immediacy the seemingly insurmountable difficulties that faced early missionaries in Africa. The writer clearly loved and respected the people amongst whom he worked and his record of more than two decades of tireless unbroken service bear testimony to the power of God as His work advanced in Central Africa during the early part of the last century.

The Publisher

October 2009

THE LOOK-OUT HUT
On the Cliff overhanging Lake Mweru

Thinking Black

22 years without a break in the long grass of Africa

"There's a legion that never was listed,
That carries no colours nor crest,
But split in a thousand detachments
Is breaking the road for the rest."

D. Crawford

JOHN RITCHIE LTD
CHRISTIAN PUBLICATIONS

40 Beansburn, Kilmarnock, Scotland

ISBN-13: 978 1 904064 87 9
ISBN-10: 1 904064 87 6

Copyright © 2009 by John Ritchie Ltd.
40 Beansburn, Kilmarnock, Scotland

www.ritchiechristianmedia.co.uk

The *Classic Reprint Series* is derived from facsimile copies of the originally published material.

At times the quality of print and typeface may have been compromised as a result of either inferior original copy or the facsimile process itself.

We are confident, however, that the vast majority of the printed content is of reasonable quality and most importantly is legible.

Typeset by John Ritchie Ltd., Kilmarnock
Printed by Bell & Bain Ltd., Glasgow

PUBLISHERS' NOTE

—◆—

THE soon-to-die Livingstone farewelled Stanley in
these tragic words :

> " On crossing the Lualaba, I shall go direct
> S.W. to the copper mines of Katanga. Eight
> days south of Katanga the natives declare the
> fountains [of the Nile] to be. When I have
> found them I shall return by Katanga to the
> underground houses of Rua . . : travel in boat
> up the river Lufira."

Alas ! the brave " Dawid " never so crossed the
Lualaba, and this volume records the fulfilment of
Livingstone's last desire.

Most of it written by the flare of the African camp-
fire, the name of this book corresponds with its nature.
The author is *thinking black* all the time he is writing
the book so named.

TO

the first lady who ever

penetrated these wilds

MY WIFE

ACKNOWLEDGMENTS

———◆———

To my friends at Bath and Glasgow for all their loyal help during long years of absence.

To Mr. Arnot, who so kindly saw us off in Bihe, and regretted his inability to come into the Far Interior.

To all my friends on the African field, including Dr. Laws of Livingstonia, the true Bishop of Central Africa.

To Miss Ada R. Habershon for her help in revision and indexing.

To Mr. Dudley Kidd and Mr. Bernard Taylor for some good photographs.

CONTENTS

—◆—

BOOK I

BOOK II

x CONTENTS

BOOK III

PHOTOGRAPHIC ILLUSTRATIONS

———◆———

xii PHOTOGRAPHIC ILLUSTRATIONS

THEN and NOW

THEN

A.D. 1889

"Wanting is—what?
Summer Redundant,
Blueness Abundant,
Where is the blot?"

Peering back through the haze of twenty-three years, behold the retrospect! There goes the West Coast slipping silently past under the port bow, and Africa (much-loved, much-blamed Africa) unrolls the panorama of her coast-line in seductive welcome. Only the other day embarking at London with a cold heaven glittering overhead like blue steel; now, here you are under the line, where sleepy coast towns lie hidden in the haze of sun.

Then comes the landing at Benguella, where the surprises are marvellously many. All your ship-board surmisings, you discover, were easy and elementary error. How little you knew of the African puzzle is seen when it leaks out that the very name ("Africa!") is utterly unknown to the negro. Africa? He never heard such a hideous word. It is a mere tag, a mere ticket stuck on the back of this poor Continent by outsiders. A perfect parable all this of Africa, the land, and the African, the man. A straw indicates the current, and if we know not the name, then we know less of the nature of black place and black person, of black man and blacker manners.

*   *   *   **

Another dawning surprise. No delirium of speed here. No catching of tram or train by the fraction of a second. There never was a taxi in all these latitudes, never was anything on wheels. Fifteen miles per day lies ahead from water to water, from camp to camp. Speed? Now it is you endorse the old definition that speed is only a mad method "whereby you miss as much as possible between starting-point and destination."

*   *   *   **

Then again. No wayside inn; no apartments to let. You must find your own hut in the woods. Why not? As Thoreau patly puts it, "There is some of the same fitness in a man building his own house that there is in a bird building its own nest."

But worse still. As a slap-in-the-face surprise comes the realisation that you, the newcomer, are not at your best; that, in fact, to come to Africa means to come "down" to Africa. Even before sighting the African coast, and while still far out at sea, we saw the whole coming problem in another panoramic parable. This time it is a romantic river reading us a lesson, and by way of warning that the confluence of the Congo might soon be expected, here is our blue Atlantic painted a muddy brown eight miles out into the ocean. Parable, surely, of the ugly fact we are soon to prove that evil African communications corrupt good European manners. There, in that monster mouth of the Congo, yawning seven miles wide, and vomiting its dirty contents into the blue Atlantic—there, I say, you see the sad and symbolic story of decadence on the West Coast of Africa. For the fearful fact must be faced that all things European degenerate in Central Africa—European provisions go bad, European fruits, European dogs degenerate. So, too, European men and women.

*   *   *

**NOW
A.D. 1912.** *And now the wheel comes round full circle. Emerging from a long shut-in life in the Far Interior, one receives quite a mental jolt on striking the first "tin town" of advancing civilisation. Where are you? have you struck the planet Mars? The long lapse of years makes it all strangely familiar and familiarly strange. One opines one has dreamed all this years and years ago. Can I believe my eyes? There, jutting out of the grass, I see two spokes of iron coming up from the South—my first railway train in twenty-two years!*

*   *   *

Then again. Right across Africa, remember, there never was a shop, so here it is, while the human tide pours along, you are all eyes at the seductive shop window of some little local Selfridge's, the tin town's universal provider. Fascinated as by a basilisk, you gaze stare-struck at this dream of past years—a shop window! There are crowds of renegade natives from the North down here at the rail-head: poor specimens these, sucked into the whirlpool of gambling and gin boosing. This is the place where the new arrival from the train can see just enough of the debased type of African to keep him from the desire of seeing more.

Booming up from Rhodesia comes the mad northward surge of invading civilisation. To use the language of Holland, the dykes are down and the ocean is pouring in on poor Central Africa. Transitional periods are notoriously times of peril. But here is a horrible, hectic-flush crisis which you can only denominate as "the terrors of transition." Carlyle is the only man who expresses the real reason of it all. "Perfect ignorance," says he, "is quiet, and perfect knowledge is quiet, but the transition from the former to the latter is a stormy one." As weird as it is wild, here you have the meeting and mixing of widely divergent men and manners, 1912 B.C. coming sharply round the metaphoric corner and looking 1912 A.D. full in the funny face. It is all as droll as though a Pharaoh of the Moses period proposed to sit down with a Cockney in a Central African forest and eat sardines together!

Here at last you have struck the uttermost man in the uttermost parts of the earth. Uttermost white man, probably, as well as uttermost black, for both races are in the grip of Carlyle's terrors of transition. Life here at the rail-head is a mad medley of natives warped from their primitive simplicity by European influence, and of poor old white men not less profoundly modified by a climate and surroundings to which they were not born.

*   *   *

Yet all the while one's heart is out of it and away off North on its own. Up past the Lufira, up past the Range, away up to one's "ain countrie."

*   *   *

Afar the Golden-Crested Crane is calling !

BOOK I

CHAPTER I

First Fears Justified

"Mombaza, and Quiloa, and Melind,
  And Sofala, thought Ophir, to the realm
  Of Congo, and Angola farthest South."

PARADISE LOST, xi. 399.

*   *   *

"The African race is an indiarubber ball. The harder you dash it to the ground the higher it will rise."

BANTU PROVERB.

*   *   *

"We negroes are one in racial unity with you whites — different yet the same. A crocodile is hatched from an egg—and a flying bird from an egg."

THE EMPEROR MUSHIDI.

*   *   *

"The Earth is a beehive: we all enter by the same door but live in different cells."

BANTU PROVERB.

CHAPTER I

First Fears Justified

WHEREIN the reader, landing at Benguella, finds himself faced with Africa's first and final law — to put down a lot one must put up with a lot.

LET us begin at the beginning. Coasting down West Africa the year of grace 1889, the first thing to strike you in the ever-shifting drama is the sarcastic significance of Milton's mention of these lands in such a poem as *Paradise Lost,* "the Realm of Congo and Angola farthest South." For, as he safely guessed, Paradise is lost, very much lost in these latitudes. There is tropical treachery even in those poor brown palms you see flitting past, for where is defeat so common for a white man as just there on those sands of the seaboard, the air all a-dance with heat? A taunting palm over a tin shanty, symbol not of victory but disaster. Each and every solar ray giving the exile two knocks : the first, *en route* to earth, striking the man on its way down, the second getting him again on the rebound from the sparkling

2

sand. Each day two burning darts per ray—and how many billion rays per day ?

Take the negro now and watch withal a curious thing. I mean that hard, impersonal stare of these bottomless-eyed natives, not the intense, penetrating thing of Europe. You might be something worked on tapestry or painted on a china cup, so impersonally does he look at you. He even denies you credit for any act of your own personal prowess or initiative, shooting for example. For if, per-chance, you draw a most careful bead on a buck and drop him flat in his tracks, he as carefully sees to it that he allocates the praise between your gun and your imaginary "medicine," fifty per cent apiece, and never, nay never a crumb for you. You are merely the spoiled and petted child of a privileged civilisation—you, what have you done ? Only taken the trouble to be born white a little north of his south—nothing more. " Beyond the sea " is their great adjective for anything newfangled or European, your very Gospel being only another "beyond the sea" innovation. "The white man's parable" is another of their ugly names for our Evangel, a taunt this with the old Ezekiel sting in it : " Ah Lord God ! they say of me, Doth he not speak parables ? "

But let us end these didactics and come to our chronicle. This is how we really begin. Ignoring the ocean voyage sailed in sameness for hundreds of years, we land on the Atlantic seaboard at Benguella. Portuguese to the core, here you find a tropical town nearly fast asleep in 1889—asleep, and no wonder. For most of these

Portuguese have been boiling in this tropical kettle for many years, with the climatic result that many have a lethargic glaze on their eyes. There is also that curious listless look on his swarthy Latin face suggestive of the well-known contemplative air of a man for whom time and distance are not. Certes, what the average man from the Tagus seems to need is a subcutaneous injection of the busy spirit of John Bull. In moments of extreme exuberance, our sallow friend from Lisbon has been seriously seen to walk, but the average attitude is notoriously one of repose. The oleaginous collection of messes which they eat from the points of their knives accounts for it all. Rumour runs that he even refuses to drink coffee in the morning lest it should keep him awake the rest of the day. A Portuguese with a long romantic moustache, lolling about on chairs in somewhat unusual attitudes, is the commonest sight in the day. Thus, with sleepy, sun-baked senses, he loses himself in long time-effacing reveries. The American version of it is that he sits as solemnly as though he meant to take root—so you see what slavery has done for the Portuguese. This Western Zanzibar, remember, is the great Portuguese entrepôt of slavery, slave labour nearly running the whole concern. And did not the Romans say, "As many slaves, so many enemies"?

Scarcely one Portuguese lady in the place. All their colonies have gone shipwreck by defying the foundation truth that wherever duty summons man, woman has a corresponding duty in the same place. Be he Teuton or

Latin, a man ever will be what his mother, wife, or sister
makes of him, an influence this that begins at the cradle
and ends in the grave. A monthly steamer in these
dismal days is the only distraction, and the black plume
of smoke on the skyline sends a monthly flutter through
the hot hole. But for many a day, alas! our expected
flutter from the Interior does not come, because the
transport road is blocked and no advance possible. Thus
you see us, here on the threshold of our long and happy
life ahead, confronted with a truly typical *contretemps* so
wholly explanatory of many a day to come in the Far
Interior. I mean that "blocked road." Now it is the
old conventional phrase in England about "your way
being opened up" assumes a sacred literal value, for the
very narrowness of the trail is itself eloquent of its
liability to be easily shut. Knocking as we have done at
Central Africa's back door of Benguella, have we not found
the said door locked? The native carrier trade is in a
state of stagnation, and the God Who shutteth and no
man openeth thereby challenges us with this loving *Qui
va là?*

Unlike the voyage inland from the malarial mouth of
the Congo farther North; unlike the long winding crawl
from Chinde up the Zambezi on the East Coast, here at
Benguella you find Africa doing a fine thing in rising
almost sheer from the sea. The hills stand out in jet
black silhouette from the humid coast, and in a few hours,
if the natives would only fall in with Nature's idea, you
could be over the mountain wall and well on your way to

the breezy uplands of Bihe. But Mr. Negro looks on
with ineffable complacency, and refuses to league with
Nature in favour of outsiders. At this early stage he
knows little and cares less for Mr. Missionary; what he
does seem sure about is that the sun rises and sets for
No. 1 alone. Yet let us give him his due. Unlike the
Saxons, Danes, and Jutes who were invited by the ancient
Britons to enter England, here you have the black-but-
comely African honestly warning you off both his soil
and his soul. Frankly saying in so many looks if not so
many words that he would rather have your room than
your company. Why should he scrape and bow to
persons with no more fingers and toes than he has
himself?

A new land, however, really means a new vocabulary,
and here with this mention of "road" in Africa we must
pause to define our terms. The substantive "road" presents its compliments to the English-speaking public and
hereby notifies a new aspect of its dictionary meaning.
For just as you throw away your Bradshaw when you
leave the land of trains, so neither Webster nor Nuttall
can tell you what an African "road" is. Though it is
the true trunk road to the vast Interior, yet the real
name for this thing is a "trail," literally a trivial trail the
size of a cart-wheel rut. And so it comes about that here
at the Benguella doorway you get your initial surprise
that this Africa for thousands of twisty miles ahead is a
land wholly innocent of roads, and boasts only this cart-
wheel rut as a highway. "Goat-walks" is the real idea,

those sheep-tracks found across the Welsh mountains.
Described at greater length anon, here at the outset it is
absolutely necessary to point out how in this serpentine
path we have the strategic key to the citadel of the black
brain. "Thinking black" this, verily. It is the African's
way of doing things as well as his way of walking, and
mentally Mr. Negro spends life carving out for himself a
theory that will fit the facts of this corkscrew path. Take,
for instance, the necessary monotonous Indian file this
same narrow trail of ours involves : there is a whole
negro philosophy of "follow your leader" meaning in
this. For as we saw, see, and shall see, the negro's "way"
of doing a thing is merely to do it as the man who went
before him did it. The slaves of precedent, they dog the
steps of a thousand ancestors, and such is the tenacity of
the negro type that to this day their whole outfit of the
twentieth century A.D. can be found perfectly reproduced
on Egyptian monuments of the same century B.C. Hence
the Bantu song :—

> "A well-worn trail is a very good thing,
> It must lead up to a very great King;
> And so with customs of days of yore,
> We do what millions have done before."

That is to say, precedent, not principle, is their black
law. And any African dictionary tells the whole tale, for
around this germinal word "path" there constellate a
dozen ideas like law, prohibition, transgression, plan, etc.

Thus glorying in this long Indian trail of antiquity,
the Bantu tribes boast the identical Egyptian kilt, mortar,

pestle, and cooking ware of the Moses period. Nor need we wonder at all this, for is not Egypt the door of Africa? Moral: A thousand years are as one day in African manners. Time may laugh at the Pyramids, but the Pyramids laugh at time.

Beware, too, of those shags jutting out along that trail—shags metaphoric, I mean, as well as shags material. There is the upstart Rob Roy ahead blocking the way with his "money or your life" ultimatum; an ugly shag he. There are those sons of Belial, the Luvale bandits, who hold you up for days and go into committee on the subject of your ransom; uglier shags they. "Gentlemen of the road" these, who egg you on to sell your soul by bullying and bouncing them. Would admire you immensely (you, a Missionary of the Prince of Peace) if all the while your index finger curved itself around the trigger of a persuasive six-shooter. Finally, there is the great Mushidi himself at the end of it all, half-way across Africa, blocking this trans-continental trail and making it a blind alley. You have Dr. Moloney's authority for it that in later days, when Captain Stairs found us imprisoned at Bunkeya, Mushidi called us his "white slaves."

But among the many intricacies of this "cobweb path" the great system of *Nkole*—the Luban word, this—makes you gasp at its ramifications. Here you have a thing spreading from sea to sea, and in this mad manœuvre you focus the real reason of all their troubles. For what is *Nkole* but only a "catch-your-pal" movement, a snatch suretyship when a harmless third party is kidnapped and

kept in durance vile for the sins of some unknown second
party? No wonder the African roads are all blocked
intertribally. Here is harmless Jones coming along the
trail, and they pounce on him as surety for the crime of
some unknown John Smith, the theory being that Jones,
one bright day, will retaliate and swoop down on Smith,
claiming damages for illegal seizure. Now try and conceive what a tangle of triangles this makes all over the
land, for in a thousand cases the stranger-surety A. never
saw in the flesh the conjectural culprit B. But what is
that to C. the kidnapper? Is not this his only way of
setting the clumsy legal mill in motion? Moral: He
that is surety for a stranger must smart for it. Take
even your best type of negro and try and argue some
sense into him on this cobweb system of native paths and
he shows not a twinge of penitence. No; unwarped and
unbiased as he looks, this *Nkole* idea he defends as a
time-honoured maxim, the treacherous triangle of the
thing being its best point—yea, is it not a triangle, and
therefore all point together?

But it is generally the Missionary who has got to pay.
Even in later days this Bantu bed-rock idea still clings to
the semi-educated African. Listen to another *Nkole* tale,
with quite a touch of terror in it, a noble white man the
victim; the author of it all only a negro body smarting
under a sense of personal wrong. The scene is out East
in more civilised conditions. Maltreated by a brother
black, this man is exasperated to find that his enemy
is too strong for him; has a sort of aristocratic status,

that is to say, "an untouchable," and therefore out of reach.

Query No. 1 : How can this nobody get his rights without committing some wrongs ?

Query No. 2 : How can a man have wrongs if he has no rights ?

And thus with much fertility of brain he concocts a fantastic tragedy with this old bugbear, *Nkole*, as germinal notion.   Laying his plans with consummate care, he singles out the house of a harmless Missionary, and this goaded black resolves to burn it down, the "surety" idea being that he has now brought matters to a head by dragging into the wrangle a mightier than his mighty foe. And, sure enough, a terrible triangle he makes of it all, for up goes the godly man's house in a blaze, thus ensuring an opening up of the whole question.   Little did that poor bush black guess how he honoured that Missionary, for, like his Master, was he not made surety for the stranger and did he not smart for it ?   But the darkest deed is yet to come.   This black stoic knows far too well what manner of act he has done, so with superior sagacity he resolves " to leave life by the back door "—to commit suicide.   Quite calmly, therefore, he scratches a note on a bit of paper explaining his "terrible triangle" plan and then hangs himself on his own club down a game pit.   Of course, at this useless point there is much *ex post facto* hurry-scurry, but all too late, for the real culprit's debt has been paid in blood and fire.   A lesson this how deeply the roots of suretyship shoot down into the bone

and marrow of Africa.   Need I go on ?   There are
thousands of such cases.

This is "thinking black" with a vengeance, and as
usual the scapegoat Missionary has got to pay somebody
else's debt.   Far from this being effete, only the other day
one of our caravans bound for Kavungu was plundered of
nine loads by the Achokwe, and all on this *Nkole* plea.
The great Portuguese Senhor (by name " Visese," a ruffian
endowed with more brains than scruples) had carried West
hundreds of captives, hence these patriots grabbing at
the first harmless nobody's goods in retaliation.   Of daily
intertribal occurrence this : take another instance.

Here, as I write, is Kaveke, a Luban, who runs in and
tells me with quick-breathed rapidity that four of his
relatives have been seized as *Nkole* or surety, and the
man of the party killed, head cut off—well-known Jones
killed for unknown Smith.   But that *Nkole* story is not
ended ; for when their father was so killed, his daughters
were enslaved and the two nice-looking girls made chief's
concubines.   Let us call Ngoi the sort of Martha of the
story and Mujikle the Mary.   Well, this latter, alas ! had
scarcely entered bondage when her brute of a master died,
and Mary, a mere slip of a girl, is now told that she must
be buried alive with her father's own murderer.   So Mary
has died like hundreds more, the only sop she got being a
farewell supper of meat and mush—a sort of black bribe
this, equivalent to the English : " If you are a good little
girl you'll get jam with your tea."   The escaped Martha
is now with us at the Mission, and poor Mary, pulsating

with buoyant life, was buried alive. Not a dying yell, remember, but only a great dry sob. O Africa!

But it were impossible to tell all. One cry there is, though, so uniform the words that it almost amounts to a horrible technical term. Reminiscent of the Epistle to the Romans as it is, you cannot resist the steady conviction that Paul must have known it too. Take, roughly, a dozen such cases known to me—I mean, the living forced to embrace the mortifying corpse. The terrible formula of their cry was just Romans vii. 24 over again : "Who shall deliver me from this body of death?" No negro could ever read Paul's anti-sin moan in Romans without a special shudder at that metaphor : well he knows what it means, for often did he hear that cry. And long may he shudder at sin, say I.

*   *   *

But nobody knows his Africa who is not on terms of intimacy with the fire-flies. Darting about bewilderingly, they flash their intermittent signals into the night, and eight or ten confined in a phial give sufficient light to enable one to write. At sundown behold a parable of your Missionary tribulation ahead, the fourth plague of Egypt. For no sooner do you light up than the thousand tribes of local gnats, flies, and moths mobilise to fight the flickering flame, each enunciating with impertinent emphasis the dictum that the fly or the flicker must snuff out. Children of night as they are, you can see them swarm round that candle in clouds—war-cry : We love darkness rather than light, because our deeds are evil.

But the faithful flame flickers on, an apostle of light, true "thinking black" parable of the Devil's battalions trying to snuff the little lights of testimony twinkling across Africa. Far-fetched metaphor though this looks, yet can we place it under the sure shelter of high authority. For did not Faraday long ago begin his famous lecture by declaring " there is not a law under which any part of this universe is governed that does not come into play in the phenomena of the chemical history of a candle "? Not that these millions of midges haven't a method in their madness. Hidden for their lives by day in the marsh, full well they know that the scorching sun would devour them if they emerged, war to the death being proclaimed between solar light and these broods of darkness. What wonder, then, at this their revenge on the poor candle, a diminutive disciple of the sun spluttering in the night, their vindictive swoop eloquent of the anti-light malice. This certainly is the native's notion, for in his alliterative language he makes a linear pun of it—calling the lamp the "Sun's little Sonny," the prefixes rhyming as in English.

This is digression, though, and we must get on with our story—but that means another chapter.

CHAPTER II

First Things First

"Sorrow and the scarlet leaf,
 Sad thoughts and sunny weather;
Ah me! this glory and this grief
 Agree not well together."

  *   *   *

 " Though ye have lien among the pots, yet shall ye be as the wings of a dove covered with silver, and her feathers with yellow gold. . . . Ethiopia shall soon stretch out her hands unto God."

Psalm lxviii. 13, 31.

  *   *   *

"There is a depth below the depth,
 And a height above the height:
Our hearing is not hearing,
 And our seeing is not sight."

CHAPTER II

First Things First

WHEREIN the reader, finding no advance possible, ponders and probes Africa's great problem of " the blocked road."

SUCH, then, is our ridiculous " road " over the hills, and lest peradventure we take too much for granted, I suppose I should explain that this caravan of ours is not by any manner of means an English four-wheeler of the gipsy sort. Really a twisting, travelling town it is, and there you see more than a hundred men, women, and boys wriggling along through the tall grass in Indian file—the "crocodile" our negro facetiously calls it. A curious hotch-potch of humanity, here you have the small tradesman and the dancing man, the musician and the doctor; these and many more all twisting in and out with the trail in faithful "follow your leader" fashion. This doctor fellow while drawing his rations as carrier has also the perquisites of his profession among his brother-blacks, the dancing man likewise reckoning that he can in a spare hour "hand round the hat" for a consideration. The witchery of this man's tongue is wonderful, for he

wheedles round the negro on his soft sing-song side, plays
his own accompaniment, and has a rich repertory of all
the tribal reels, strathspeys, and laments.   Often overgrown with thick grass, the trail is lost below it, and the
terror o' mornings is to squeeze your way through this wet,
matted tangle.   The drier the season, of course, the greater
the deluge of dew, and all to be negotiated in the cold,
callous dawn.   Often, too, you get out of your blankets
only to discover that another thick blanket of mist lies
across your path, the cheerless sun looking through the
fog like a snowball.   Real malarial mist, pale with
the awful pallor of death, and no wonder one prefers
the famous pea-soup fog of London.

But the weakest go to the wall in all this, and your
big black carriers push on the shivering youngsters ahead
to dry off the clammy dew on their bodies.   "Human
brooms," they are called.   Take your stand against an
intolerant tradition of this "dew wiping" sort and you
will be worsted, for they argue that such is the tribal
mill, and had they not all to go through it?   So here you
have a literal case in which "a little child shall lead them,"
mere babies driven on first to brush off the dew.[1]

Have you caught the idea?   No Factory Acts here.
Mere babies goaded on ahead for the drenching dew
of this 13-feet-high grass to pour down on them spray-

---

[1] By a conceit of etymology the word "pioneer" is coined from this very
idea of such an one being a "human broom" or "dew drier," and a fair
English equivalent is to call a Burton or a Livingstone "Mr. Waterproof,"
because he braved the inclement days of pioneering and got drenched that
we might go dry.

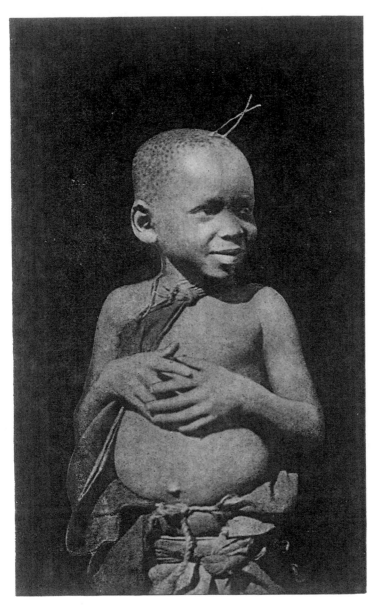

A TYPICAL DEW-DRIER.

bath fashion. This grass, of course, is so dense that it hides the tiny trail, so each step is a squeeze forward into the unknown, the said squeeze being equivalent to the turning on of the tap on our little 36-inch-long nobodies. But there is a law of compensation even here. Oh yes, these nobodies become somebodies with their resultant revenge. I saw one such diminutive "dew drier" go straight up to mamma and let her have a sounding smack in the face. Angry? Not she. Dissolving in smiles, she looks at her offspring proudly : " What a splendid warrior he'll make ! " Pushed on ahead in the dark dawn, of course, these little bits of black humanity run the chance of a hungry old hyena or leopard lurking by the way to nab first comers. Too well are they aware that even the smallest contributions are always thankfully received by the Carnivora. And thus is evolved Africa's *enfant terrible*, the sad stuff, forsooth, out of which Mr. Missionary has got to build the poor little African Sunday school. Ragged schools, one might indulgently call them, only the problem is to produce even one rag sometimes.

But all this is to anticipate, for it is easier to talk about the trail than to use it, and we are forced to settle ourselves down on the sickly seaboard like a man in a railway station condemned to wait the next train. Heigh ho ! here it is you learn that patience must be your pet African virtue, and here, too, you first face the dangerous yet delightful fact that you are wholly in the negro's hands for weal or woe. For if those expected carriers of ours don't come out of the hills one of these days and

pick us up, we cannot budge, a rueful reflection this, quite
a wholesome corrective to British bluff and swagger.   So
here on the baking Benguella sands we pass the long
electric nights longing for the climbing of the great
"African Divide."   That straight, shy glance we constantly cast at the brown girding hills is full of desiring
with great desire to pass on and into the Far Interior.
We long for the uplands and brisk breezes that will blow
new ideas into the brain.   Only to get a start, only to
get on our legs, this is the sole African solution of
stagnation.   *Solvitur ambulando* was the cunning little
Latin maxim of the thing, and the Luban has the exactly
equivalent epigram : "It is settled in walking."   Days
grow into weeks and still another red sunrise with no
carriers to hand ; only that solemn booming of the great
Ocean on the sun-smitten sands.   In these dreary days
Browning (!) in three luminous lines supplies the diary
data for as many months :—

> "The sun looked over the mountain's rim,
>   And straight was a path of gold for him,
>   But the need of a world of men for me."

Thus you see how the African scores such an easy first
in his own land.   Even this vaunted pioneering of ours
he looks down upon in a most amused and patronising
manner.   Not that this ox-eyed black is lacking in many
a word of cheer when you are jaded with the journey ;
indeed, he rallies you with the cheering reminder :
"Hurrah : the first along the dew-damp path in the
morning (*i.e.* the pioneer) dries off on his own body the

wet grass, for the benefit of those who follow him." A perfect parable this of grand old Livingstone staggering down South to his Ilala grave, for did he not endure all his discomforts that the men following might reap a harvest of travelling tranquillity? Hence the negro song, dedicated to all pioneers, which I translate thus—

" Lead thou the way in the wet grass drear,
Then, only then, art thou pioneer :
For Mr. First must get all the woes,
That Mr. Second may find repose."

Called technically "The Path-Borer," a pioneer of the old school is almost canonised by the negro, and all who follow in his wake are his younger brothers. Even to this remote day, all around Lake Mweru they sing a "Livingstone" song to commemorate that great "path-borer," the good Doctor being such a federal head of his race that he is known far and near as *Ingeresa*, or "The Englishman." And this is his memorial song—

" Ingeresa who slept on the waves (*Lala pa Mava*),
Welcome him, for he hath no toes !
Welcome him, for he hath no toes !"

That is to say, revelling in paradox as the negro does, he seized on the facetious fact that this wandering Livingstone, albeit he travelled so far, had no toes, *i.e.* had boots, if you please !

And as Livingstone, so yourself. Here it is, sitting in the penumbra of the camp fire, you hear much ambiguous whispering, the changes all rung on one wonderful word they have coined—your new African name, nothing less.

3

Often only a much modified adaptation of the old one; oftener still a nasty nickname for a nastier man, this awful Africa, so unlike Heaven from sea to sea, impudently lays down the laughable law that you must have a new name in this land. The spade is at last called a spade. Without a pang of pity they rob you of your old patronymic, all the Europeans in Africa, like a band of burglars, being hidden behind the mask of an *alias*. Sorry to suggest, this just suits many of the riff-raff, for as nobody is shy at a masked ball, many a Portuguese under the mask of a *nom de guerre* raided Lubaland, his identity lost in a nickname. Again and again have I been baffled in tracking such murderers, all the fearful facts genuine, but minus the necessary name. So you give it up—fooled, fighting a phantom! Not one new name, mind you, but many; for the bigger the criminal the longer the list of *aliases*.

Mr. Negro, too, like the changing town-names in a Map of Africa, is quite as bad. The changing man has changing names. Here is a lad at my elbow with a pensive air; wants an advance of pay, he says, to buy a trifle —to buy a name, be it known. This means that a name is a serious part of moveable estate and is as much legal property as his gun or dog: witness, this youngster proposing to go shares with another man's name, and solemnly buying it for £ s. d. And unconsciously quotes Scripture in the translation : "A good name," says he, "is better than riches !" So he pays the price and gives the riches for a good name. Of course, he has one already, but opines that his birth-name is too juvenile; was it not given him without his permission and therefore purely conjectural? Should not a name be an appropriate photo of his character? He alone knows that name. So he argues and so he acts, and this is the reason why the question of native names becomes a perplexity, a hate, and an amazement. For as the ins and outs of his life go like his river in twists and turns, even so each new aspect of life means a new name. In this respect the long sinuous Congo has the same history as a Congo native, a dozen new names for the dozen new twists down stream. A mere Smith or Brown cannot exist in these lands, for there is the real article, a Mr. Smith really worth the name for he works in iron, and an equally real Mr. Brown as brown as a berry. No wonder, when you tell the African that in Heaven we shall have a new nature, his rejoinder is, "Then we *must* get a new name." New nature equates new name.

But the worst part of this Benguella story is yet to come.

CHAPTER III

Far, yet not Farthest, In

"Atticus! . . . the stupidest and ugliest slaves come from Britain."   Cicero.

*   *   *

"I'm king to-day," said the dying slave to the king who killed him.

*   *   *

"Here in Lubaland a goat costs four yards of calico, and a woman-slave is also sold for four yards, *ergo* a goat = a woman."   Kavovo (Luban chief).

CHAPTER III

Far, yet not Farthest, in

WHEREIN the reader is invited to call a spade a spade, and return a true bill against Portuguese slavery, the black ivory being proved to carry the white ivory out to the Atlantic.

FOR here, in this trail debouching on the seashore from the Catumbella Hills, you have the most famous slave track in Africa—yes! And all persistently passing under the nose of high constituted authority, remember. His Excellency the Governor is there in Benguella, while beyond that dignitary, away far out at sea, an occasional curl of blue smoke indicates a passing British cruiser. The port-holes look exactly like the clenched teeth of a bull-dog longing to bite the Portuguese slaver. Yet the confusion and degradation of thought is such that for more than a century there has been a tacit conspiracy to wink at it all. But the God Who has cursed the man who winketh with the eye is not indeed mocked, and " Cursed Catumbella " is the awful alliteration of this sad story. For if inter-negro slavery

be a bad black thing, then *a fortiori* white *versus* black
slavery is worse.   But if high constituted authority winks
at it all, then, *a fortissimo*, cursed is the said Government that winketh with the eye.

As far as can be done in cold print let me say what I
saw.   My date is in August, the location a forest in
which Latitude 12° South is intersected by Longitude 21°
East.   Who could ever forget the nightmare of this
monster slave caravan we meet in the Chokwe country ?
Flying as we both are in opposite directions through the
hungry country, you are bewildered and exasperated to
see this staggering mass of captive humanity heading for
the West Coast.   Through desolate marshy lands have
they come ; across the burning sands of the Kifumadzi
flat have they dragged : Lunda and Luvale lands are now
passed, but the Ocean is still a weary way off.   Already
months on the road, hunger is gnawing at the vitals of
the whole cruel caravan, and dozens of hectoring brutes
are clubbing on their "moving money" (*olombongo*)
from behind.   The coldest-blooded creature south of the
Arctic circle could not contemplate that *via dolorosa*
without revolt, for here is the "open sore" streaming
with life's blood before your eyes.   Spring expostulat-
ingly on one of these obese and orthodox slavers in the
forest and he tells you with alacrity that the Portuguese
buy them all up.   Yea, further, with engaging frankness
this brutal black gives you the name and address of
reputable merchants in Benguella and Catumbella who
snap up as much black ivory as possible : are they not

going to ship them over to San Thome for the cultivation
of cocoa ?

Look, then, at this caravan, taking nearly three hours
to march past, a horde of eight hundred souls, all doomed
to exile for life. Some tottering old men there, mere
shrivelled sacks of bones who at any moment may
need to lie down by the roadside and die. Dozens of
women there, staggering along with little babies born
and unborn, for this famished " hungry country " demands
a rushing speed for the caravan. *Item:* One mother,
the grief-lines furrowing her face, goaded on with baby
just born that day by the roadside, maternity conval-
escence, say, one hour and a fraction. Saddest sight of
all, crowds of little emaciated boys and girls all sold for
a song in the Congo State, the little legs at last giving out.
Yet only four months before every one of them had
radiant youth bubbling in his veins. Who can forget
that, Lubans born and bred as they are, these same little
souls sing a song in their own country about the joys of
a jaded piccaninny on the trail when nearing home at
last ?

> " If toiling on a journey dreary
> A little toddling child is weary,
> One whisper of the magic ' Home,'
> How strong the little legs become !
> No longer weariness they feel,
> For they are stiff like bars of steel."

But here they are, far from home, that long wriggling
horror of a slave track before and behind them, so thin
and hollow-eyed you can only think of them as a moan

materialised into flesh. Heading for the slave-pen at Benguella there is no such magic word "Home" to stiffen their back in resolve to reach it. One of these girls had fallen behind, strength gone, load of rubber thrown on the ground, so, emerging from the bush, I was just in time to see her owner club her head, yelling out a threat with each stroke. This was more than I could stand, and as Christ saw nothing worse than that among the Temple dove-sellers I sprang at this burly Bihean with a stick to administer unto him a not undeserved trouncing—but of course he showed a clean pair of heels. One tiny girl I redeemed from a dark death by the roadside, a girl who is now a happy Christian mother on Lake Mweru.

Item: Literally sold for a song was one such little boy whose name became Sikispence, his market value one coloured handkerchief at 6d.

Item: A native named "Truss of calico" bought one youngster for 1s. 4d. ; a cheap chattel this, stolen while mother was off in the field.

Item: Dilunga's child, too, was sold for an old waterproof coat.

Item: Ndala was a boy who fetched, as market price, a small bag of corn.

Item: Musole and her child were also sold for grain, two small bags for two human beings. "Man eats corn, but corn can eat man," their proverb runs.

Proof positive ? Here is a blunt fellow who has done the thing for years, no Portuguese he. Quite a prodigy of obesity for the climate, he has bought and sold many a

SMOKING INDIAN HEMP,

slave. In his ample mouth there is an ample pipe, and
between the puffs he boasts of his slave-trading ; two
slaves for one rifle, is an instance. Committing himself,
as he did, to an IOU for the accessory cartridges, here
you have frank fact and no fiction. Daring to marry in
after years, this union was so degrading that when he
died, his widow, on the 18th of April 1907, sold off seven
slaves, two going to Snr. "Katavola"—to give the name
of place for persons. This Senhor, of course, offered good
prices for some girls she had. Figures are not at all
difficult to get at, for often a blunt question receives as
blunt an answer, this especially with the "old timer," a
high-and-dry Tory. A slaver by principle as well as
practice, he does not believe in exposing too much of
the white of the eyes on this subject of slavery. With
Dickens' policeman he believes that "words is bosh," and
the polite modern "serviçaes" is too fancy a word for
him. Asked point-blank to give the percentage of slave
mortality *en route* to ocean, this out-and-outer makes a
careful calculation of the losses. Far from parrying such
a preposterously pointed question, " Well," says he, " they
vary a good deal ; from some districts they are hardier
than from others. If we are lucky we may get *six out
of every ten alive to Bihe, and if unlucky, perhaps only
three out of ten.*"

The first draft of the programme for our route ahead
is very simple. Two hundred miles inland is our first
stage to the kingdom of Bihe, and our roaming Bihean
is the man who holds the key to the Far Interior. The

accurate African analogy is found in thinking of Benguella as the sort of Western Zanzibar, and busy transport Bihe as the Unyanyembe of these latitudes. This Bihean, though, scores off his Eastern brother in having more commercial initiative, whereas in the prowess of war— "clash of arms" they call it—the poor Bihean is as famous a "woman in war" (*sic*) as the Arab Rugaruga is a historic horror. The very grammar of the story tells this tale, for the proper noun "Rugaruga" became ultimately the proper verb (and improper, alas!) meaning "to murder and loot," all around Lake Mweru. Both of them professional slavers, the Bihean in the West found himself in the grip of a much more keen economic process than the Munyamwesi man out East. For unlike the Bihean's Portuguese master, the fastidious and aggressive Arab kept commerce in his own hands, disdaining a delegate. On the other hand, the lethargic Portuguese threw all the initiative on the bold Bihean, of course throwing at him at the same time a few hundred pounds' worth of guns, powder, and calico. The black factotum thus armed with a curious power of attorney in the form of a huge Portuguese flag disappeared "over the hills and far away" for a nine months' pacific (!) penetration of the Interior. No sedentary Portuguese, as a rule, even followed him to ask nasty questions, and if the man from Lisboa ever had any curiosity about the Interior it very seldom seemed to have crystallised into active exploration —Silva Porto of Belmonte the great exception. Thus it came to pass that in a quarter of a century the Bihean legend spread far over the Interior, and in the solemn matter of slavery these "black Portuguese" became the great knights of industry in the land. Even when a young boy Bihean really finds his legs, off he is drafted East, across the Kwanza River, to be trained like a young bull-dog to show his teeth at the slaves. At six years of age the busy little commercial brain of Master Bihean has long ago learned the market prices of human flesh and blood, man-slave, woman-slave, child-slave, and baby-slave all assorted and ticketed in his head.

At glad last—and thanks to kind Mr. Woodside—we climb out of that loathsome littoral one lovely evening in July. Casting a last long look at the Western Atlantic disappearing in strange apocalyptic glow among the Catumbella Hills, ours it is to take the first faltering step on our way. Not again shall we sight the salt sea until one remote day the wide continent is crossed and the Indian Ocean flashes into view at Chinde. The "boring" of Africa is the native's technical term for this crossing from sea to sea. Working out to the sea after being shut in to the long grass of the Interior for nearly twenty years, the first sniff of the Ocean ozone dilates the nostrils with the subtlest of all human joy—the prickly breath of the salt sea driving deep down into the panting lungs. Louder than the thousand Greeks of Xenophon you can utter the long-pent-up shout, "Thalatta! Thalatta!" on sighting the great green sea—

" The sea ! the sea ! the open sea !
The blue, the fresh, the ever free !"

The climb up to Bihe is the first stage of our long
journey, and the three opening days see us covering a
curious switchback arrangement in mountains, the Ekonga
and Kañyon presenting the worst difficulties. Probably
a section view of the former might show eight rude
angles of nearly 70°, and until the ridge of Mount Elonga
is gained on the seventh day and an altitude of 5000 feet
reached, it is persistent ascent all the time, the chill tonic
mountain air biting the cheek. We cross, too, numberless
little perennial streams spanned by bridges, both creaking
and rickety, and only two rivers of any magnitude—the
Bailombo and Keve. The Bailombo, the size of an
English trout-stream, is fairly fordable ; the Keve, a deep
rapid thing, you must negotiate in a leaky little bark
boat (coracle, rather)—one man, one voyage. You feel as
safe as if you had put to sea in a washtub, and about as
dry. But to have a lively sense of the saving humour of
things is one thing, and to indulge that same sense half-
way across this washtub voyage is quite another. You
recall the old saying that "a sailor has never got home
till he has had his dinner," and a slip between this cup
of a canoe and that lip of a river bank is a daily, deadly
occurrence. If ever there was nothing in a name, here
you have it in this bark bundle called a boat. Too truly
you embark. That bright red shell cracked all over and
puttied with mud proclaims this to be her maiden voyage,
so be sure of it the whole situation is abounding in
ludicrous possibilities. Squeezing into the thing, you
wonder desolately where your negro paddler can contrive

to come in ; already, sufficient unto the canoe is the cargo thereof. Truly a trial trip ! But if he cometh not this cargo goeth not, so our funny friend lurches in feet first, the intelligent idea being that if these really frightful feet find room his meagre body can easily follow. Already filling fast before you start, you are almost as wet as the traditional drowned rat, and away you wobble on the river. The water is now as much in the boat as the boat in the water. Circling in many a creditable curve, you long " to be over yonder," a negro glued to your back, a brand-new boat and a brand-new experience. It is a remarkable fact—and fact it is—that old Kasonkomona, on the Lufira, used regularly to capsize his canoe at the precise point where, on the morrow, he would dive for the lost treasure—of course, after his half-drowned passenger was well on his way to the next camp. A strong swimmer, he always dramatically saved the sinking voyager, the greedy glitter in his eyes bespeaking salvage operations on the morrow — guns, spears, beads, all harvested from the river bottom.

Another detail. At each of our camps we are forced, gipsy-like, to build a culinary Ebenezer, not one but three stones necessary for a pot-rest, each new bivouac appropriately demanding its new Ebenezer. " Hither by Thy help I come," these sermonising stones seem to say every time the pot mounts the memorial heap, and looking away back out to the Ocean I see a long row of Ebenezers, almost enough to build a Temple. That British tinsmith who manufactured my camp copper kettle little guessed what a prophetic touch he added to his work by graving "Ebenezer" on its handle—the very stones and cooking-pot crying out to God in the desert. Indeed, the whole long story can be told in the exact terms of Bunyan's allegory : not a mere playing at "Pilgrim's Progress," for we were pilgrims and we did daily make progress. Many a "Hill Difficulty" lying across our track; many a "Slough of Despond," too. Many a time we laid up stores of future anguish in a supper of uncooked beans. Often and often we braved the perils of pea-nuts and green corn before turning in. Yet another handful of pea-nuts Likewise a handful of pea-nuts. And so on and on. Just that. ON AND ON.

Then we get on our legs. Break camp in the silence and solitude of the moonlight, wide awake at every pore, the grey and ghostly light outlining weird forms of fallen trunks and decaying roots. Ours the tip-toe of expectancy, enjoying the two distinct thrills of a cool starry night merging into the reddening dawn waking up the forest. Mark you, only sixty minutes separate prospective blaze from present blackness, yet one hour hence these forest glades glimmering in gloom will seem things of years ago, a far-off memory and dream. Have you caught it? The mere minutes separating 4 a.m. and 5 a.m. are few and flying, yet once again fancy fights facts, making each of these minutes seem a month. For the awful antithesis yawning between the nocturnal and the diurnal, between the gloom and the glory, defies you to measure it by mere minutes. The antagonism is too abysmal. It is like

getting up in December to break your fast in June.   Even
the negro has caught the identical idea when by way of
sunrise greeting—his way of saying " Good morning!"
this—he puts to you the phrase, "A night's a year!"
The ghostly gloom is now a gleaming palace of life,
and the eerie stillness of the night is blotted into
oblivion by the million cries of the morning.   The battle
of the day resumes.

So on and in we go.   Picture our pleasure on finding
at Bailundu and Bihe a splendid type of mission worked
by our friends the Americans.   Pioneered by one of the
"Bible" Bagsters, how suggestive that the family that
flooded England with Bibles should also have sent out
a living epistle to Africa.   Messrs. Sanders, Stover, Fay,
Woodside, and Currie were men both winning and wise,
and they fought slavery here at its hard headquarters.
No wonder the Portuguese were exasperated, for as you
drew near these glad little centres of testimony, while
yet a long way off you could hear the Missionaries' names
fondled as a household joy; the names "Sandle" and
"Kole" being passwords that work like magic.   The
same old song this, we ourselves afterwards found in
the Garenganze.   For, in the teeth of many a hard-
mouthed denial from white men, the Missionary, having
advanced the claim that the African has as soft a heart
as his body is tough, must perforce prove his point.   And
according to his faith on this "negro heart" subject, even
so is it unto him.   Mr. Missionary wins the hearts of the
whole countryside, and that, too often, to the chagrin of

his resident officials. I had an amusing debate with an exalted personage on this very tender subject, the dialogue being as short as sharp.

"Why have you Missionaries all the natives around your Mission Station, and the Government scarcely any?"

"The Government say 'Allez!' and the Mission says 'Allons!'"

CHAPTER IV

Our African Apprenticeship

"And Moses sent messengers to the king of Edom : Let us pass, I pray thee, through thy country : we will not pass through the fields, neither will we drink of the wells : we will go by the king's high way, we will not turn to the right hand nor to the left, until we have passed thy borders."

NUMBERS xx. 17.

*   *   *

"And he said, Thou shalt not go through. And Edom came out against him with a strong hand. Thus Edom refused to give Israel passage through his border." NUMBERS xx. 20, 21.

*   *   *

"A famous man is Robin Hood . . .
And Scotland has a thief as good,
An outlaw of as daring mood ;
She has her brave Rob Roy."

CHAPTER IV

Our African Apprenticeship

WHEREAT the reader yawns at African delays, and discovers that patience must be his pet virtue in this lazy land.

POOR old gin-soaked Bihe! There it was Joseph Lynn, young Dr. Sparks, and others in later days poured out their lives for the land. Paul-like, ready to be accursed rather than not save souls; Knox-like, ready to die unless God give him his Scotland. There are few who have done so much, and talked so little, as these dear martyrs, battling on in hard Bihe among drink-sodden slavers. But we restrain ourselves, and laying our wreaths upon their graves pass on.

That cry of Grog! Grog! Grog! Not content with their thriving export slavery, the Portuguese resolved to make sure of this bad business by forging a second slave-chain of rum, vulgarly called "nigger killer." And soon Bihe began to fill up with gin-distillers, every other little stream boasting its hell-trap. The liquid sold was such wicked stuff that it could almost corrode a paving-stone—what then happened to the negro? Result, a

4

blear-eyed Bihean who would sell his soul and *his family* to get a drink.

Quadrupeds first, of course; then follow the reluctant bipeds, one, two, three fashion. Oh yes, he pauses in the process, for he likes his family, but likes the fire-water best. He even fights the temptation for a week, then all is lost as the first flow of liquor stings its way down the alimentary canal, tearing at his vitals. Wipes his lips now with the back of his hand and—and starts to sell the family. No wonder Scripture, away back at the beginning of the world, kindles for Africa such a beacon of wild warning when it reveals the negro's ancestor naked in his tent, and drink the cause of it all.

No wonder the pawky English tongue insists that gin = an inebriant and gin = a trap. In Bihe, the sovereign specific, when the supply of slaves languishes, is the rum business. Here it is that slaves are "made to order"; slaves literal, I mean, as well as slaves moral. A man ran in to one of our Missionaries and said that his father had sold his own son for rum, sold to Senr. ——. First enslaved morally by his "fire-water" thirst, the next move was one of frank literal slavery; sold his own flesh and blood for the fiery fluid. Such a sure source of enslavement is this, that the commoner wile is to advance sundry "modest quenchers" on credit, the sure slavery of thirst ultimately demanding a deal in slaves for liquidation of the liquor bill. Take Senr. Z. of *Ohwa*; he gave one Bihean just enough drink, not only to drown the man's wits, but also to drown the drinker at the Kunehe River

crossing. Remorseless as destiny, down swoops this gin-
seller on the drowned victim's next-of-kin, claiming his
pound of flesh. And gets it, too, in two qualities : flesh
of man and flesh of beast, an ox and a slave, Katumwa
his name. History is silent on how these bereaved
Biheans weathered the financial sea, for if they borrowed
the slave they would need to pay two for one. *Kapapelo*,
their gin-drunk nephew, lost his balance and was drowned
for it; here is a Portuguese — reader, forgive the
sneer!—resolved not to lose *his* credit balance at any
rate.[1]

A weaker word than "fascinating" would therefore
describe the Portuguese methods in Bihe and farther East.
Dominating and dwarfing all other issues is the Fort, and
round the average Commandant you have a ring of
rascals, "Ovimbali," white man's personnel. "No one
hearing, one cannot speak," so said Cicero long ago, and
so say these hangers-on who buy and sell justice to the
highest bidder. Not a mere case this of "having the
ear" of their master ; they are his ears and they are his
mouth. Coleridge described it all unerringly when he
said that "a dwarf sees farther than the giant when he
has the giant's shoulder to mount on." Hemmed in by
injustice of this sort, the wise native is the man who
sanely and shrewdly steers clear of it all. *Kan* was
one such, and wronged though he was, he snapped his
fingers at it all : "Why should I go to the Fort for help
against the Fort? Why go to the Chefe? Is it worth

---

[1] See Mr. Swan in *The Slavery of To-Day* for substantial corroboration.

while to ask the river to champion your cause against the lake, when you can only get water from either?"

The *Kofwali* case will illustrate Fort methods, and establishing as it does a really regrettable precedent we must hoist a danger signal. The thunders of the law roared on poor Kofwali's head because in his own person he dared to confess to being the *nephew* of a man who when alive was the *neighbour* of a man who had committed the crime. Judgment: that the said Kofwali, nephew of the neighbour of the accused, be fined two slaves, one ox, and trade goods thrown in. The coloured sergeant got one slave for settling the crime, the claimant had the other slave, the white officer who had given the man a severe beating with the *chicotte* got the ox for his exertions, and the soldier some of the trade goods for feeding him whilst he was a prisoner, as such are not fed free in the Fort.

But the hateful exigencies of this story demand an ugly realism. That this foul official often falls foul of the Seventh Commandment is too glaringly undeniable. Mr. Swan's facts are unarguable and must really be repeated to mark the depths of disgrace to which some sink. A woman's child is at the Fort and, straight as a needle to the pole, that woman heads for her bairn; of course, under the escort of a friendly native who is due there on a visit. Here at headquarters the woman is seduced by the Commandant, and here, too, a roar of rage is heard from the official's own paramour. Alas for prestige! Now begins a Billingsgate broil, concubine

versus Commandant, the legal lion bearded in his own
den by his own negress consort. Piqued by the storm
in his own household, the Chefe calmly seeks a scapegoat and finds it in the harmless escort who courteously
brought the mother after her child. Chuckling with malice
and determined to come out of it with colours flying, the
Judge on the bench (who should have been prisoner at
the bar) condemned the scapegoat to pay two slaves,
because—I quote—he having brought the woman and
the woman having tempted His Honour the Judge, therefore judgment must be entered accordingly.

But the really profitable part of this bad business is
" the runaway slave " department. Here you have stay-
at-homes who often make more out of it than the zealous
man-hunters of Lubaland. Take Senr. Z., for instance, and
work out with him this spicy little sum in slave arithmetic. Problem—how to make one slave produce
twenty-three other slaves *plus* oxen, rubber, and pigs
thrown in. Now this subterfuge is really as simple as it
is common, for he sets the ball a-rolling by so maltreating
this one slave that run away she must, and now woe to
all who harbour her! She darts into a hamlet, and
breathlessly elated, Snr. Z. darts after her, for that townlet
must pay, yes, cash down, ten slaves *plus* ten *ipako* (*i.e.*
any other legal currency). Our peppery old colonial rubs
his hands with glee at this brisk business, but he is on for
more. (Reader, are you working out this sum in awful
arithmetic : one slave has now captured ten more,
including etceteras?) Next move is nothing new, the

same old bait slave is going to catch more. K—— is the man who is next mulcted, and he pays one young woman, a pig, and a load of rubber ; business is not so brisk, you see. There is better fishing farther on, however, and the village of Lak pays up two slaves, two oxen, and two loads of rubber, all on the vile old plea of harbouring Onesimus. Can we not now strike the grand total and get done with it ? No, we must include a closing (?) item. Farther along there was an open gateway, and this hunted-down slave darts in, only to doom the villagers to a final fine—ten slaves, cash down! Now you may strike your terrible total. Twenty-three slaves *plus* two oxen *plus* one pig *plus* three loads of rubber for one runaway slave. Plain arithmetic all this, not rhetoric. Deduction : The Portuguese put a premium on the maltreatment of slaves. Therefore the old specious pro-slavery argument, running "The man who treats his horse badly is a fool," etc., this argument, I say, is as rotten as is the audacious analogy between a horse and a human being.

But there is worse to come. Take another vile expedient having the same sad objective, I mean, the swelling of this Westward-going stream of slavery : the "Shylock system" among the natives. Here is the trader's chance, and the borrowing native is soon involved in a quagmire of trouble, to wit, a 1000 per cent extortion on the borrowed goods. (Not an E.O.E. invoice, by any means, for this arrogant Shylock never makes an error and never omits anything.) Snr. —— is a case in point : as usual, he does not want his calico back, he wants payment, not in cash but kind, and that kind the best kind, yea, the human kind. Therefore this knave grabs at nine women as against his debt for goods, an account this the natives stoutly refuse to pay because they have *already paid it in blood*—be it noted the blood of the bulleted debtor, killed by Shylock. Appealing to the Fort, the Chefe votes for his compatriot creditor, arguing that as Shylock has spilled the said blood a few miles beyond the Fort's jurisdiction, obviously the deed must be ignored and the nine slaves retained for the debt. Mark you, here you have blood shed and blood winked at. The Sekeseke case is akin to this : a gentleman he, known to his Catumbella friends as Senhor P—— B——. Beating a slave for days into a pitiful pulp, of course the said slave died, and was buried at midnight in the corner of his garden. Was Senhor P—— B—— punished for this murder, and if so, when, and where, and by whom ? Now for the swing of the pendulum.

Not that such slaves learning from such masters are much better : how could they be ? Pouring into Bihe as these streams of slaves do, here in the villages you have the great mixing bowl of West Africa ; and a slave in a few years takes on the Umbundu polish, aping their twang of speech to a nicety, but tripping to the last over an M = V. *Will* say Monjo for Voujo, and so forth. Inter-negro slavery, however, is here seen to be a humaner thing ; at least, the slave gets a curious chance among his own colour. Indeed, the ascendancy of many of these freedmen is all very like a page of Gibbon, a master often being indebted to his slave in the meeting of his lawsuit liabilities. For like all "woman" tribes who dread blood-spilling, the great Bihean terror (and substitute for blood) is this network of *Ovimbu* = lawsuits, the curious complications arising being a prize conundrum in jurisprudence. Certainly if colour has ever been given to the statement that slavery has something good in it, the most specious side is the domestic servitude. It is a bold assertion to make, but such is the equipoise of events that it may be asserted that the average chief is almost on a par with the average slave. Rex sleeps on the same sort of reed mat as his Onesimus : Rex drinks the same beer : Rex wears the same apology for a garment, and eats the same sundown supper of mush. Nay, the scales go tilt on the wrong side, for often at nightfall a slave slips in a red-legged partridge or parakeet to his guidwife ; contrast the chief who has gone to sleep on vegetables, and his slave sneaking a late game supper ! The same abundance of firewood, too, for master and bondsman alike ; same cooking utensils; same blend of tobacco, with a communistic whiff from the same gourd pipe. Flowing like a tide, the royal slaver pours into my left ear, defying me to gainsay the fact that his slaves are freer than their lord : "Has not a slave only one master, and is not a king servant of all ? " Besides, the slave has a hidden weapon all the time in the institution of *Okulitumbika*, *i.e.* the choice of any master he chooses. Here is an instance where a leathery-lunged slave, "The Creator," they call him, yawned and said he had had quite enough of his master's

insolence. So casting around him, he picks out as ideal a
master as he can find, gravely goes across to this new
master's spirit temple and breaks one of the sacred gourds,
thereby snapping the old chain and welding a new. Does
not the owner of the broken spirit chalice claim the slave
as damages? Law : Damage an article and the damager
pays himself in as damages. But one day will see his
boldest stroke of all. For, quickly accumulating a small
capital, this slave awaits the day when he sees his master
in financial straits, and forthwith turns the tables on his
lord, actually buying up his own taskmaster.

Now for the darkest despotism in all slavery ; I mean,
the ex-slave ruling the ex-lord with an iron rod. And all
this according to that most ancient of sayings passed
along in whispers from one bondsman to another : " If
thou art an anvil, be patient, O slave my brother ; but
if thou art a hammer, strike hard ! " One such ex-slave,
called " The Python," ultimately lorded it over our huge
caravan, and instead of being abashed at his slave blood,
he was precious proud of it : " O white man, you are
proud of your descent, but I am proud of my ascent,
was his idea. Coleridge it was who wrote of "the pride
that apes humility," and our friend " The Python " had it,
for if not pride of race it was pride of place. But make
it a rule never, oh! never to argue with such a fellow—if
you fight with a sweep you cannot blacken him, but he
may blacken you. Tantalising though he often was and
worthy a well-merited wigging, there he stood, head and
shoulders above them all, a go-ahead boss just "up from

slavery." He did not cringe to us, and did not mind running risks with his bread-and-butter. Wise, too, with a corrosive sort of wisdom, some things he said were a clever echo of Epictetus (and who by the by was he, if not a slave?). Even Horace would pardon me for calling him eloquent. (Horace, too, who was he if not a slave's son?) Yet this man finally became as tame as a friendly mastiff, although all the time a snob to his fellows. And a slave snob, remember, is king of all the snobs; proves it, too, by kissing the feet of the man above him on the social ladder, while he kicks the other who is below him. Himself a slave by purchase and with a commercial instinct quite in accord with the best traditions of Bihe, he would sell his own father and mother for an old song. Q.E.D.: The Romans were right, "As many slaves, so many enemies"—bad slavery makes a bad slave.

Why forget that for two centuries and a half the Mamelukes or white slaves of Egypt ruled in luxury farther North? Slaves though they were, did they not excel in art and poetry? In later Rome, too, what about the educated slaves who earned large profits as writers, lecturers, bankers, physicians, and architects?

But all this is not lost time, for these days of delay in Bihe are really full of African apprenticeship. Pushing on alone as I had done, Mr. Currie kindly gave me sanctuary in his little mud cabin at Chisamba, and many a happy day we spent together. Dieted on raw native mush and beans, this good man (by calling a Missionary, and by necessity everything) was the Canadian outpost

of our American friends.   Here, all alone, he camped on
the edge of a wood, making a beginning by felling tall
trees and roughing out of the thick bush a clearing for his
future site.   Soon the songs of the wind whistling through
the woods were answered by the songs of Zion, and thus
at long last the story of centuries of heathendom was
ended and a new chapter begun.   The large modern
Chisamba of these later days was long ago cradled there
in that tiny mud hut in the woods, and I should be
insolently ungrateful were I to forget these early days of
promise, eyes ranging over the Eastern skyline,

> " Yearning for the large excitement
> That the coming years would bring."

But the negro must really be seen in his own compact
and cramped stockade town, and I shall never regret
beginning my life in Africa in one such village on the
Kunje River.   Cooped up inside the same stockade, air
stale and sour, we black and white lived together for
months, the same beehive huts and porridge our portion.
" Chenda," or Pilgrim Town, they called the village, and a
kindly old grandmother saw to my comfort.   Feeble and
wrinkled, this genial body was only one of the withered
old " hags " of the modern explorer's book of travels, yet
as the days passed and we got on family talking terms,
here was a seemingly repellent old negress developed into
a charming dowager armed to the finger tips with finish
and polish.   Listened to your verb *Ndu Pandula* (Thank
you) with a pretty pleased old blush.   With her old hard,
corrugated hands she stirred my porridge day by day

cooking all the meals with the alacrity of a girl in her teens. Beaming with simple truth, the more this old lady talks the more the scales of prejudice fall from your eyes, and you begin to see her striking resemblance to some English lady you have known.

In Lubaland I met another such dear granny whose intention was better than her attainment. A beaming lady, seventy at a guess, she claims to be the champion cook of the country ; tells you, moreover, that she is the Chief's cook. Proof positive this, that being Chief's cook she is chief cook also. Has cooked in her day all manner of messes : fat snakes, soft snails, and many another menu item that would look more polite in French than in English. Boiled dogs, she tells me, are her speciality, and according to this authority the Lubans pet their famous dogs for the greedy reason that the very dog that was so friendly before he entered the cooking-pot might still agree with them—in digestion. Well, this kindly dame it was who came poking around my pots and pans, emboldened by her " Royal Letters Patent " to believe that she, poor soul, could even cook a dainty dish for " he of the boots." Finally, my boy gave me hopelessly away, by hinting that I ate eggs, a very debased sort of diet to a Luban, for in that egg is not the chick yet unborn ? (And if we must eat eggs then, *ex hypo.*, why not wait until they are just old enough to hint that there is a semblance to a chick inside ?) My boy, however, coming to the point with praiseworthy directness in two terse, patronising words condescended to tell this Chief-because-

Chief's cook that she had merely to break the shell and the thing was cooked in a minute. So away trotted my Queen of all the cooks, this and this only ringing in her ears as a kind of key to the new recipe, I mean the advice to break the shell. And break it she did. But watch with what kindly concern she washes that shell—and what do you think? In best cocksure manner she now gets a stout stick, smashes it up shell and yolk together, the resultant omelette being studded all over with jagged shells sticking out like carpet tacks. Nor did she succeed in putting us off eggs. "Emperors' diet," we call them, even in Africa's dirtiest hole, for when the negro manioc palls, when their meat is tainted, when the cooking oil is rancid, every time you crack the shell of your breakfast egg in a heathen hovel, you equal the crowned heads of Europe.

But, as I have already hinted, strange though such doings seem, the doers thereof almost resemble your own flesh and blood, the Bihean peculiarly so. This, too, applies to the young darkies who crowd around; every lad of them suggests his English "double." You feel a bolt shot back in your memory, and get quite certain it is only the lack of a white collar and tie causing them to disresemble their tow-headed English twin-brothers Tommy Jones, John Smith, etc. Coarse fat pigs are the national riches, the said snorters being also the village scavengers. This killing of the pig is a big function in the Bihean family, when there is quite an infectious quiver in the air, and he is gobbled utterly up.

The roar of the rejoicing is such that they even beat the Chicago packer's boast that everything about the pig is tinned except the squeal.   Yea, they surpass even the America that is great in all things, great even in exaggeration.   For in Africa the noise is so loud that the negro seems to have swallowed the squeal along with the pig.

Listen!   Across stream there goes the maddening drum, a knot of young fellows having started the music as a signal for the girls to join them, this rub-a-dub roar being really a sort of sweetheart's call.   The local crickets have learnt the same trick, for that shrill cry from a thousand cricket throats is merely the male insect rasping his wings as a reed instrument to attract the lady cricket to his side.   The frogs with rolling eye are identical, for all their mad croaking is merely Master Toad in yellow waistcoat and tight green trousers wooing his lady with weird calls from the marsh.   So Messrs. Negro, Cricket, and Toad are all at the same game on the same night around the same marsh; all alike in their resolve to use the same African moon with the same noisy music for the same amorous assignation.

But it is cruel to beat a cripple with his own crutches, and you must not forget that this bewitching moon is the negro's only candle, his only fleeting chance of an evening out of doors.   It is not my intention to argue here the ethics of the thing, but let us try to understand before we judge.   Taking it all in, cause and effect, condemnation and excuse, who shall throw the first stone?   The

lurking leopard or hyena forces him into his few feet of
stuffy hut during all the waning phases, so now or never
is the chance when it looms large like a new half-crown.
Right through the night that dance froths and bubbles
along, the whole negro from head to heels mad with the
moonlight—the Devil's St. Vitus dance!

So ingrained is this jigging that even a sedate negro
convert to Christianity has still got it in the very bones,
"dancing before the Lord" she would call it.   Here was
a thing to be seen and never forgotten, the Devil's jig
consecrated to the Lord.   The soul of delicacy and discretion, I spotted an elect lady dancing out her Christian
joy as a solemn duty, not a smile in her antics, no thought
of the burlesque, yet to me, a new-comer, what a gazing-
stock !   The amazing, maddening mix-up of the prayer in
the heart and the prance in the feet !   Asked her what it
meant at all at all, and she quaintly replied, "Oh ! it is
only *praise getting out at the toes.*"   Then she actioned
this new idea to me—this praise-getting-out-at-the-toes
idea, I mean.   Making a diagram of her own body, she
first of all put her hand over her heart as indicating
her central source of joy—"the generator," she called it.
Granting then a heart pulsating with joy ; with her crooked
old finger she now traces on her body two opposite thrills
of joy, one shooting up and through her mouth in vocal
praise, the other darting down to her feet—praise getting
out at the toes in dancing !   A confession this with a
moral, surely, for how much of God's joy is allowed to
evaporate by the mouth in mere talk when it should

descend to the feet in real walk. Hamlet's answer too often covering all results, " Words ! Words ! Words ! "

Again, I say, I am glad I went to school with the negro in his own town. The mere globe-trotter gets a poor enough chance of getting to know the real African. It is only here, stuck in amongst his own hovel huts, you at last reach the region of hard fact, and a few months of such "slumming" is worth years of monotonous "Station" life. On a Mission Station the black boy is often only a false eager echo of the white man, whereas here, in his hamlet, you are verily *chez lui*. Lying awake for hours, note-book on pillow, you can listen to their talk, talk, talking, this cheeky chatter you hear being the natural and normal idiom of the native, not that "wooden" Anglo-Bantu so common even among Missionaries. True, for the first few days they are tongue-tied, and excruciatingly bored by your spying presence; let a week pass, however, and then you are truly and technically " in." This is what the African means when he sings to the white man the little couplet—

" Oh, come near,
And I'll hear."

Sleeping inside their fenced town, the awaking at sunrise is a weird business. There is no daily newspaper for the daily dose of information, so dream-telling becomes a serious substitute. To-morrow's news, that is to say, is more important to them than the stale doings of yesterday. And just as night only blots out a world to reveal a universe, so, even so, dreaming by night is a bigger business

than working by day.   For to Mr. Negro a dream is an
avant-courier from to-morrow, a whisper out of eternity
for the guidance of men.   Farther East I came across
a proof of this.   Coming out of the grass, I met a band
of solemn-looking men with a curious old-world look in
their faces.   Wonder of wonders, they were a "dream
embassy," said they ; had travelled a long way and were
afoot on a kind of Missionary journey from one great
chief to another, his friend and faithful ally of years.
A "dream embassy," mark you, God having spoken to
their chief in a great dream ; and the solemnity of it all
had so sunk into the monarch's soul that he sent off these
Missionaries of his dream to warn his dear friend, a
brother-king, of the ways of God with man.   So serious
a thing is this dream-telling that they have coined a
special verb (*Lotolwela*), "to expound a dream."   Not in
the temper of mere expediency did I listen to their sacred
story, the negro *tête-à-tête* with the Infinite, men on the
march for many miles, their theme, God ! God ! God !
Picture me there a dazed Missionary listening to these
dream-tellers — listening and wondering, listening and
wondering—as with uplifted hands they point skywards
and paint it all so vividly.   Telling me of the stately
goings of God in their far-away marsh ; how that He
challenged their king as to his dignity ; how that the
king responded with his long array of titles ; and how that
the more he vaunted before God the less did his strength
become.   Yet again and again did God so ask him who
he was, and just so often did their king make this foolish

5

boast of dignity—only to find his strength oozing out of
his body.   But just as in painting light is brought out
by shade, so this king learned the secret of power from
this very secret of weakness.   For finally God said He
would " make an end," and this word " end " was the
beginning of bliss.   Said the monarch : " King ? no king
am I, but a worthless slave.   All kingship is Thine and
all power ! "   Then it was the wondrous tide of power
flowed back into his body : the weakling now a giant ; the
abject a strong man made strong out of weakness.   Mere
dream though it was, it has solemnly crystallised into
dogma, and here am I a Missionary stumbling across these
other " dream " Missionaries in the grass.   In our zeal
for God's written record we are too apt to treat all this
as a weird and doubtful business—mere misty dream.
Forgetful of the fact that God's own Book it is that
declares, " in a dream . . . He openeth the ears of men."
Forgetful, likewise, that if England does not get these
divine dreams it is because England, a land full of Bibles,
does not need them.   Forgetful, finally, that God may
speak to those to whom He does not write.

In Lubaland, one old man, " The Snuff-maker " by
name, beats the whole land at length of hair, and this
because he has bound himself with an oath never, nevermore to get his hair trimmed.   He dreamed a dream,
but the dream played him false ; and, as the head is the
dreamer and not the heart, he doomed his head to the
endless rebuff—of nevermore visiting the barber.   A great
punishment, indeed, but so, too, had that dream been

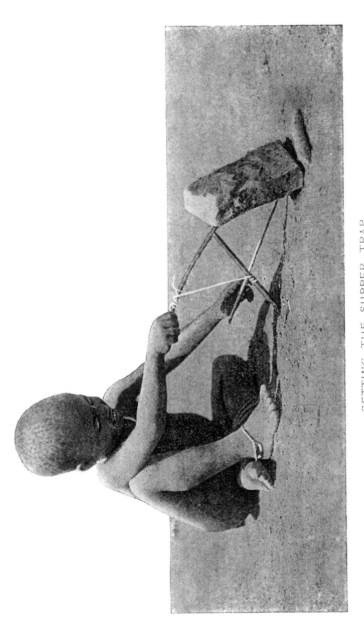

SETTING THE SUPPER TRAP.
Query: A Bird or a Rat?

great, a gorgeous vision of royalty and riches. Vividly in his sleep, old Mr. Snuff-maker saw himself acclaimed king of the country, loud rang the cheers as he ascended the dream-throne, and then—then broke a grey chilly dawn to undeceive and drag him down to dirt and poverty, "a fading away inheritance," he calls it. But the stout old soul could not go back on the word that had gone forth from his lips. So the days grow long and the hair grows longer, but onward he must go on his unchanging way. What an opening for me to bring out my Gospel wares and offer this old dream-duped man "an inheritance that fadeth not away." His riches came in a dream and went the way they came.

*   *   *

To revert to our stockade hamlet, scavengered by pigs and vultures. Your mode of getting "in," remember, is quite akin to the way you get into their huts. This negro doorway is so low that you must double up like a half-shut pocket-knife before you can effect an entrance, and so, too, with the metaphoric doorway of the black brain. British bluff is of no avail, and only by stooping can you wriggle into both Africa the land and Africa the man. Now is the time to consult Alice's famous "book of rules for shutting people up like telescopes." It is the old story of harvest gleaning. Good gleaners must be good stoopers even in this harvest-field of black beehive huts. You don't bow to the negro, but you must bow to his dwarf doorway—" stoop to conquer," in fact. As narrow almost as they are low, these same door-

ways of course debar a hurried egress. The story goes
that the advent of a rare white skin one day caused a
stampede among the frightened female population, one
well-aimed rush being made for a very narrow but very
inviting doorway. Unfortunately for some of these
swarthy bipeds, a very stout dowager stuck fast in this
rat's hole entrance, effectually blocking the ingress of her
sauve qui peut sisters behind her. The narrator of this
event in African history relieves our anxiety by informing
us that the lady was eventually extricated from her
uncomfortable position, and would doubtless personally
supervise the building of her own front door in future.
Deduction : You dare not (because cannot) rush the
African town of Mansoul.

    To ask for anything in the Portuguese loaded-revolver
tone of voice is to shut yourself out by bolts and bars,
and all the facts and forces of the negro's life will be lost
to you. Be sure of it, to be "Farthest In" is a poor
enough thing if it only applies to the mere elementary
geography of Central Africa. Yet is it a pathetic fact
that many a man can live a long life in the land and
never be really in Africa, and such a man regularly reveals
his personality in the curiously candid confession : "Yes!
I can speak all right to the native, but cannot catch what
he says." Now, where does this land him ? It means, of
course, that as the years pass his ears are shut to the
steady stream of black speech that should be daily flooding his ears and washing out of the brain his purely subjective ideas. The result is obvious, and here you have

a man who will never really be *in* Africa because Africa never really gets into him.

But mere negation is not the worst part of the story. For positively here is a white man who must be somebody in Africa, so, dissembling this much-lacking in-streaming flood of pure negro ideas, he pumps up his poor English counterfeits from the deeps of his British breast. Thus, too drearily often, English idiom is domesticated on African soil, and the user of it, though he lives for fifty years in the land, will never really to his last day be *in* Africa. "Bantu of the boots," is their phrase for this wooden Anglo-African speech.

CHAPTER V

"Boring in" Farther

"Jog on, jog on, on the footpath way,
　　And merrily hent the stile-a;
A merry heart goes all the way,
　　Your sad tires in a mile-a."

＊　　　　＊　　　　＊

"Still with Sound of Trumpet
Far, far off the daybreak call:
Hark! how loud and clear I hear it wind:
Swift to the Head of the Army,
Swift, spring to your places:
　　Pioneers, O Pioneers!"

＊　　　　＊　　　　＊

"Sometimes a light surprises
　　The Christian while he sings;
It is the Lord Who rises
　　With healing in His wings."

CHAPTER V

"Boring in" Farther

WHEREIN the traveller reads his first lesson in "thinking black," and discovers that to be in Africa the said Africa must be in him.

BIG with fate as these early days in Bihe are, the great event of our real start is now looming in the near future, and our prospective caravan gives us a lot of work. For here in Bihe we find out that the launching of a Far-Interior caravan is as ceremonial a function as the sister ceremony in connection with a British battleship. It seems that just as God gives us the stars and we all make our own astronomy, so Mr. Genus Homo Africanus seizes on a hundred humdrum events and drives the monotony out of them by some formal, fashionable function. This setting out of a Far-Interior caravan, for instance, is one such event, and so orthodox in character that you must begin by ceremonially "going into camp," as the phrase goes. Now, this only means that you formally shake the dust from your feet, by leaving your village hut, and, picking out a bit of forest, you hoist your private flag on the highest

tree : the solemn "Blue Peter" this, notifying all comers
that your land ship has already set out on its long voyage.
Yet, as a matter of fact, the real start is many a month
ahead, but deeds are the only eloquent words in Africa—
and have you not, after all, gone a few formal yards from
village to forest? So, there in the woods, you build a hut,
and out to that camp your prospective carriers troop,
spending the dragging days quizzing you as to proposed
route and destination. One-sided enough this heckling,
for you must be precise and pertinent in your answers,
whereas the negro only responds to your questions in a
vague, non-committal voice. This policy of make-believe,
however, has an excellent effect on the raw negro, who is
all eyes and no ears, and the result is that right off, the
news goes buzzing round the district that the "big devil"
(*Ochindele*) really means business at last. Then comes
the first crowd of volunteers. Be sure you write in pencil,
though, not ink, for generally a few negro wags lead off
by making counterfeit overtures to join your caravan, the
false names being eagerly recorded by the impatient white
man. Merely the "lead pencil" men these, who turn out
to be as visionary as the Secretary of War's "spectral
force," and this crowd soon thins to a trickle of "faithfuls."
One by one your real *Olongamba* (carriers) reluctantly
permit you to write them down, Ham, "the servant of
servants," being for once wholly the master of this situation,
and you of Japheth his grovelling suppliant. His whole
talk in these preliminary days of negotiation is flavoured
with a good spice of negro condescension, for did not this

very black man pick us all up on the Benguella seashore
and carry us, like mere baggage, on and into his own
interior? No wonder, therefore, the whole district from
which you recruit your carriers is converted into a huge
"penny in the slot" machine, for you must put in your
money before anything can be got out of it. Moreover,
this note of independence struck so early and so frankly
in Bihe is continued through the long journey until at
Kavungu there is a real revolt, mine and countermine,
repulse and attack for days. Thus you see what a
masterful mind this Bihean of ours has, the real
"pioneers" being these old blacks, who are not bashful
in reminding us of the fact.

These, moreover, are the needy days when to your
profit and loss you solemnly invest in a "Man Friday."
Cook, Treasurer, and What-not of the caravan, "boy" he
is called, even to his fortieth year. Nor is this compact
between you, his master, and him, your factotum, so
quickly sealed and settled. Fixing you with his fathomless
black eyes, with appalling candour of comment he leads off
by inquiring stonily if you mean to cheat him as the last
Portuguese did, and generally "heckles" you as though you
were a prospective local M.P. His fatal facility for jabber
is such that he almost argues you into the belief that you
will cheat him, his theory of this solemn compact being
that it is all a mere speculation, on the principle of "heads
you get paid, tails you work for nothing." However, after
half a dozen inapposite questions ("temper-testing," it is
called), you close with him, and Man Friday, very conse-

quential, annexes your pots and pans with much slamming
and banging.   A child of earthenware utensils, what sweet
music there is to him in the bang of an iron pot.   This in
fact is the very thing that makes him careless, for with his
own fragile native thing he must be high-strung and careful even to trembling.   But a donkey must be coaxed
with carrots, and this culinary compact is generally signed,
sealed, and delivered by a sort of " taking the shilling " on
his part—calico, not cash, being the currency.   It must be
white and not dark in colour this fabric, otherwise you
will have symbolised sorrow and not joy.   So you go with
the tempting tide, and having conciliated your friend the
cook (" your mother " is his phrase), off he swaggers to the
native quarters, all glorious in a loin-cloth as white as
the untrodden snow.   You can see that his very way of
donning this white prophecy of happiness is, on his part, a
sort of flourish in the face of fortune by which he, the said
Wanga, defies the future and the fates.   Indeed, as if it
were all a page of Homer, has he not consulted the
" Omens " for a favourable start ?

Does this story drag ?   Blame our negro and let us
move forward—Eastward Ho !   Watch now the rule of
the Far-Interior road.   Yonder a thousand miles from the
Ocean is your objective, and the farther in you " bore "—
that word again—your pilgrim kit necessarily assumes an
austerely simple aspect.   Like ballooning in cloudland, the
higher you want to ascend the more ballast you must
throw out, and even so with this Far-Interior caravan
of ours.   At the Mildmay prayer meeting did not that

pious lady whose house had been burgled the night before return thanks to the Lord that "He had made her lighter for the upward flight"? And we too had been robbed, not by person but by place, for our last and nearest bank lay far behind on the Benguella shore. Praise Him, £ s. d. is demonetized in those early days, and the only cheque-book you can reckon upon is God's own blank cheques, your Bible. Did not Billy Bray love to say, "The promises of God are just as good as ready money any day"? So the fact gradually soaked into our souls that we could only run the race set before us as we laid aside every weight. Such surely was the pinch of this particular party. Narrow indeed is the way that leadeth into the Far Interior. In this exceptionally hard year the Garenganze trail is indeed a narrow cork-screw thing, and our far-off goal can only be gained by a minimum of "dead loads." Two pairs of boots, two shirts, and (oh luxury!) just two or three humble handfuls of tea for the long journey and longer imprisonment ahead. The pity of it, such a pauper provision of tea for the days of acclimatisation lying in wait for us. At first, this terrible tea was reserved only for the high solemnities of our vagabond life. As the days of depletion advanced on us, however, and the tea nearly finished, it was only by the feeling of a sudden plunge into profligacy we dared to drink a coward cup of straw-coloured tea. Crouching like a devotee at a shrine, before a smoky fire, your Missionary, in the most appropriate of kneeling attitudes for such a function, brewed his "cup that cheers" with all the solemnity of a high priest offering an oblation.   Even long after that last tea-masking had given out, we were still, with a tragic intensity, boiling and reboiling the useless leaves, for the sixth time certainly.   Nor did we fail to get at least white steaming cups of best "Memory Blend," for the tea was so weak that it had to be imagined.   Long afterwards we roasted a native pea into supposititious coffee, but to the end this poor substitute was a doctor's dose, not a "cup that cheers" but a sort of pharmaceutical preparation.

But our real problem is not Africa but the African. Wouldst thou have a key to "thinking black"?   Then look at him.

Paul was accused of turning the world upside down, but if you mix enough with these natives and use your eyes a bit, an hour of it will suffice to give you the notion that you are standing on your head, life is all so upside down.   Yonder is a ferryman in his boat, but see the black turning tables on the white by placing his back to the stern, face to the bow, and off he starts paddling as though he were stirring his porridge, not his canoe. Laugh you first, but he laughs last; for to him, what sense is there in a white man looking one way and rowing another?   Wise?   Nay, he shakes his head and opines we Europeans are wise, but our wisdom is rather showy than exact.   The black man, he thinks, is wiser than he seems, and the white one seems wiser than he is.   No wonder this looking-one-way-and-rowing-another attitude of the white man becomes the negro's parable for an inconsistent Missionary. Why does he not go in the direction he looks ? Why preach this and practise that ?

It is now raining, be it noted, and the problem stands how to save his bare black body from the cold; very adroitly he draws into shore and dips deep in the water to get out of the wet. For the fisher law is that being wet you must get wetter in order to get dry. Watch now the same man land in the reeds, donning his clothing. Out there in the piercing cold he was as bare as the blast that stung him, but now ashore when the sun scorches he can be seen sporting not one but two sets of garments, the whole surmounted with a mighty blanket of many hues. Now watch the same man beginning to cultivate. There he is gripping his spade, and digging away in the opposite manner to ours—that is to say, he digs towards and not away from himself. Of course, after sending the earth flying at this rate, he is now dirty, but that means he is white; for a negro is black when he is clean and white when he is dirty.

Give him, if you dare, a book to read, and he will surely hold it upside down. Watch him with a pencil affecting a fair and clerkly handwriting, and he is sure to begin the prank from right to left. Ask him now for a drink of water, and being the very pink of courtesy he must take first drink, the gourd-cup receiving a loud labrose smack as first gulp. Reeking of resultant *aroma Africanum*, you may now have *your* sip, for has he not guaranteed the said water pure from poison, as saith their proverb, "Drink first, die first"? Even the almanac turns somersault, for here is an African winter as hot as an Indian summer sweeping over the country like a fire : a conundrum in human speech, "a fiery freezing winter." Watch now the same negro produce a pair of ancient boots, and carefully as fastidiously lace them up with bark rope—surely this time he is going to be normal at last. Not he, for quite solemnly he produces an old pair of socks and wears them outside his boots. The same man again sports a starched shirt once white, but now unredeemedly vile, a vision of smudges. Down dips the sun and out come the stars, but the tale of topsy-turvyism is not yet finished. There is your old Northern friend the "Great Bear" on the horizon, but this time he is upside down. Sprawling on his back in a manner most undignified for a respectable constellation, he is one more instance of the somersault ways of this queer land.

(*Later.*)

But stay. These upside-down doings are not yet complete.

The scene again changes, but not the subject. Enters a young slip of a girl who has been beaten for no fault of hers, yet never a tear does she shed : no tears mark you, and no crime did she commit. On plying them with questions, I find that far from her innocence being conjectural they blandly admit she did nothing worthy of stripes. Yet she got them all, forty *plus* more, and the curiously candid confession is that because she was innocent therefore was she beaten with many stripes. It now comes out that the African can wriggle out of even this injustice, the explanation being that the girl is a twin, and as her sister did the deed they must be beaten in pairs ; not either nor neither, but both or none. Twins they were born and twins they live and die. So mad are the Africans on this twin subject that even when Miss First gets married, the bridegroom is forced to marry her twin-sister Miss Second on the same day. (Although these sisters are slim little things, yet literally their names are Miss Elephant and Miss Hippo, all twins being forced to take these two traditional titles.) There was a case here where twin-brothers were forced to marry the same lady, so inexorably operates this dogging law. Right up from birth each has ever haunted the other, their food being scrupulously divided into two, the twin bairns with twin portions. In proffering them a gift you must sternly make it a two-handed one, simultaneously holding out both arms to both recipients. When a twin sickens mortally no doctor may be called nor any medicine administered, all mourning being deprecated. God, they say, did this deed of creating "terrible twins," and God must kill or cure them. The only way to wish them well is by cursing them, and these cursings the complacent twins receive as choice compliments. The hapless father and mother likewise get all the town abuse, each vituperation being a sort of upside-down blessing. Yet these are the very folks who would throw the old anti-Paul taunt at us about turning the world upside-down. Dare to suggest to them this, and Mr. African at once engages in a very unfavourable

diagnosis of the mental state of a " white " who can
hazard such nonsense.

(19th June 1890.)

Here comes June, and the time to be up and off.
Across a brook, on the third, we[1] wave good-bye to kind
Mr. and Mrs. Arnot, and away East we go, off and out
of Bihe.   Just in time, too, for war is brewing, the
Bihean bent on giving his last national kick at the
Portuguese.   More than that : this brewing storm breaks
behind our backs, and we are swept before it, not out
to the Ocean—that has storms enough—but into our
long-loved, long-lived-in Interior.   My old friend Senhor
Silva Porto, Capitao Mor, seeing trouble ahead, resolved
on sudden suicide, and blew himself up with gunpowder.
A dramatic death this.   Six barrels of gunpowder lined
out as deathbed, the said six covered with a drapery of
Portuguese flags, the old Portuguese topping it all as sad-
hearted sacrifice.   Up went the famous explorer in an
explosion, and down went the old Bihe dynasty in that
same smash.   For this death of Silva Porto must be
avenged.   Too long ignored by his own nation, too long
despised by the Biheans, here is his solution to force the

---

[1] *Peccavi !* I find I have been remiss in my introductions—who are the
" We "?   In the sequence of seniority the names are Messrs. Thompson, Lane,
and "the writer," a mere boy in those days.   A threefold cord not easily
broken, we were utter strangers to each other at the start and represented
the three nationalities of our race.   Yet I can recall with delight the splendid
lives these good men lived before my eyes, the consummate fellowship being a
treasure.   Mere rules and regulations in Africa are a poor enough guarantee
for a tranquil time, but if love be the fulfilling of the whole law, then love
guided by the Word of God is better than any code of laws.

THE ETERNAL PROBLEM:
"How to Cross."

Government's hands. And, sure enough, Bihe was broken : Captain Paiva's joint expedition of Portuguese and Boers came on the scene, the king captured and carried off to San Tome. There the wild Atlantic is Portugal's surest sentinel on that lonely isle ; there the slaves find themselves so hopelessly locked in for life that they eat earth for suicide.

This is how we take the great plunge. An Ombala, or Chief's town, rests upon the top of the rather steep slope slanting down to the sandy Kwanza beach, crowded with " dugouts." But this ramshackle village is so very much the key to the crossing that you must enter by its front gate, wriggle through the huts of the malodorous town to effect your exit on the shore. We don't stand long, however, ere there files down to the beach a long trading caravan, waving the big flag of little Portugal, and this with ours makes a fine babel in bidding for canoes. Meantime, Messrs. Thompson and Lane have crossed to receive our loads, while I remain for three mortal hours to direct the crossing. Then (Heaven-sent chance !) the old broken-backed chief comes down, and we sit cheek by jowl chatting Christianity. With one foot in the grave, here is a withered old man treating you to a long, disconcerting scrutiny, and quizzing incredulously as to our Garenganze Gospel venture. We yet await classification, it seems ; we are not traders, nor raiders, therefore he cannot get at us, cannot " place " us. The only category he can conceive is that of the " people who live by doing nothing." The Vachokwe tribe, next-

6

door neighbours but one, kindly allowing for a probable touch of African sun, called us the *Afulu*, or "Softies," this because we refuse to point a business-looking revolver at their nose. Farther East still we were dubbed "The God-ites" because we preach the Gospel, and sometimes "The Feminines" because we refuse to spill blood. With his bunch of charms round the neck, you can see it is all—Church of God, for shame!—so bewilderingly new, newness being naturally the bar sinister of African thought. Antiquity in Africa means sanctity, remember: a tremendous affair this antiquity, a religion almost. "An old well-worn path must lead up to a big chief" is their way of saying that their millions of a majority ("the well-worn path" of precedent) has out-voted you and your Christianity. You, a mere Mission-ary in the microscopic minority of one, where is your well-beaten track of precedent inspiring the traveller's confidence? With your white skin and creaking boots, he looks at you as though, perchance, you were the denizen of another planet. Oh! drop with me a tear for the poor old men and women of Africa who hug their fetishes, and whose hearts are the dwellings of night. They have a weird way of waving you off, as much as to say, "Too late! It is not for me." Can their idea be, that as the grave is so soon to receive their dust, why should they offer Christ the wreck of their souls? The sad old tell-tale faces seem each to say, with a wail :—

> "Look in my face: my name is 'Might have been';
> I am also called 'No more,' 'Too late,' 'Farewell.'"

It is in talking with all such that the Missionary hears the bugle call of the long-coming struggle ahead—I mean the lack of conviction of sin. Unlike a man in England, cradled in Gospel privilege, here we meet thousands of souls who cannot feel remorse, for they are only the children of their dark ancestors who lived and died in darkness. Ask such an one if he is at peace with God, and he, a negro who was never sick or sorry in his life, will answer with alacrity that he never quarrelled with Him. No wonder that peace had to be "made" for such, apart from their opinion on the matter. They themselves say of true conviction of sin, "A shivering man does not need to be forced to the fire," and this is the reason there has been no authentic weeping for sin in any African Mission until a preliminary period of evangelical witness has been passed. Then the tears begin to glisten over personal (not tribal, this time) responsibility.

(Later.) [1]

Across the gulf of twenty years, ours is the pure untarnished joy to see many such old folk rejoicing in the evening of life. Their morning broke grey and their mid-day was dark and stormy, but the glory of this evening sunset blots out the memory of their gloom. When one beholds the sacred sight of a group of grey woolly heads in a meeting, listening with a glaze over their eyes and a fog over their souls, one feels stirred anew to press on. They

[1] Occurring, as it does, quite often, this " Later " indicates that the section of the narrative it introduces is subsequent in time but similar in character to the conditions of the context.

believe, some of these old dears, believe with aged bodies
and childhood hearts.   Summer has come late to them,
no doubt, but it is the summer of God that knows no
winter.   There they are, crooning an old "Golgotha"
song of Christ's dying pangs.   Pitched on the wrong key,
notes all out, yet I defy you to deny that they are
singing sense into that holy hymn.

(20*th August.*)

It is notorious that our African is a congenital liar,
and here comes an example.   Breaking your way along
the trail, any native travellers you encounter make
strange temporising manœuvres until convinced you
come peaceably.   A party of six carrying food signals
us a long distance off, and their plan is literally to
"hedge" us.   Immediately all the baskets are in hiding
in the grass, along with five of the party who lie flat
with bated breath, while No. 6, a bolder spirit he, comes
slowly along the path till we accost him.   His story is
always a stupid concoction of lies, not at all cleverly
spun, but palpably false; not mere "embroidery," that
is to say, but the lie circumstantial.   When, however, you
divulge your identity as peaceful nobodies, away to the
winds go his fears, and he coolly whistles up his friends
in hiding, utterly regardless of the lie-direct this ugly
appearance of theirs gives to his sheepish story.   Nor is
our rascal ashamed one tiny bit.   For with eyes liquid
with mirth he—just a plain everyday liar—enjoys it all,
and sees no sting in the suggestion that he is one of the
greatest tale-tellers within the confines of the solar

system. Suggest that he is a silly liar and he will soon
prove that he is a master of the art by arguing that there
was no "cuteness" in thus frankly owning up : is not the
man who sticks to one lie forced to invent twenty more to
maintain that one ?   So there is a method in this madness
after all.   (Remember the sub-title of this book should be :
"The Blacks as bad as the Whites.")   When, however,
the English negrophobes proceed to prove from this that
such a long liar cannot be a man but a monkey, then it is
—just then !—this very negro proves from his very mode
of mendacity that he is a Britisher's own brother.   For,
baffling personality though he be, this black man backs
his lie with blasphemy, à la Whitechapel, dragging down
the name of God into the mud of mendacity, " As sure as
G——! " the famous formula of his sin.   Why is it that
lost blacks like "found " whites all sharpen the point of a
lie with the name of God and thus drive it home ?   Yet
they inconsistently laugh at our preaching about God.
There is no God to worship, no God to serve, no God to
pray to—only a God to swear by.

   To prove that this is no mere subjective notion on a
Missionary's part, this black link with England becomes
realistic when you see that same negro draw his finger
across his throat, the accompanying formula being that
old refuge of lies : " As sure as death ! "   Verily the
whole world is kin, for here is a black man sighting a
white skin for the first time in his life.   Watch, too, that
parting quip he throws at you just as he disappears into
the grass.   Like a naughty British schoolboy off he goes,

pulling down his brown eyelid with mock-anxious solicitude as to there being any green therein.

*   *   *

We now swing from melodrama to grim tragedy, and
here is a stern old priest who has just killed his young
brother, yet not the least concerned. A famous decocter
of poisons, his brother was chased into his own village by
some neighbours who accused him of theft. The grim
old priest listened to his brother's protestations of innocence, then, spreading out his hands pontifically, said in
really a relieved voice, " Oh ! then, if thou art innocent,
thou wilt drink this poison ordeal to justify thyself."
So, suiting the way to the words, this son of the witch
of Endor, with the blind and magnificent enthusiasm of
their cult, asked his beloved younger brother to enter the
house, passed in the lethal cup, a few minutes sufficing to
kill his man. Meanwhile, love or no love, here is the old
priest spurning that very corpse of the victim-brother, his
belief being that inherent righteousness is so mighty that
it can neutralise even the deadliest drug. His brother
beloved, therefore, died with a lie in his breast—" We
can do nothing against the truth," is the saying of these,
the world's greatest liars. In plain English, here you
have the impudent paradox that where lying abounds
there, even there, truth—in theory—much more abounds.

So here comes the conundrum : How can a nation of
liars consistently believe we can do nothing against the
truth, locked up in a falsely accused man's breast ? If he
is innocent he will not die. Plied the old priest with

questions, but at the end we were no nearer than the poles, for he stuck to it that neither fire, nor water, nor poison could kill by ordeal a really just man. So, instead of burial, the body was condemned to what is called "witch cremation," the smoke and flame ascending "to feed the stars." With the slight stammer that gives a charming emphasis to his remarks, here is an old liar preaching to me a homily on the Truth, a subject he knows very little about, for sure am I his telegraphic address is not "Veracity, Africa." The Arab's version of this negro inconsistency runs thus : " A crow exclaimed, God is the Truth." "Then," quoth the listeners, "the dirt-scraper has turned preacher."

(Later.)

See how the Devil outwits the Devil. Two hours antecedent to my pitching camp, there had been a foul murder. Constructive, premeditated butchery, the very devilishness of this deed created quite an atmosphere for my message. The long-smothered tribal conscience begins to assert itself, and for two long days they hang on my evangel, the whole being uttered in a conciliating I-do-not-talk-to-you-but-with-you kind of tone. They now actually wince at the very thought of death, they, the wantons, who otherwise would have been nonchalant. Every mention I make of it is a jag to the murderers, and if they are not prepared to think of death they are not prepared to meet him, for if the shadow alarms them what of the reality ? Yes, murder will out. I came on the trail of a butchery of three travellers, husband, wife, and son. A tiny thing proved the clue, and soon this hidden horror was heard crying out to Heaven as loud as the blood of Abel. The whole thing would have been hid— one of the many mysteries of the marshes—had not a young woman died at Chisenga, the usual Ñanga being called in to consult the oracle as to cause of death. This old " borderland professional" (their local title, this) was not lacking in the true bloodhound instinct of scenting a trail. Ringing up the underworld for information, the oracle himself replied that the girl had died a natural death, yet some other dead people were crying from the ground for vengeance. And now the " devil-doctor" turns fierce on his clients and upbraids them for hiding even a little from him : " Confess and I absolve," cried he. " Look at the poisonous cassava we eat as tribal diet : by soaking it in water it loses its deadly effect, and so, too, with that bitter secret of murder in your breast, pour it out to your priest and it will lose its sting !" But still they are obdurate, so the old doctor snaps his fingers at them, says that he is a man of many means, and again rings up the oracle, with the result that it all comes out. For during her illness that dying woman had received kindly care from her husband, and among other things he robed her in a fancy red shawl. " Now," said the wily Ñanga dramatically, " that shawl was a blood-shawl." And sure enough in two ticks he pieced together the genuine data of a triple murder and plunder from this shawl clue. (If one may speak of the light of conscience, then they have got it —just enough to light them to Hell !). The murderer was a canoe-man who found out soon enough that dead men can chase the living both above ground and beneath. These three strangers had come to the ferry seeking a crossing, and soon they were shooting across the creeks to the other side. But as the time passed, the ferryman slowly and surely found himself in the deadly grips of this murderous idea to kill his passengers and grab their goods, particularly that red shawl, *yes, that blood-red shawl.* So he did the deed, speared the lot, and threw the bodies to the crocs. But watch how heaven, earth, and water are leagued against him and sworn into the service of justice as sort of special constables to patrol the lonely marshes. Incredible it all looks, yet you can shudderingly guess what happened—the crocodiles refused to oblige the murderer, and kept well up river near their favourite promenade, the confluence. Next come the quick currents on the scene as sort of Scotland Yard detectives, and away they go at full speed, the three corpses sailing straight for the murderer's own fishing-hut hard on the shore. At dawn, out comes Eugene Aram Africanus, to be confronted with his victims, the long accurate voyage perfectly piloted by God Almighty's own currents. Tableau! N., S., E., and W. that murderer looked before doing the deed, looked everywhere—except UP. And, of course, this is only half of the story, for the expectant hostess, seeing the days pass, suspects foul play. There are currents on land as well as on water, and people's tongues will wag. And just as the river currents brought the corpses home to the murderer, so these land currents of gossip brought the charge home to him too—was ever man so hemmed in by a fence of his own contriving ?

*   *   *

The monkeys, scared off our route, are rare as small : you must push East with us to the Lufira Valley to see their frolics. There it was I found a whole town in the terror of a monkey battle, big yellow fellows who stand up to a man and fight him. With all the ready resources and fine tact of his tribe, this long-tailed monkey apes the biped in many things, particularly the deft breaking off a stick to thrash a man. Yonder in the dark grove of trees fringing the cornfields, the whole yellow regiment have mobilised for three days' campaign —sort of anti-corn-laws crusade, call it. The trouble is, however, that in monkeydom they are not all birds of a feather who so flock together, and when they are not fighting the natives they are having a wild time together, monkey *versus* monkey. One chap, two inches taller or two ounces heavier than his fellow, must have a wipe at his junior—the old tale this, that the common attraction drawing them together makes them less attractive to each other. Beaten off a hundred times from the ripening corn, there they are with a chastened optimism still entrenched in the grove for a night sortie, and the moon high in the west will see a victory the sun denied them. The field-owners are so philosophic over this annual attack that they call it the monkeys "tithing the corn." Followed up to their grove, these animals know so well the rules of the game, that they greet the negroes with

showers of stones, some of which strike home.   But there
is a monkey ambulance idea, the most human touch of
all.   When a negro wounds his monkey with an arrow,
in a jiffy the army-surgeon of the quadrupeds whips up
the wounded monkey, spits vigorously over the spot, tears
off a morsel of bark from a tree, and rubs in the resultant
medicine, spitting and rubbing again and again for a
cure.

But the biter often gets bit in this business, and
during the lean days of famine I found Master Monkey
himself make excellent emergency eating : have enjoyed
dozens of them soaked in banana vinegar.   Nevertheless,
a long good-bye to monkey stew.   Never no more.   The
last I shot got his bullet in the breast ; but standing bolt
upright, he tragically put his hand on the red oozing
blood, and three times thrilled me by pointing indignantly
at his wounds.   Like a K.C. for the prosecution, "*J'accuse*," those three mute but eloquent appeals to his
wounds stabbed me with remorse.   To recall the re-
proachful glances from the large, liquid, mild eyes of a
dying antelope is bad enough, but here is something with
vastly more sting in it.   Another and cuter monkey
avoided death and the subsequent dinner by—what do
you think ?—point-blank theatrically refusing to be shot.
Seeing the gun levelled at him, he puckered his brows
with incredulity, and waving his arms with indignation
defied the hunter to commit such an unheard-of crime.
" Me ? who ever killed my kind ? " he seemed to say.
Needless to add, down came the unshot barrel, and off

stalked Mr. Monkey, an easy winner. Why not? He alone of all the forest fauna has learned the law of the lever : he alone uses a stick to prise open a box-lid.

I wonder, in a way, if these negroes learn their gestures from the local monkeys. Amid all the jabber of rival dialects the best because most eloquent sort of lingo is this language of negro gesture, arms waving in the wind like semaphores. Not the zigzag movements of an excited Frenchman this, nor yet the impoverished expedients of deaf-mutes : here, I say, you have a serious vocabulary of gesture, with deep abstract ideas stinging you with sarcasm. The mechanics of African speech this, so to speak ; the pulley and lever and screw of conversation. O that magician wave of the negro hand ! With it they demand, they promise, they call, refuse, interrogate, admire, reckon, confess, repent, express fear, express shame, express doubt, instruct, command, unite, encourage, swear, testify, accuse, condemn, acquit, insult, despise, defy, disdain, flatter, applaud, bless, abuse, ridicule, reconcile, recommend, exalt, regale, gladden, complain, afflict, discomfort, discourage, astonish, exclaim, indicate silence, and what-not ; with a variety and multiplication that keep pace with the tongue. And yet we, the progeny of John Bull, dare to talk for hours with hands down in the pits of our pockets ! Take, for instance, such an everyday thing as the pointed finger thus : ☞ What is the true African idea of such a gesture ? Well, here's a thing so deeply abstract that it could drown you in its depths of irony. Certainly you will be very chary of

A TYPICAL "MOP" HEAD-DRESS.

pointing your finger in future. For in this action what do you do if not point *one* finger only at the black man, and *three* at yourself? So ho! you are trebly as bad as the man you point at. Else, why point *one* only at him and bend back *three* on yourself? Here, then, is a gesture you must solemnly schedule in your lexicon as The-Hypocrisy-so-vile-that-it-accuses-another-of-an-evil-it-itself-possesses-three-times-stronger.[2] The moral of all this is that the Missionary who goes round an African village pointing his accusing finger at the negro ☞ is really accusing himself in a three-to-one degree. Are they ungrateful? Then we the finger-pointers are trebly so ☞. Do we warn them to forget not all His benefits? Then our very gesture is a threefold warning to do likewise.

(Later.)

Cut off from your nearest shop by hundreds of miles, what a fuss there is before you shoot supper. Emerging on our last stream for the day, we find it, not flowing, but only dilly-dallying through a green meadow dotted all over with red buck. Corresponding with, but by no manner of means resembling, an English butcher's shop, these *qui vive* antelopes out on the plain are the only chance we have of filling our pots for supper. A sort of local "penny in the slot" meat-machine this, warranting rich, red cutlets. Only instead of the unknown penny, you slip a cartridge into the slot of your rifle and, click! drops dead your antelope. So much, and no more, for the local

[2] ☞ ! ! ! ! ! ! !

meat-shop; now for your Luban bedroom. Yonder it is hidden discreetly on the edge of a thicket in the same old sixpence of a hamlet built on pestilential soil, and there, in the dust, we must sleep the sleep of the just. The deepening darkness, however, forces us to postpone our supper-shot till the morrow, and lying down genuinely "meat hungry" we dream of a morning fry of juicy venison "fixings." The sun rose, and so did we; but our brave butcher's shop has vanished in the night, dashing for dear life. For in the moonlight ("There goes our breakfast," thought I), wuff! wuff! came a pack of jackals scurrying through the meadow, chasing those antelopes for their lives; miles and miles they pant, heaving flanks and gaping, dribbly mouths telling how terror-struck are the buck.

Nothing reminiscent of England here; no copse and hedgerow, no down and moor, no slate roof and grey spire; a wilder, denser look everywhere, and just so much more interesting. Farewell the gas, glare, and paint of thy shops, O Albion! Shops, did I say? The African never dreamed the shop-idea, and only very grudgingly will he be so kind as to barter you an evening meal, kind for kind. But—shop or no shop—fish I want and fish I resolve to have, for their tell-tale bones are strewn all over the town. The Chief tried to brazen the matter out, but with stony severity I met his every no, no, no, with my sanguine yes, yes, yes. " All right," said he wearily, " if fish you must have, fish I must find, so just wait *till I poison some for you.*" Right off he picks

the beans, then powders them with a pestle, then shuts
off an arm of his river, throwing this poison-powder
therein, then in half an hour, behold! fifty white-bellied
fish floating dead to order in the poisoned pool.   Fish we
wanted, and fish we get.   But not now—by no means
now.

CHAPTER VI

Eastward Ho!

"I hungered for Hell. I pushed into the midst of it in the East End of London. For days I stood in those seething streets, muddy with men and women, drinking it all in and loving it all. Yes, I loved it because of the souls I saw. One night I went home and said to my wife: 'Darling, I have given myself, I have given you and our children to the service of these sick souls.' She smiled and took my hand, and we knelt down together. That was the first meeting of the Salvation Army."

GENERAL BOOTH.

•   •   •

"But all through the mountains, thunder-riven,
    And up from the rocky steep,
  There arose a cry to the gate of Heaven,
    'Rejoice! I have found My sheep!'
  And the angels echoed around the throne,
  'Rejoice! for the Lord brings back His own.'"

CHAPTER VI

Eastward Ho!

IN which, at last, the reader is up and off over the Kwanza River, thereby taking the formal "header" into the Far Interior.

To push far beyond the Kwanza from the seaboard means that vast savannahs are encountered that could easily swallow a hundred missions. Thousands of miles rolling ahead, and all guiltless of gates and hedges; a land that could swallow up millions and still wait open-mouthed for more. Scarcely one lock and key in the land, the usual means of opening a door being the butt-end of a gun. Rather like Sir Thomas More's "Utopia" this : did he not stipulate that no door in his ideal State should be locked? For years and years, fancy sleeping with unlocked doors in Africa : how does this tickle the conceit of England with its bolts and bars? In one backward glance you see that England as a parish is only a spoilt and petted child of privileged preaching. Your roots are merely in a flower-pot, and not in a real roomy soil. How different the feeling when this wide, weary Africa begins to open up before you in yawning expanses of Gospel silence! But note withal a curious thing. This advancing into Africa seems to have a strange reciprocal effect on a new-comer. Day by day, what in fact is happening is that Africa invades you a metaphoric mile, the Dark Continent flooding your insular English being at every pore. The first thing to haunt the Missionary, for instance, is the silent sarcasm in the relative disparity of mileage, Africa *versus* England; and the mental map you find yourself making of the huge land has always at the bottom corner an ironical inset of "England on the same scale." To make a good picture, remember, you must come back far enough to catch the true focus, and here in the black bush we certainly seem to see our tiny, much-divided England in true perspective.

Let me say it a second time—that 16th of August will ever remain a red-letter day among our African dates— we crossed the Kwanza River. For here is our real Rubicon, the great line of tribal cleavage, and at this point we take the technical "header" into the Far Interior. So sharp, indeed, this line of demarcation that the first native you meet on the off-bank is labelled "a heathen or Gentile" by his own pot-black brother the Bihean. *Ochingangela* is the term, and there is sting in it. Curious solidarity of the race this preaches, for here we discover the black sons of Adam to be such born Pharisees that each African tribe thinks its neighbour only a coarse "Gentile" mob. Tit for tat, right across

Africa, and thence right round the globe, these taunt names are passed along the line, each tribe sporting its rags of righteousness at the expense of the other. Of course it is always the next man who is the alleged "bad 'un," nay, never, never No. 1. The Bihean eats dogs, and the Luban eats snails, therefore each reviles the other on this touchy point of tribal diet. The true trade-mark this, of all negro Pharisees—

> "Compound for sins they are inclined to,
> By hating those they have no mind to."

The Luban, in order to eat man more comfortably, calls outsiders Vahemba; ask him if he eats "man," and he will say, "Oh no! I do not eat man; I only eat Vahemba." That is to say, only the Luban is a man, and a Gentile a Muhemba. No random idea this taunt title, if you please, for you may choose your coast of entrance, East or West, and find Africa full of a Pharisee who never saw Jerusalem. The abrupt first day's climb of the West Coast or the gradual ascent of the Zanzibar side in the East; yes, choose either, for the whole world is akin. First comes the sleek Swahili man, as black and as negroid as any. Now in his raw estate was he not altogether lighter than vanity, and did not the Arabs from Muscat call him a Kaffir? And did he not meekly and mildly swallow the dose without a murmur? And being immensely pleased with his own dear self, does not this pride in himself make the usual demand on the "other" man? Therefore, being a Pharisee of the good old international stock, he, scorning a contaminating touch, dubs all Interior natives beyond the pale " Wasenshi," the flouting glance of the negro eye being the best lexicon-meaning of the word.

On and inward we travel, following our "will o' the wisp," ever following but never finding the "heathen" man of our quest. The Munyamweshi, for instance, is ostensibly one of Mr. Arab's "Wasenshi," but this burly Interior man denies identity — phew! the imaginary envelope has been misdirected evidently. Take this man, now, for a guide to find the unfindable "heathen" and note what befalls you on the westward journey. Himself called a Musenshi by the snob Swahili, he too swallowed the dose meekly as mildly, and now prepares the potion for the next man. Listen to this often chanted word Munabushi he is using, with a lordly sweeping gesture; don't, please, yawn as I tell you that this is the same old sing-song of Pharisaism, heathenising everybody except himself. And so our old friend " Barbarian " rolls on and on, black tit answering black tat with mournful monotony, for every Roland an Oliver, for every Quid a Quo. What! even the cannibals? Yes, even the Lubans do not differ; for across their Mupaka, or tribal border, they throw the epithet "uncircumcised" at all comers; *Muhemba!* is the shot they fire at you.

Reflection : The Missionary in preaching does not need to dig up the famous old fossil Pharisee of Jerusalem as a relic of antiquity. He has the real and genuine thing all around.

(*25th August.*)

Do we sleep in tents? Nay, but we creep into our tiny grass huts at sundown, and roll out our rugs on a Robert-the-Bruce mattress of fresh grass or leaves. Far, far cosier than a flapping tent, the wildest tornado in the night roars past, leaving you snug asleep in your grass den. Contrast a poor " Edgington " rocking in the gale like a ship at sea, the fly ballooning in the breeze. Besides, the wild wind swishing through, with the rattle of the rain on the tent, rousing you out of sleep. The necessary fireless-ness of a tent, too. Therefore for snugness *plus* security *plus* the faggot fire in it, give me a grass hut. In a few minutes you can get snug with the knowledge of an old campaigner, and your weary carriers have the same jaded joy. I heard one of these drop his load at sundown, saying :—

" Hurrah ! welcome, O night !
I don't need to carry the night."

But don't misunderstand, please ; I am only arguing for a roadside hole to sleep in, and not a house as domicile. For years—and more of this anon [1]—we have fought the negro on this housing question with almost incredibly successful results. Their average beehive hut is a verminating hole, a den of disease, and indeed the most valuable characteristic of that heathen hut is just this impossibility of living in it : it drives you into the fresh air. Prefer the hut, and you will be bitten all night by large fat—— but need we discuss the exact zoological

[1] See p. 445 *post.*

designation of these creatures ? These pests are legion, and what with our own creeping pace of travel by day, coupled with these other creeping things by night, I dreamed two nights in succession a curious jumble of a dream—a vision this of a large roomy railway station placarded all over with monster advertisements, "Keating's Powder." The railway, one opines, stood for a rebuke to our caravan's creeping pace, and "Keating's" was—well, for the other creepers.

But "he jests at scars who never felt a wound," and I would hereby emphasise the fact that a tent is next to necessary for the inclemencies of the rainy season travel. Even as early as the 9th of July surprise rains caught me in a forest with not a yard of canvas for cover and not one straw of grass for a thatch. The annual grass fires only the other day had roared through the land, licking up every stock of long grass suitable for hut-thatching— all, all swept off the face of the country, only green leaves remaining, under which we crouch for shelter. Down pours that ruthless rain, until the most promising of fires soon goes clean out,—first red, then yellow, then the bleak little blue flames, your firewood finally ceasing to smoke. What next ?—muse on your miseries ? Why, of course, sing :—

> "It ain't no use to grumble or complain,
>   'Tis just as cheap and easy to rejoice ;
> When God sorts out the weather and sends rain,
>   Why ! rain's my choice."

However, even an African cannot sing for eight hours,

and in fact, a few hours later, misery is depicted on his plucky black face, for he sees no prospect of an evening meal ahead. Everything for miles around soaked and as unignitable as asbestos. Caught in the rain, and five miles in the rear, my poor old bed-man is sounding the depths of desolation, crouching under a leaky umbrella-like tree, the dark night settling down on him in the cheerless forest, *sans* fire, *sans* food, *sans* hope. Philosopher to the last, this old man could even defend that pertinacious pour lashing him in fury. "We had a race for it," said he, "the rain and I, but the rain got home first." This July downpour, however, is quite rare, and the Garenganze rule is that only after October the African sky is too damp a ceiling to sleep under. Blue, serenely blue, for a solid six months, here is a sky never once out of temper, never once sulky and sour like your English one.

Have we tinned provisions? Not a box. We make old Africa produce its coarse meal—remarkable neither for its quantity nor quality—and *nolens volens*, on this repellent "mush" one dares to dine. No cook on earth could make what might be indulgently called a loaf out of this meal, and in order to manipulate that sodden cereal properly what was needed was the far subtler mysteries of a magician, not a cook. (Ladies may well smile at this statement, for as a matter of fact the deft white fingers of the first lady to penetrate the Interior made delectable pancakes with this very meal!) With a daily diet cut down almost to the level of a black slave's, our imperious appetite makes us long to seize this Africa by the throat and wring a few of its menu secrets from it. But, alas! Africa, beyond the boast of a heady, frothy beer, has no culinary secrets to hide. In later days another of the impatient expedients was the boiling of triumphant bush dumplings, "Jack Horners," for if you put in your thumb you could not pull out the proverbial plum. "Go to! let us have a 'sinker,'" was the pathetic prophecy of indigestion ahead. Nevertheless, ours it is even here to build an Ebenezer by each of these cookery cannon-balls, and to record thankfully that we who did partake of them are still alive and well. So unlike Paul in all our other ways, it is delightful for us to think that just here we have stolen a march on him—I mean that, unlike ourselves, Paul never left his natal climate zone or average national dietary.

(26th August.)

Day by day, this African looking through you like glass. Day by day, that relentless negro stare. Thus you see us confronted with a painful and even awful aspect of this winning of first-generation Africans for Christ : I mean the innocent way they take you for their walking and talking Bible : "an epistle, known and read of all men." They read you off like a page of large easy print and come to quick calculating conclusions. At least Mr. Aboriginal has two eyes in his head, and behind the said eyes he has just enough brains to suspect that a Missionary's life and lips should agree. "So we preached and so ye believed" is only half of the story, for they copy you *in toto*, the very gesture and the twang reproduced with a fearful fidelity. Quite unconscious of the trend of the thing, you have in Africa hundreds of little groups who are unwittingly " the Smithites " and " the Jonesites " and " the Brownites," according to the varying names and fads of their various and varying Missionaries.

*   *   *

A vile negro calling you " O Lord God ! " is a reminder that the deepest wound a Missionary regularly receives in Africa is when his good is evil spoken of. Take the late sainted Benjamin Cobbe as an example. Here was a holy man sent from God, if ever God sent a man to the Garenganze. Welcoming him to the country, I met him at the Lualaba crossing, a white, fragile-looking traveller, with a Pauline gleam in his eye. " Have come to pay my debt ! " said he, with a winning smile, and there you have the whole story in two words—that white fever face trying, but failing, to kill that glad smile. This Africa of ours, mark you, is far too captious on the subject of what kind of body you bring into it—the same sorry Africa that cares not one little bit whether you have a soul at all.

And so, short and sharp was the course Cobbe ran, for it is quite true what the forest proverb says : " The straightest trees are the first felled." Calm and cultured, he was not one of the boisterous " Oh-be-joyful ! " sort of saint, yet did he walk with God, and got the heavenly face. His motto was : " To grow up, you must grow down "; and a fine thing, indeed, God got out of him.

Watch the sequel. This holy man, if you please, had drunk so deeply of God's wine of joy—the new wine that came to him last in life—that it kept him going at high pressure right on to the end. The new wine, in fact, was busily at work breaking up his old bottle of a body, for when these two meet in Africa then one of the two must be lost, but that one thing will never be the new wine— that is hid with Christ in God. So the fragrant saint died at his post, the " old skin bottle " broken in a ferment of fever. Africa got the holy dust, and God received him into glory. He foresaw it all—saw certain death ahead, yet resolved to pay his debt to the heathen. So endeth Phase No. 1.

Now, far from this being a *de mortuis nil nisi bonum* panegyric, here we come to the curious sequel. I have called his a fragrant life ; but as the years passed it began to dawn on us that the perfume of Mr. Cobbe's piety had stolen far out beyond our sphere. That gleam of the life eternal so often seen to shoot out of his hazel eyes was far more eloquent than long-winded speech. And, travelling one day in Lubaland, I was appalled to find out that a negro, whom I met, had promoted Mr. Cobbe to the literal rank of a " god." After a few exploring remarks, I ferreted out from the sealed sanctuary of his black breast a little private scheme of salvation he had concocted for his own particular benefit.

And thus, even thus, did the uncanny thing run.

Yes, he had known Mr. Cobbe in the old days— fragrant and holy in word and deed. The memory of

the heavenly things he saw in this saint never left that
negro, and away he went back to Lubaland with " the
living epistle" graven on his mind. " Look up, for we
are going up—and oh, so soon!" was a fond phrase of
Cobbe's, so this negro thought much and long, and knew
that the saint had really gone to God. *That* thing he
had actually seen in him could not be killed by fever.
He had only died into glory as the stars die at sunrise.
Hence the daring idea of this poor benighted soul to
evolve a private religion of his own with Mr. Cobbe as
central " saviour." " Ah!" said the negro, " when I am
in a fix in life this is what I do, I just send up a prayer
to Bwanna Cobbe as mediator, and he will arrange it, for
he has a big say with God." " He will pass it along to
God; he will have a big say with God!" Of course, I
righted his wrong theology. Of course, I deplored and
implored that this was the unkindest cut of all—that this
was stabbing him, not kissing him. But oh! the bitter-
sweet reflection notwithstanding—this that a mere dust-
to-dust man should be chosen as a daysman between God
and his soul : " a living epistle"—a walking and talking
Bible. They saw—may I dare the phrase?—the gleam
of the life eternal shooting out of his honest hazel eyes ;
they *saw*, I say, and they believed in a man of God.
How much more will they believe in the Man in the
Glory, the Man who is Jehovah's Fellow ?

Little wonder that Paul could even hope that " much
more in his absence" the young church of Philippi would
prosper, for, like many an African Missionary, might not

Paul's princely personality attract too much of their gaze ?
Is this, too, the reason why Philip and the first negro convert of this dispensation were so quickly separated from
each other ?   At least neither Paul nor Philip gave them
a wrong start by permitting them to think that they
could lean on them long, for they soon left their young
converts.   Certainly too much coddling of converts on
the Mission Stations has fostered sickliness of soul, the
flippant defence of many a backsliding black at the mines
or Bulawayo being that because there is no Mission there
can be no godliness.   This poor parroty brand of black
is, alas ! too common, and resembles the famous parrot
out on the Tanganyika Plateau who changed masters and
manners twice.   No. 1 was a trader who taught the
bird to swear, and No. 2 a Missionary who taught him to
sing, poor Poll muddling up the swearing and the singing in his old age—out of the same mouth blessing and
cursing ; therewith blessed he God, therewith cursed he
men.   Like Rowland Hill and the drunken man who said
to him, " I'm one of your converts."   " I believe you," was
Rowland's arch reply, "you look like my bungling work."
Far from such negroes having no religion, their Mission
veneer proclaims them to have too much of it—in fact,
the only sensible thing is to tell them that if their religion
does not change them, they should change it.   For if
prayer does not surely make an African leave off sinning,
will not sinning surely make him leave off praying ?
Ignoring Christ's rule of sending out His disciples two by
two, these renegades generally go off alone and pay the

A TYPICAL SOLDIER'S WIFE.

penalty. For the same wind that blows out a candle, only fans two faggots into a flame, and wisdom is thus justified of her children.

(Later.)

Hats off to the African lady, she—brave heart!—is a wonder. Undeniably she is stamped sterling. The negro may laugh at a woman because she has a few ounces less brain than a man, but very often the daughter of Eve makes up in muscle what she lacks in mind. Witness, a woman at the salt-pans who killed her lion as deftly as a man, howbeit the method was quite *à la* Mrs. Beeton. Out on the salt-pans the big earthenware pots are kept boiling all night, with someone lying out to tend the fire. A widow she happened to be. Past midnight the fires had gone low, and the lonely watcher awoke from her doze to see a large lion on the opposite side of the pot proposing to grab her. Slightly scared as all lions are at a blinking fire, this very delay on the beast's part was the widow's choice opportunity. Well, and what did that homely housewife do if not drench the lion with the scalding salt water—yes, drenched it dead! Mrs. Beeton could not have given clearer instructions how to scald and salt a prize lion, and she was a local Luban heroine for a week.

But that is only incident No. 1, and the curious coincidence of the second affair is that a woman and her water-pot are again the central facts of the history. This, too, is a woman whose life is under a cloud : witness her slinking off after sundown to draw water from the well.

Late hours, though, in Africa have their penalty, and just
as she stooped down into the well to draw water, behold!
as in a mirror her own face in the same reflection with a
leopard's. It all happened in the lightning glance of an
eye, the leopard on the other side starting to spring on
her at the simultaneous second when she saw his head
mirrored with her own in the same pool. (And, remember, the only shield and buckler she possessed was
Mrs. Beeton's glory, a housewife's water-pot.) Well,
happily for the poor woman, she instinctively, on the
edge of the well, covered her body with this homely
utensil to break the leopard's spring across. And not in
vain. The success of this manœuvre was triumphant.
Just enough to cow the beast a very little, this little
meant such a lot that the leaping leopard missed a foothold by one important inch, fell down the well with a
splash—and now there is more need for the water-pot
than ever. Thus begins a long game of hide and seek,
woman above and leopard down that well. Once, twice,
twenty times, the woman and the leopard played at blind
man's buff down the hole, and every time the beast attempts to climb the well, this negro Mrs. Beeton claps
her water-pot over the mouth of the pit, thus cowing her
enemy. All the time, of course, she has been shrieking
in the direction of the village, and at last some men running up reward her bravery in the spearing of the wild
beast. Yet this woman had only 2 lbs. 12 oz. of brain as
against the men's 3 lbs. 2 oz., but the margin lacking in
brain she made up in biceps.

(29*th August.*)

Heat increasing as we push on and in, the quicksilver hurrying up the glass towards grill heat by 10 a.m. At daybreak taking up of the fragments of supper that remain a pocketful, we are off on the wings of the morning, pushing far ahead of our crawling caravan. Chancing on a rippling river intercepting the trail, you sit down on the shiny, moss-covered bank and perform a much more serious toilet than your fugitive cat's lick in the dark camp. (*N.B.*—A tooth-brush over a running stream, this is the cream of all tramp joys.) Then, at last, behold our crawling caravan emerge from a hurst, the Union Jack bearer leading the way. As we have given them the slip and pushed on betimes, this is our first encounter with our own men, so when the Indian file marches past each man has his morning to give, followed by some droll remark. Then one perchance starts a song, the whole line of leathery lungs taking up the howling chorus : this particularly when at the end of a long fagging journey. Sirs ! what singing, the whole harmony not unlike the tune with which a rusty old coal-cart tries to solace itself when crawling down a hill.

How do we travel, you ask ? Have we carts or horses or donkeys ? No, we have none of these, howbeit a kind English lady was so concerned about our delays that she asked the touching question : " Did the wheel of your cart stick in the mud ? " Alas ! the only " cart-wheel " we have to do with is the aforesaid rut of that name, and a few months of this gipsying on the road makes you agree with Ruskin that railway travelling is not travelling at all. It is merely being sent to a place, and very little different from becoming a parcel. Your alternative to tramping it is a lazy lotus life in a Portuguese *machila*, wherein dozing is the retrograde rule. Bowling along in your carriage and six (hammock and six stalwarts) while the honest blacks are sweating it out. Although a good ambulance arrangement, this humbling hammock can easily make a man as lazy as he is limp and lifeless. On the contrary, marching under vertical rays is delightful up to the sixth hour. When, however, you push for a camp eight hours off, all the pleasure goes out of a tramp after that solemn sixth hour. The lovely glimpses of the picturesque in the earlier and brighter hours all vanish, leaving you dull and dead, a mere walking machine, unpleasantly conscious of a hole in one sock, and discussing in your hot head how far to camp.

CHAPTER VII

"Own Up and Pay Up"

"Christ the Son of God hath sent me
    Through the midnight lands,
Mine the mighty ordination
    Of the piercèd hands."

*   *   *

"All Christians are altogether priests; and let it be
anathema to assert there is any other priest than he
who is a Christian; for it will be asserted without
the Word of God, on no authority but the sayings
of men, or the antiquity of custom, or the multitude
of those that think so."

LUTHER.

*   *   *

"You might as well attempt to measure the moon
for a suit of clothes as tell what sect some belong to."

GEORGE WHITEFIELD.

CHAPTER VII

"Own Up and Pay Up"

WHEREIN the reader continues the perilous process called " boring in," and encounters along the trail sundry sons of Belial.

BUT how ridiculous all this trekking seems in retrospect, when we see to-day this same Central Africa quickly becoming a gridiron of railways. Against our weary retrospect of thirty-two months from England to the Garenganze, Sir Douglas Fox now offers a prospect of three days to the same goal from Benguella. Ah me, as the curtain of memory lifts, it is incredible to think that within two decades the pant and puff of the red-eyed engine will be heard rumbling along our old trail. And, remember, we are told that double band of steel linking the Ocean with the Katanga will mean the commercial-traveller stage of existence—ambassadors for Canadian whisky, Scotch tweeds, English marmalade, packed in the sweltering carriages and making the country hum. Not far down our Congo the very cannibals who hurled clouds of arrows against Stanley's canoes are to-day them-

8

selves firemen and engineers of the river steamboats, perspiring over their engines with lumps of cotton waste in their strong dirty hands. Malemba was one of them, and I chatted with him to-day in our *lingua franca*, Swahili.

(30*th August.*)

Watershed country as it is about here, this means that the rivers have not yet time and place enough to form yawning ravines, consequently bridging is easy and almost nominal. Dead level as the land looks, you soon discover that this very flatness is a mere artifice and trickery. For here, under your very nose, great river-systems are silently worming away in diametric directions; here is cradled the mighty Congo of the future; here, too, slumbers the source of the Zambezi : so hypocritically small here, so haughty yonder. To a Missionary there is Gospel as well as Geography in all this, the same Gospel I preached later on when crossing Kundelungu Range. Sharp on the watershed I halted my men and preached a three minutes' appeal—a short enough sermon, but if they practise all I preached they will find it long enough. Standing by a tree, I showed them how one half of the branches dripped rain that flowed far West, while the Eastern branches shed away to the Luapula. And there you have the very pointed moral of their position, as good theologically as geographically—every man of them standing on the watershed of life and called upon to make an irrevocable choice : one momentous move this way or that meaning endless joy or endless woe. Of all the dunces beneath the patient heavens there is none like the man who denies that the Gospel of God is Africa's true solace and salvation. Here is a man who says he has gone to the extreme of sin, and here is a Missionary saying that Christ has gone to the extreme of atonement. What more does the sinner want? What more does the Saviour?

The villages encountered are still of the same verminating pattern first met near the Coast. As clearly as the shell of a snail indicates its species, so the Chokwe[1] has his typical hut. Having no chimney, his roof is a long needle-pointed spire, their protest this against the smoke blearing their eyes. Hence height of roof to induce the smoke to curl up inside, not outside, the cone. Experience grows, however, and you soon see that more than mere sounds of the forest are invading the negro home. For taking another glance out of his ash-heap of a kraal, this time, your nude negro saw, or rather did not see, one straight line in Nature, so once again out of sheer servile allegiance to his Nature-creed the crooked negro has a crooked town, the black beehive huts scattered all over in a most random manner. Now, as that hut is itself only a clump of cut trees tied together with bark ropes, even so he still drags in forest ideas into the stockade, and the haphazard growth of a clump of trees is the planless maze of this grass town. A lighted arrow shot into the place would send it up in a blaze.

[1] Some years later the first to open in Chokwe were our American friends Messrs. Loutitt, Maitland, and Dr. Morey. Then Mr. and Mrs. Taylor and others followed and began farther North.

That old-as-Adam circular hut of his, be it noted, is the seed plot of all his " thinking black " ideas, for when natives gather in a meeting they crowd in a circle ; then, in true sarcastic sequence, they think and talk in a circle. The eye is circle No. 1, and looking out on the landscape of life it is a case of like eye, like landscape, 360° every time.   He rambles round in a circle of speech in the same way as he sees the circularity of seasons in Nature, or the day and night cycle of sleeping and waking.   His carved stools and utensils are all circular, and he borrows from Nature the idea that rotundity is the only safe shape of things.   A chief argued with me for a week that by making a square house I had at once created four points of near or remote breakage—a circle has no weak point, so he argued.   The fact is the whole prospective puzzle in connection with our black man is, how to make him, a round peg, fit into the square hole of civilisation.   You go roaming around Africa sighing for one straight line and lo ! you find it not—a parable all this of black morals as well as of black men.

(31*st August.*)

The sun-baked trail stretching ahead is still going due East like a long snake, twisting and turning now to the right now to the left with a whole foot-path philosophy in the thing.   Nor would you prefer it severely straight like a Roman road, for this corkscrew with its secrets ahead possesses all the pleasure that is born of accident and surprise.   You turn an ant-hill and know not what will confront you ; squeeze through scrub, then out, pit-a-

pat with expectancy, on a green grassy glade. You know
not what is ahead, nor do you want to. Here your "thinking black" negro moralises once more, and insists that
this track of ours is like the way and walk of life. The
veil that covers the face of futurity is woven by the hand
of mercy. If you knew a month's happening ahead, you
would grow grey in a single night. Day by day in this
same cart-wheel rut, however, has a curious effect on you
the traveller : it gets on your brain, precisely as this
sinuous trail has made an equally sinuous African. He
gets a twist too. With chameleon consistency the negro
has utterly become like his own zigzag path ; it is his
way of doing things as well as his way of walking. In
speaking—say—this slippery native can only twist in and
out of an idea precisely as he twists along his path :
" Going, I went, and speaking, I spoke, and doing, I did,"
being the average formula of your wriggly black. An
adjacent lion is called a "dog," and a friend asking a
friend to drink beer is vaguely invited to drink "water."
Hence the famous fact that our son of Ham will never
come straight to the point, but hedges and temporises—
"meandering to the point" he calls it. Depend upon it,
too, this gentleman has got to learn that a straight line
is the shortest in morals as in mathematics : is not their
twisted itinerary exactly like their twisted morals ? Why,
for example, is it that your savage prefers to take a long,
roundabout way in murdering his man, lingering and
lavishing the finest touches of the art of murder on him ?
Round the corner of the cook-house you can catch Mr.

Chef excruciatingly murdering your supper fowl, plucking it while yet alive. The same boy's father, too, in killing a prisoner would with a refinement of cruelty insist on first digging out the heart. The same devious course of devilry is seen when they catch an eagle raiding the chickens. Oh yes, they release the captured culprit, but it is only with one leg cut off, one eye gouged out, then away the regal bird flies in misery, maimed for life. Yet so daring are these vultures that, at Molenga's, one successfully swooped down on the plate passing only a few yards from cook-house to table and carried off the savoury meat thereon !

*   *   *

What next ? The *ex post facto* Chokwe "hungry country" is a relative joy compared with the treatment we receive from the Luvale people. The staple product of this road-blocking tribe is a wealth of Rob Roy bandits who live on loot. Squeezing through the grass is a small concern compared with squeezing past these stand-and-deliver ruffians. This is what the phrase "boring in" means. Small ragamuffin sovereigns, let us call them, generally this type of negro is the greasiest and the dirtiest that ever defied soap. "Water rots the skin," is their saying. Samikilenge at Peho is the worst of the gang, then comes Kalunga Kameya, and then old Kangombe. Every man of them nurses a private grievance and demands "cash down" for seeing the light of His Majesty's countenance. Most of their towns, too, more prominent on the map than on the planet earth.

To judge from their dirty appearance they seem, at one time, all to have suffered from hydrophobia and never completely recovered from the dread of water then inspired. These and many more form a band of black rogues who fatten on honest men : witness Livingstone in these very latitudes in 1854 and his perilous plight. By way of temporising, a common proposal from these road-blockers is a delay of some days for the *Kasendo*, or blood covenant of friendship, between the travellers and the lord paramount, a mere trick this, of course, " to bleed us" in a dear double sense. The idea of this one-sided covenant as unfolded is a sort of " Mutual Accommodation Society Limited," and I assure you it is limited —strictly so—our upstart Chief being sole beneficiary : he wants everything, even a literal suck of your blood. Every few miles means a new embarrassing case of a blatant Kinglet demanding your money or your life, yet most of these nobodies only dreamed in one night they were kings, their proof of regal succession being as weak and visionary as that of the Pope being the fabled successor of Peter. But patience must be your pet virtue in Africa, remember, and now, oh now, is the time to produce your pet. Calico and beads are their £ *s. d.*, but mere current coinage is the least and last thing in their despotic demands. Our prudent shabbiness, in fact, is a necessary boon ; for they want our boots, want our shirts, yea, they must have the only iron cooking-pot we possess —perhaps. And all this under splitting vertical rays, the precious dry season quickly speeding past with our

Garenganze goal yet a long way off.   These fine folks do not measure time by means of little machines carried in their pockets.   No need in this easy land to catch train or tram by a fraction of a second.   There is not one time-piece in the vast country, their only watch and eight-day clock being the accurate sun who faileth never.   To say, therefore, that " punctually on the stroke of six " our caravan moves out of camp is an error, unless you apply the phrase to our slavers, who can only get their bondsmen off after a sixth whack with a stick, "punctually on the stroke of six," indeed.

(8*th September.*)

But we have an anchor to windward all the time. Here are your September and October rushing past, I repeat, the punctual rains due at any time, like an express. And here, too, are your hot Africa and hotter Africans trying hard to make us a broken-spirited jumble of dis-traction.   But we meet our Rob Roy's hang-dog look with the genuine and exultant retort that though indeed empty-handed we are not empty-headed, and therefore cannot give what we do not possess.   Well, this demon-strable denial of ours is, as I have said, a real anchor to windward, for the African has a curiously hard-headed way of judging things by practical proof.   But, mark you, until in some way you have paid this man's demands, normal relations with the tribe in food-buying are not supposed to be established.   You are boycotted, and neither by charter nor barter can you get anything from them.   First things first is the idea in this preliminary tribute wrangle, and the demand really amounts to the astounding idea that we must pay for the very faggots we break in the forest; must pay for the very water we drink; yea, finally and fearfully, we must pay for the very air we breathe.   Pay for the very air we breathe, and if we don't " stand and deliver," then—why, soon we will be breathing no air at all.   Ah, these road-blocking days are the Missionary's terrible times, when the feelings are at flash-point and not at all improved after a sleepless night of native drum-dancing.   You seem to awake with the feeling that you have not slept for a hundred years, and with a complexion like uncooked pastry. Content as these negroes are to drone through life, they glory in thus blocking the road with their delusive and abortive demands.

Let me introduce you to this fiery friend of ours, Mr. Rob Roy.   For a moment you think the whole thing must be an optical illusion.   A globular personage, with the voice of Stentor and the build of Falstaff, here he comes mincing along to the rhythmic music of tight new boots—bought from the slavers.   Personal remarks in Africa are permissible, and you will perceive that Rob is dressed in his Sunday best for the occasion, to wit, an utterly abominable soldier's uniform, probably now entering its teens.   Fat and fifty, our friend is obviously bursting for relief, for the rag-shop red coat is giving him a claret-coloured face.   With every button straining at its fastenings, observe how the tight-unto-choking collar makes his ox-neck overflow in waves of fat.   After many

a strange vicissitude of fortune, and originally fitting
some thin, trig T. Atkins like a glove, this coloured coat
inflicting slow tortures is seemingly not at all adapted
to our bandit's middle-aged development. The head-
dress is quite as remarkable too as the nether garments.
H.R.H. as substitute for a crown walks carefully balancing
a caved-in No. 6 policeman's helmet on a No. 10 head.
But, alas! the head can be empty that fills a hat. Look
now at that tall and gawky youth strutting at his side
wearing a wild waistcoat, a-graduating in the Luban
school of manners. This, be it known, is Rob Roy junior,
playing local "Prince of Wales" to his father's rôle of
Rex, an "heir-apparent" he, more heir-presumptive than
"heir-apparent," for his presumption is appallingly
apparent. Burton was right. Mere barbarism rarely
disgusts : it is the unnatural union of civilisation with
savagery that makes the gorge rise. The incongruities
are not grotesque enough to be amusing : they are merely
ugly and painful.

(Later.)

What, then, is this negro's programme for the day?
"Drink beer, think beer," is the old African saying that
describes it all. For with tipsy hilarity he promises you,
by the graves of his ancestors, that you will be released
to-morrow ; but his precious promises are like proverbial
pie-crust, only made to be broken. Thus you see our
Rob Roy glorying in his old game of the blocked road,
his glory our shame. Each dragging day of delay he
celebrates with one of his all-night dances, the nude

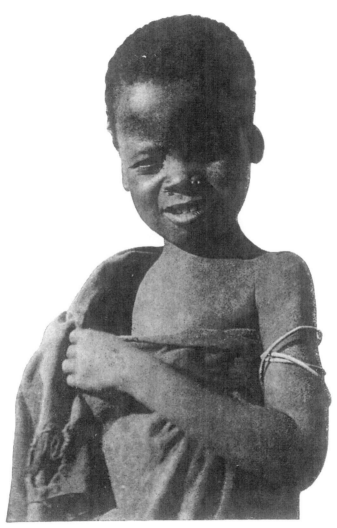

A PRECOCIOUS PRINCELING

celebrants roaring themselves hoarse under the fig-trees. Though they dance in their nudity under a fig-tree, they seem quite unconscious of the ancient application of fig-leaves, and certainly they have more need of a covering of fig-leaves than fig-trees. Enemy of daylight and decent living, there goes the midnight noise of the drums echoing to the roar of the dancing Luvale, and the native proverb hits off the dual emptiness of both drum and drummer : " A drum only sounds because it is empty." Nor is this music mellowed and harmonised by distance. The native has his drum so near that it seems to be stuck in your drum of the ear—a pandemonium of music. Be vigilant, for this midnight drumming is on the same principle (or lack thereof) that a band of thieves burgles a London house while one of their " pals " plays an Italian barrel-organ at the gate to draw off attention. Again and again, these Luvale folks have unthatched a hut under cover of the noise and decamped with a truss of calico. At Nalingombe we lost, not merely a bale of calico, but also the next needy day of delay " talking " the theft palaver—bale lost, day lost, temper lost. Tried in a lull to barter some local curios, my predilection being for combs and bead-work ; but they edged away, glancing with open animosity, after almost closing with my offer. Depend on it, in Luvale a collector of curios seems to the native to be himself the quaintest curio in his whole collection.

(13*th September.*)

What is all the delay about ? The answer is that what we are really doing is " buying the road." You

cross one Coilantogle Ford sort of boundary only to find
that the Roderick Dhu you have just escaped has a dozen
cousins of the same ilk farther ahead. Often a coarse
English ballad is a truer snap-shot of African life than
more pretentious poetry, and if a coarse land needs coarse
description then here you have Luvaleland in modified
English rhyme :—

> "There's a king on every ash-heap,
>   There's princes not a few,
>   There's a whole raft-load of potentates
>   On the road to Timbuctoo."

Thus you see the divinity that hedges every tiny chief
has to be propitiated with *Ochivanda*, or tribute, and the
galling fact is that this nobody has all your own men in
the hollow of his hand. He has marked you for his
lawful prey. Perceiving you in perplexity means that the
iron is now red-hot, so he strikes with a will and like a
wild one. "Keep the trail white for us to return" is the
catch phrase from your traitors, and at every turn they
deplore your lack of deep respect for all constituted
authority. They nag you and they jag you with the reminder that all the chiefs will loot any further transport
following us in, if we fail to make the path "white" by
paying exceptionally extortionate tribute. Proverb-logic
again routed us, and this time the reminder was that
"the key that opens is also the key that locks." Nor
was this all. Our Biheans rushed to more mad metaphor
to make us yield. "Look," said they, "at this long road
in from the Ocean : like the human body, lo! what is this

road but the gullet? Out yonder on the Atlantic sea-shore you have the mouth open to receive supplies. Now you white men (literally, "you big devils") are going far into the stomach of Africa, but linking mouth and 'peptics' (*Chifu*) is this long gullet-way which must not be blocked—block the gullet-trail and you will starve, for the mouth is cut off from the stomach." Thus we surrendered at discretion, swallowed the affronts in a deplorably double sense, kept our mouths shut, and our long line of supplies open. For what again saith the proverb? "If, O exasperated one, you are tied up in ropes, the more you tug, the tighter the knots become."

N.B.—In Africa a Missionary is like steel, no use if he loses his temper. By every trick and device, the Devil tries to lure from you your song, and the only safe man is the Psalmist sort: My heart is fixed, *I'll sing*—*i.e.* I am going in for singing as a habit of life in Africa. "The happiness of duty" is a blessed old belief, no doubt, but far, far better in Africa to reverse the motto and make it run, "The duty of happiness." "Chance sparks kindle chance tinder," runs the proverb, so beware!

(Later.)

Mere "Bible and walking-stick" campaign as ours is, no wonder the natives call us "The Softies." But again and again it is Mr. Softie who gets them out of a hole. For example, let me here record as legitimate history an olive-branch victory farther East that opened the Luban road. We are twisting along the trail, a great band of Mweru-bound emigrants numbering nearly three hundred

souls. Very weary and very dreary that great crowd is;
witness this worn-out mother whose baby was born to-day
on the long march. Born in the woods, this biped baby
is treated like a little antelope and must travel two hours
after he has seen daylight. Christened after the forest
that cradled him, this title clings to him all his life;
imagine an English baby with no cradle but a travelling-
trunk, and travelling with the trunk as soon as it is born.
We are pushing on for a river camp before nightfall;
some have snatched at a dry faggot, remembering the
needed fire ahead; here and there mushrooms put in an
appearance for the prospective supper, but we are all
weary and pinched. Duck, a welcome sight in the
morning, is the last thing we want to see now, for a duck
means marsh, and marsh means weary wading, wet socks,
and a shiver-and-sweat fever. Afar—oh the music!—the
voice of our terminal river begins at last to call, beckoning
us on, and at last we come out of the forest with a shout of
relief, for there ahead is our river—green Jordan, call it—
beyond which is the negroes' promised land of—of camp.
And soon we have negotiated the deep dark thing over
an acrobatic bridge, and soon the axes are out felling a
spacious bivouac. An odd enough company, to be sure,
for ten tribes are represented, which augurs not discord
but the contrary. In the old Mushidi capital stranger
met and mated with stranger, the man from the North
with the woman from the South; and the family tie was
often shown to be the merest calico concern, wearing out
with the calico that bound it. Our camp every day is

like a good-sized village, the loud after-supper hum from
the fires being rather pleasant though a little bit noisy.
The sweep of stockade is fully 150 yards in circumference,
in the centre of which is my big hut, where I sleep with
my personal boys. This palisade is so built that it forms
at the same time the huts of the people, each man having
so many yards of ground to stockade before he joins on
with his neighbour, who comes to meet him half-way.
Only one gateway is allowed, owing to the dangerous
state of the forest, and, with all their instincts up in arms,
the men look out jealously that no one leaves a gap. It
is now broodingly dark, and most around the fires are
looking with a hungry, glassy stare at the supper-pots,
when a shrill whistle startles all—a shriek-whistle known
too sadly well; and then! And then, as a matter of
plain, unpleasant fact, some red toucan feathers appear
over our stockade. Everybody's jaw drops, and, in a
flash, we know that war is in the wind, red war that has
painted the African map from ocean to ocean. Where
then, to be definite, are we? Into what trap have we
fallen? "Oh no," say the emerging warriors, "we have
nothing against *you*, but to-morrow *we* begin." In a
word, we have put our foot in it, have arrived just on
the eve of a great inter-tribal battle, a wild Waterloo.
The old tale of the hereditary hatred of the clans and
the Highland Mac's sending round the fiery cross—fiery
feathers in this case. A long quarrel has been in soak
for years; boundaries have been dishonoured, clansmen
kidnapped, ivory tribute stolen; and now at last for the

final argument of kings. And is God not going to have a say in it all, the pitched battle raging itself out? And will they die like dogs without knowing that He has an argument with both of them?

Yea, here again (and blessed be our Rock!) we may write on earth what God has written in heaven: Bible diplomacy, olive-branch pleadings right through the night, and with the day-dawn came the truce of God; a red sunrise to a "white" day. We were as bland as they were bitter, but we won. This is how it was done. Halving a group of elders, the one section went off to preach peace in Chona's war-camp, while the other half carried the olive branch into the rival Mac's. And although at first they were greeted with a pelting storm of refusals, the great armistice was at weary length assured. Not a mere truce, not a patchwork peace, but a sterling pact that has held on through nearly twice ten years, and ensured an open Western road. These, be it known, are the Luburi bog tribesmen, whom a whole park of artillery could not dislodge from their amphibious retreat; "human otters" their title. So, even so, we open the way, under God; a few burning words of daysmanship, a longer pleading for soul-escape as well as body-escape, and lo! the rainbow in the cloud. The Western road! What pioneer memories of the olden time are in the name; of weary days when we bored our way far, far into the interior: yes, we purchased that long weary trail, bought (with kind, not cash) a passage with our meagre belongings, an old shirt here, an older pair of trousers there—and so we moved on our pilgrim trail, nightfall seeing us minus a rag or two and a day's march nearer home. Fools for Christ's sake Whose is the princedom of peace, we tried to meet all comers with a Gospel smile, listened to their Rob Roy intentions, paid their free-booters' levy as though it were Cæsar's shekel of silver, and laid up treasure in Heaven according to Matt. vi. Even Rob Roy, I presume, comes under the heading "There is *no* power but of God." Nor does one find it difficult to wave a welcome olive branch in the face of long-drowned tribes who are weary to death of war's deluge. Peace has balm right round the globe, and you bless the Prince thereof that such is your calling, to bring men out of the midnight into the sunshine.

CHAPTER VIII

Dark Doings in Luvaleland

"To do as all men ever would,
    Own no man master but their mood."

        ❋   *   *

"The fact is that the running of a tropical colony is, of all tests, the most searching as to the development of the nation that attempts it; to see helpless people and not to oppress them, to see great wealth and not to confiscate it, to have the absolute power and not to abuse it, to raise the native instead of sinking yourself, these are the supreme trials of a nation's spirit."

SIR ARTHUR CONAN DOYLE.

         *   *   *

"In Africa the animalistic, self-indulgent white man approximates yet nearer the animal; the intellectually active, destitute of the stimulus of conversation and encounter with diverse opinion and nimble wits, becomes an intellectual fungoid."

BLACKBURN.

CHAPTER VIII

Dark Doings in Luvaleland

*I*N *which the veil being only partially withdrawn, the black man is seen to have black manners.*

(17th September.)

ALL these days our old friend Latitude 12° is running East and West on our right, more like a hand-rail fencing us in than an imaginary map-line. So East, endlessly East to the sun does our road run, that the way-faring man though a fool shall not err therein. The rivers are elusive and uncertain, wriggling across our trail for a few minutes like a shining serpent, then darting off, lost in the bush. Not so loyal Latitude 12°. Say, nearly as far as Longitude 22°, it is a faithful friend all the way; now river, now jungle, now flats—but come river, or jungle, or flats, the 12th parallel unifies them all. "Sourcing it" is their participle that gives the geography of our route. On our far left the baby Kasai is babbling like a brook, and the 1st of September sees the far-flowing Lumese born a little after we left Tenda. One day more and a sharp turn East reveals the baby Luena, a poor trickle of liquid mud made up of a few ponds linked together. Long sandy slopes all the way, the green shoots of the rubber root often the only speck of relief in the trail. Farther back in Chokwe country the hills were huddled too close, their V-shaped hollows giving quite a jolt. Only after a long series of complex tumbles did we get out of it with meal-bags that had been empty for two years—days, I mean. But the pitcher that goes often to the water will at last surely be broken, and at Kasenga one of our men, a tough old roadster, lay down and died. Two days ago he gave the warning that this travelling blend of jolting and hunger would kill him, the honest hazel eyes of the fellow proclaiming that his was no shuffling cowardice. So there in the dead of night we were forced to dig up the floor of his hut and bury him like a dog, lest the natives got wind of it. Only dare to die in their country, only dare to cover the face of your dead on "ashes to ashes" principle, and at once they pounce down on you with the old nagging lawsuits. *They* don't bury their dead, oh no! they, grandees excepted, merely stick the corpse up in the forest between two trees, and they demand damages for all burial.

Read this. Albeit prompt payment is the Luvale theory of lawsuit assessment, their excessive extortion really frustrates quick settlement : witness a man to-day dunned for the debt of his great-great-grandfather. Yet generations ago the first instalments were paid to account, and dribbling down the years it has been pay! pay! pay! all the time, "the white chalk" acquittal (receipt) denied

"No chalk, no clearance" is their formula. *Milonga!*
Milonga! is the cry, and off all the young lads are carried
by their uncles to go the round of the courts and learn the
tricks of legal blood-sucking. Like a small pea in a very
big pod you have a mere boy trained in word-wriggling
and munching mouthfuls of legal terminology. This is
the reason why a Missionary can scarcely keep a bright
young scholar about him. The uncle is sure to turn up
and drag him off, willy nilly, for this legal education. If
you expostulate, the retorting relative only expectorates,
and away they sail out through the Mission gate, the
uncle dragging the nephew like a big steam-tug making
off with a dainty sailing yacht. No new ideas are allowed
to build their nests in the young Luvale's brain. Nature,
always fertile in analogies, gives a good example of all this
in the dozens of dogs nosing among the garbage of their
own filthy towns. Even so, Mr. Luvale rakes up the
mud-heaps of memory, and at last having found his quibble
as a dog his bone, he straightaway bows to his victim with
awful politeness : *Linga! Veta!*

Nevertheless, prompt payment is the tribal ideal, and it
is only in the "death damages," or *Chipeshi*, they hit on a
gruesome expedient to make a man pay up. A husband,
say, is bereaved of his wife, so he must be mulcted heavily
by the relatives ; calico, goats, and oxen all going to
appease their counterfeit wrath. Now is their cruel
chance for "cash down," so, like Sinbad the Sailor, they
shut in the man with his conjugal corpse and let the days
drag past to their extortions. Meanwhile, of course, rapid,

revolting mortification is going apace, and weeks after it
is all over, debts paid, " white chalk acquittal," he emerges
to the sunlight. Semi-starved, too, all the time, only
water and gruel his allowance. So very sad, bad, and
mad is it all that every tiny detail is clutched at to make
delay : " We bury only bones," is their phrase (*Natu
mbila vifuhwa kaha*).

This bereaved husband, for instance, had a long preliminary wrangle with his kinsman in the mere notifying
of his wife's death. For, be it known, " to notify " means
that you send a personable bit of live-stock, a goat but
preferably an ox, and only thus can the news of such an
unlikely thing as *this* death get home to the man's intelligence. Sent a big goat in the first instance, this kinsman
looked askance at the animal and said that its very smallness told him his cousin had not much wrong with her—
dead she certainly could not be with only a goat to
announce it. People don't notify deaths per post-card
even in Luvaleland, and to send a huge ox is the African
equivalent to sending a black-edged mourning letter. A
goat is a mere post-card. Here, then, is his chance to
make vexatious delays, the preliminary trouble being how
to get the relatives even to believe there is a death at all.
A full week has run its course before they even dream of
gathering for the *Chipeshi* (wake ?), the initial fees of
notification being now paid. Then, one by one, the
bereaved kinsmen trickle in, all armed to the teeth, all
vulpine in greed, and all resolved at besting each other in
their demands. A mere cousin though he be, the long

list of items in his funeral bill is stolidly fought for day
by day : "death damages," the most complicated of all.
For—and note this—death to a negro is indeed dissolution
of life's pleasures as well as dissolution of a mere mortal
body, and all the details of that woman's wedded life must
now be paid for. Of course, she cooked his food, so now
for paying the total cookery bill. She fetched firewood,
milled the meal and drew water, now's the time to pay up,
ay, pay for every drink of water and every faggot of
fire. Mark you, pay up for every item to every kinsman,
all at once and once for all. One item in this incredible
invoice naturally makes you laugh, for the thing itself is
about laughter : " To the much laughter you enjoyed for
years when conversing with your late spouse, our legal
cousin—total value, one goat." Not much to laugh at
now. And so on and on, the post-mortem invoice runs,
many a shameless (because nameless) item haggled over
on a money basis, £ s. d. as to its very initials being
suitably equivalent to Law Suit Damages. Alas! the
higher you ascend in the social scale the lower things sink,
the worse and wilder the extortion. The great Queen herself, Nyakatoro, is the lewdest of the lot, and the occasion
of her grandchild's death was the scene of a loathsome
Chipeshi. Weeks and weeks dragged past, but no burial,
the mourners forced to nurse the putrefying corpse on
their knees on the Luvale " we bury only bones " principle.
Meanwhile, the shameless Queen is conducting an inquiry
into the death of her *Musukulu*, a " who-killed-cock-robin "
sort of investigation this, in which she unblushingly

reveals the names of her many paramours, all of whom must now pay damages for the grandchild's death.

*　　　*　　　*

Here is a strong healthy stream we must tackle. And being strong, not sickly, how can you expect it to be always confined to its bed? Winding and rewinding like a watch-spring, we follow the twists of our river round the great S, then out we go together, both river and traveller, out on a pancake plain. More marsh than plain this becomes, alas! for its old orderly up-stream flow is now impossible; and although no doubt, like ourselves, this river entered on this plain with the very best intentions, the flat bankless marsh has now forced the poor stream to break all his good up-stream resolutions—a floundering bog, nothing less. Yea—and note this, gentle reader—we too end in bog, just as sadly and badly. For you cannot canoe it, so you resort to the "double man" of exploration— that is to say, aloft is your traveller, pickaback like a Japanese acrobat, on his negro steed, hands clutching at the woolly pow, legs twisted tightly round his neck. Not that this "double man" is doubly a man—oh! no, for the more inches you go up in the world the lower you descend both in imagination and in reality. Each groping step in the pitchy, stinking mud sees you nervously clutching at the negro's head, knees driven into the neck and ever mindful of the white knight's fate in "Alice's Adventures," to wit, a beautiful parabolic curve, head first. And then for the sordid sequel. Gathering up what little shreds of dignity are left to you, you roll yourself up in a blanket, while your shabby shirt tied to a tree branch is dancing itself dry in the wind. But the cold cuts like a carving-knife, and a blanket is inadequate. So, to finish the folly, you are facetiously forced to keep the shirt company—you dancing yourself warm, while it dances itself dry. Of course your comfy negro, *per contra*, likes all this splashing, for he never wore boots and never felt damp with the clammy cling of wet stockings.

(Later.)

The extraordinary insalubrity of the Luvale flats is appalling. In later days, it was in these sweltering plains Cyril Bird and brave young Copithorne poured out their lives for Luvaleland. Characteristically and cardinally men of deep love for souls, they gave their all to a tribe that listened for years to the Gospel with sharp antagonistic ears. Once Bird left for the Ocean, ostensibly to take a much-needed furlough, but the haunting need of that vile Luvaleland dragged him back, and the end was soon reached. Life like a spent steed panting towards its goal, the Pauline gleam in his eye and praise on his lips. Black-water fever they called his mortal malady, but he died of a broken heart, yes, broken for a tribe of robbers—a holiday at last, furlough in Glory! Weary and worn by the vertical rays, what a whiff of joy in the thought: "Heaven's ahead—hurrah!"

Remember, there is no deep valley but near some great hill, and that sowing in tears culminated in others reaping with joy.   Days grow into months, and months into years, and then a lady can tell of a whole town of Luvale[1] turning to God by Jesus Christ : men, women, and children, who at last look beyond the Missionary to the God Who sent him.   Oh ! ye binders of other men's sheaves, remember the weary Birds and Copithornes of the African field.   Let us not therefore judge "another man's servant" in this resolve of Cyril Bird to die in and for Africa.   Much can be said *pro* and *con*, but probably more *pro* than *con*.   Would you desert your own infant in a foreign land when desertion meant doom ?

Under English laws it is a misdemeanour punishable with five years' penal servitude to abandon or expose an infant or child under two years so as to " endanger its life or to inflict permanent injury, actual or probable, upon its health."   How much more the crime committed against the new-born African soul in exposing it to the vicissitudes of a pastorless existence !   Too well this brave man knew that mere " marking time " is of as little value as counting beads in worship.   Too well he knew, that if we speak a dozen African languages with the tongues of men and angels and have not love, then Africa only claims in us one more of the mob of sounding brass and clanging cymbals.   Ay, even if we give our bodies to be burned with African fever and have not love, we are nothing.   Nevertheless, it is just here the Roman

---

[1] Following Mr. and Mrs. Bird came Mr. Schindler, Dr. Fisher, Mr. and Mrs. O'Jon, Mr. and Mrs. Cunningham, and many other noble men and women. Kazombo was the first branch station, then Kalunda, then Kaleñe.

Catholics, farther East, make the cosy Protestants blush, for while we are famous "furlough" folks, they burn their bridges and stick to their posts. Both nuns and priests dedicate their lives to the land, never hoping to sight Europe again, while we parade England with lantern lectures! These Romans laugh at us for so deserting our posts, and say that we are like a soldier who runs out of action to go and try his skill at a shooting-range. The real battle and real bullets are in here, in the bush, while away yonder on a far English platform is the amateur shooting-range. "I felt like a fireless chimney in summer," was the testimony of an old "deputation" Missionary in England.

(19th September.)

Unless, however, this record is to remain hopelessly tangled, we must mention sundry Luvale traits that block our road. Like chief, like people. Copying the Wagogo on the Zanzibar road, here you have a whole tribe spreading its nets and lurking by the roadside for loot. Legal loot, though, this claims to be ; for when the word is passed along the path that a caravan is advancing, there is a tribal flutter, and this news draws them like a magnet. Sea-lawyers every soul of them, they flood your camp and pack in so tightly that the perfumed crowd exhales the noxious smell of a bad drain. Dr. Johnson's remark about Scotland is really applicable to odorous Luvaleland. For when they informed him, travelling by night, that he had entered Scotia, he retorted, "Yes, I could smell it in the dark !" (Fie ! Dr. Johnson). Having the blood

of good old Scotland in my veins, it costs me quite a
patriotic pang to repeat this anti-Scotland slander, but
the words, false then, are true now when applied to the
Luvale—you literally smell your arrival. You smile,
too, at the crowd of women perfecting the work of nature
with dress and face smeared with red dye. Yet, after all,
what is the difference between these and an English lady,
who daubs two big spots of rouge on her cheeks? How
true it is that the vices we laugh at in others, laugh at us
in ourselves. Ponder the whirligig of time. In the
Apostle Paul's day at Rome, was not this the very taunt
to restrain Roman ladies from dyeing their hair and
painting their faces, to wit, that they would become as
ugly as "the woad-stained Britons"? Yes, we were the
"niggers" of those days. Did not Propertius try to
frighten Cynthia out of cosmetics by likening her to "the
coarse blue-eyed Britons"? And did not Cicero write
to his pal long ago: "Atticus! . . . the stupidest and
ugliest slaves come from Britain"?

In a second, with commendable promptitude, the business begins, jabber, babble, twaddle, cackle!—all baiting you
like a bear. Then they break into a whirl of questions,
who? why? when? where? whither?—and although once or
twice you make a wild dive for a probable answer, it ends
in your wearily resigning all pretensions to deal with them.
These Luvale ladies have a limited dress allowance:
fancy one of these sable sisters of mine wearing *à la mode*
a mere four-inch ribbon of calico. Pointing her black-kid-
glove finger right in my eye, she called me "Softie." It

is *Chindele!* this, *Chindele!* that; and so they prattle on, all of them talking the proverbial nineteen to the dozen, yet peevish and perverse withal, and—depend upon it— just waiting for an opening. Yet something must be done, so throwing etiquette to the winds, after enduring it all with exemplary meekness, you gesture them off. But (wolf!) dare even push one, dare even flick one across the face with a handkerchief, and the looting law-suit begins. We are caught as neat as a rat in a drain, everything now ripe for a row. Fishing is the best simile for this thing, however, and one of our Biheans is the first foolish fish to rise to the Luvale fly, the possible lawsuits now being legion.

(Later.)

Be sure of it, from the Atlantic to the Indian Ocean, these lawsuits in Africa are legion, the be-all and end-all of their lazy lives. From prince to beggar they have resolved to trade on the local sanctions and punishments of society. Take this big black, shedding not the tears of penitence but revolt; he blundered into litigation by running into a hut for shelter from the rain, and the housewife has the law on him. Plea: "You came dripping wet into my domicile, and these thy raindrops betoken much weeping in my house." Verdict, the wet man must pay for his ominous action. Next comes a pettifogging action because a man called his fellow by the wrong name: "How dare you call me Mr. Tree when I am Mr. Baggage? If you name me Tree, then you thereby saddle me with all that individual's legal responsibility." Verdict for the plaintiff, because law is not logic and logic is not law. But worse than all this comes a long string of cases, each plea amounting to the effrontery that it is wrong to affirm the right, the accused's error being that he made no error. A man named "River" has blood on his arm and a passer-by draws his attention to this fact, and in he goes among the meshes of the legal drag-net. Penalty: Mr. River must be paid for the accused's error in not committing an error. Another negro of the same ilk finds a legal grievance in the fact that truth has too much sting in it. Crossing the river with a fellow-traveller, a leech clings to his leg, and the lawsuit arises out of this friendly and kindly reminder that the leech was clinging to him. Leech indeed! the real blood-sucker is this litigious black who cries, Give! Give! Of the same sort is this third man; "Scar" (*Mukofu*) his name and scar the subject of his legal action. He is an old warrior, has a healed gash on his body, but instead of being proud of it as a kind of Marengo medal on which Napoleon wrote the lone words, "I was there," —instead of this, he runs a man into "the judgment circle" because he congratulated him on his cured wound. "Why mention the scar at all?" snapped the warrior; "'tis mine, not yours." Don't ask the why of some of these lawsuits; could mortal man tell? Here is an individual who invited another to eat porridge that has lain over-night—why make a lawsuit out of that? Here is another passing a few graves in the grass, and he goes over the names of the various occupants of the little graveyard—

why a lawsuit for that? Or this man who out of sheer kindness warned his neighbour of impending danger— why have the law on him for that? Can you wonder that the black man will not believe the Gospel of Grace because it is all too incredibly good to be true? What does he know about Grace? Here, too, you learn the reason why your emancipated African under modern European laws is such an inglorious disappointment. For the transition is all too abrupt, and the same African who formerly had tribal manners rammed down his throat by legal code, now thinks he can lapse into *grossièreté* and indifference to details. Take, for instance, that stern old law of theirs against random spitting: was he not penalised for this? Alas! the new white régime has no such penalty, and one negro cook I knew, having run out of wash-up-water for his dishes, calmly sent in to his master two courses, all the plates of which had been washed (dare I write it?) with his own African saliva.

*　　　　*　　　　*

As in Bihe, so, too, farther East, all the hamlets we peer into are of the same pig-sty sort. Imagine a land of huts from ocean to ocean; a land in which not one noble castle ever lifted its grey towers above the ancient forest; a land of holes and hovels, the huts built in a few days and lasting about as long. How true it is that the African leads off by debasing his surroundings, and then his surroundings take revenge by debasing the African. When you stumble across one of these in the woods, and send an inquisitive glance round inside, it is only to see what a long start the Devil has of the Missionary. The sin is all sinned in the noonday glare, the kind of thing spoken of by the prophet as "sin drawn with a cart-rope." The same old source of troubles, too, is this tight packing together in a filthy town. For the greatest enemy is internal: first the enemy of his own heart, then the enemy of his own household, anon the enemy of the next hut, until, finally, the enemy of the next tribe reads them the old lesson that a house divided against itself cannot stand. Born in their chains, they live in them and die hugging them as they rush over the precipice into the abyss. These chains are physical, and spiritual, and hereditary. In an African village you can lie awake all night pondering pitifully the needs of the land, and during that long vigil hear the snuffles and hoarse cries of a dozen little babies. Poor youngsters whose skin hangs loosely on them like an ill-fitting garment, cursed with the syphilitic curse.

> "An infant crying in the night:
> An infant crying for the light:
> And with no language but a cry."

These are the poor little bairns who, as Bishop South sadly said, "are not born into the world, but damned into it." To illustrate: Take this life-history of one such moaning and whimpering cherub. Mother loves her bairn, but she must be off to the woods for firewood, and baby cannot go. What's to be done? The dilemma is solved by a neighbour woman, one of the black barren type, who plots with deadly intent against the life of her neighbour's child. Here, then, comes the hell-born thought. Now is her chance. So, dissolving in philanthropic smiles, she hypocritically offers to nurse baby in the mother's absence—consequence : murder. The human fiend rubs into the gums of baby the virus of a loathsome and nameless disease, and the cherub dies a horrible death. Even the local black poet is horrified at a thing of this sort, and composes a Luban dirge which I translate :—

> "What is a baby's dying groan
> To the barren who have none of their own?"

Decidedly, we are in Luvaleland. The young boys about here are called the men, and the elders are called the "old boys," and no wonder. For these youngsters begin to live at full gallop when they are more babies than boys, and thus early sowing the wind they reap a roaring whirlwind : at twenty years of age they are weak and can scarcely trot, much less gallop, without the spur of stimulants. Borrowed beer, and preferably borrowed than bought. Sneaked tobacco, and the more he sneaks the pleasanter the smoke. Hemp paid for, ay, paid with the uttermost farthing, for this last lashes him with passion. And so the three wicks of the lamp of life soon burn out in blazes, the brain, the blood, and the breath. "Soon ripe, soon rotten," is the proverb that tells the whole story, for if he must be a man at fourteen then he is sure of being a boy at thirty. An African lad knows everything too early, and therefore can learn nothing when it is too late.

CHAPTER IX

The Desert Journey

"God hath His deserts broad and brown,
A solitude—a sea of sand —
On which He lets Heaven's curtain down,
Unknit by His Almighty Hand."

*   *   *

"Then Israel sang this song :
Spring up, O well; sing ye unto it."

NUMBERS xxi. 17.

*   *   *

"Long the blessed Guide has led me
By the desert road ;
Now I see the golden towers—
City of my God.
There amidst the love and glory
He is waiting yet ;
On His hands a name is graven
He can ne'er forget."

CHAPTER IX

The Desert Journey

WHEREIN the reader crosses the desert, and finds Zebulun's portion awaiting him, yea, he "sucks of treasures hid in the sand."

(Later.)

BUT in this impudent lawlessness is there no law-giver ? Not now, but (here let me anticipate) a little later the Portuguese pushed in a line of forts as far as Nakandundu, this last link in their chain of Commandants being a terribly typical affair. "Africa begins at the Pyrenees," said Napoleon long ago, and here is a Portuguese who proves that Portugal is as bad as Africa. A prince of brigands, this official is a noonday slaver · instance, his sending out 12 kilos of powder to buy a boy. No boy marketable for the moment; so in lieu of the masculine gender they drag in a young woman and baby as equitable equivalent. But this petulant Portuguese must have his boy; so a black soldier, knowing his masterful man, offers to barter a boy for the baby and mother—done ! You, of course, call this spoiling the country, and Senhor

Commandant heartily agrees with the idea; spoiling is the very word, only he makes this poor participle do double duty—he spoils the country by extorting the spoils. Across the way, the Mission is a wakeful witness of it all, but this Chefe scorns intervention, pouring out fluent anathemas against the English. Prejudice, remember, is only another way of spelling "prejudge," and the blood flames in such an official's face like a danger signal whenever the Missionary expostulates. But there is impending change. Soon this political Apothecary discovers a fly in his ointment, the British and Belgians advancing simultaneously. Up from the South-West come the former; West from the Garenganze come the latter, both bent on combating this Portuguese slavery, both encroaching up near this Commandant's door. Time was when all around was no man's land, unlimited territory meaning unlimited despotism. Now comes the check. A hunted-down Luvale man runs across the border seeking sanctuary on British soil; how can the Portuguese chief get at him? Very simply. Salimi is "wanted," but he is snug under the shelter of the Jack in N.W. Rhodesia. But — mark this conjunction — Samusole is his brother-in-law, and he is on Portuguese soil; so his village is surrounded by night and S. dragged off to the Fort. Beaten every day by *chicotte*, he pays up some slaves, yet still they dun and whack him— all by proxy, all for that mysterious other man who is enjoying English protection across the border.

This Salimi, I have said, is "wanted," but for what

and whose crime ? He has a hamlet annoyingly across
the frontier, you remember, and to this man's place came
three roaming Portuguese slavers one day.   Out of the
grass spring three Britishers, and the three slavers are
imprisoned.   Then the clannish Portuguese over the way
gnash their teeth, and now it's " Salimi this " and " Salimi
that," until in sheer exasperation they pounce on the man
who dared to marry such a being's sister.   The old ghost
of *Nkole,* you see.   No wonder the natives are bad.
Yet as a matter of fine fact the best defence of this
oppressor is made by these very negroes who are wronged.
As a triumph of terseness they read off another " thinking
black " lesson from their old Book of Nature, and find that
a dozen trees all growing in a clump together dart up like
needles to the sky.   Whereas, *per contra,* one solitary tree
has the tedious tendency to be crooked.   The letter S—
that's the twisty shape isolation makes many a lonely
white man.   Six or sixteen of the letter lllll in a cluster
—lo ! the crowding together of civilisation straightens out
all their S-shaped crooks and cranks.   This, then, is their
defence of the white man cut off from all his race, and the
Bantu song runs :—

> " Oh ! crooked lonely forest tree,
>   Yes, crooked because lonely,
>   How very different things would be
>   If only comrades two or three
>   Could break your lone monotony."

One could probably travel far across the fields of
literature and fail to find a better metaphor for the

benefits of mutual help derived from dwelling in a community—ten trees in a clump shooting up like needles, and one lone tree twisted. Moral : Don't be a hermit, or you will be crooked and cranky.

(1st October.)

And so, as the thirty days in September pass, one is endlessly reminded by this negro babble that Africa and the African are merely convertible terms. Each is mutually and monotonously explanatory of the other. Here on the march, for instance, you are daily rubbing shoulders with a negro whose naked speech is first cousin to his naked body : nude negro = nude speech. Even in English, why forget that *custom* and *costume* are the same word ? Therefore in Africa the funny formula runs, nude costume = nude custom, and naked negro means naked speech. Call it objectionable this, by all means, but call it also consistent on the negro's part. For precisely as Mr. African's soul is clothed in its only black suit of bare skin, so too that same soul clothes itself in equally nude speech.

Another key to "thinking black." Take this great African sun as a formative factor in our negro's character. Here you have the pulse of the whole black race. There in that fructifying, sterilising sun their hard history is epitomised, for in this hopelessly dry season so sharply contrasted with the luxuriant wet, you find the source of spasm in the negro's very bones. This time the formula runs, " Like seasons, like African "; and just as Africa goes to sleep for half of the year, the very tree-sap dying

down into the tap-root, so, even so, with our dozing negro.
He copies his own Africa and is as lazy as a log, hibernating like a hedgehog.   The reason, this, why there are so
few moody Africans and why per million they are of one
humdrum type.   Just as from king to beggar they are
all N., S., E., and W. dining on one absolutely uniform
porridge and beans, even so for thousands of miles they
have all the same sort of sun-baked weather, same yellow
outlook, same six-months-on-end blue sky.   No use here
for that prop of introductory conversation in England—
the weather.   Contrast the moody Englishman for whom
Nature creates a new mood with the changing weather of
each new day, John Bull groping through the mist of Monday
to greet Tuesday's sunshine, and anon waking to the rattle
of Wednesday's rain.   Weather is a notorious formative
of character in man's moods, the spirits rise and fall with
the mercury, a varying barometer making a varying type
of individual.

Not so, however, when the first loud crack of thunder
heralds the farmer's rains ; that very sound seems to
startle him from his winter sleep.   His two seasons make
the African into two distinct men with two distinct
manners, for here comes their great annual miracle of the
blossoming of Aaron's rod.   Nature's hurried growth
is now a type of his own spasmodic haste, and he has
caught the infectious quiver in the air.   Some, indeed,
do snatch at the closing weeks of the dry season to travel,
for this is their only chance to see the face of their own
continent after the grass fires have swept the vast land

bare. But the first roar of the advancing rain acts as an alarm-bell to call in all stragglers who have wandered off for a journey, and now you can behold a model negro, hedgehog sloth all gone, stooping to his hoe in the morning mists. That bobbing back of his might be made of cast-iron with a hinge in it, so pluckily, so ploddingly does he bend to this farming business. The rising tree-sap seems in some sense to be a picture of what is happening in the black man. Ah! if he would only treat his soul as he treats his fields, all would be well.

(Later.)

Ten years ago I passed along the edge of a field, and there was the owner toiling at the hard soil, a drought having baked the red earth like a brick. " From the passing a passing word " is the local proverb, so I comply with tribal courtesy, bawling across the corn-field a regret that the soil is onerous and intractable. But the churlish clay has made a churlish cultivator. Back from my gruff friend comes the gruffer blasphemy : " Yes! a hard God has hardened the soil by denying rain."

Ten years pass, years that see this graceless man with many a graceless anti-God growl, a hard heart blaming a hard God. And now comes another instance of " the dramatic neatness of God's methods "—ten years have passed, I say, and here is the same man in the same field and the same passer-by. The rich red loam is no longer refractory, two successive days of rain have soaked the soil soft, the old growler's face wreathed in smiles. " From the passing man a passing word," and once again I smile across a remark about the child's-play hoeing under such simple conditions. Saved and knows it, what does he now answer—this same man in this same field to this same passer-by? "Truly soft," says he, "is the soil, for the God Who softened my heart also softened the hard soil : He has rained on my hard soul as well as on my soil." Do not blame that simple soul because he did not see the coincidence, for he did not. No calendar has he, no notion that here—or nowhere—is divine drama. Ten solid years ago, the same field, same man, same passer-by : a hard heart and hard soil then ; a soft, saved heart and soft, saved soil now. The old graceless growl is gone, and now for the note of joy—a full octave, a grand diapason. Having both a canoe and a farm, this saved soul is as much sailor as landsman, and can literally fulfil Clement's word in the second century : " Praising we plough ; and singing we sail."

(20th October.)

A formidable feature of our inland journey is the crossing of the weary Kifumadzi desert in the Luvale country. A curious bit of the earth's crust this to crawl over. In old maps here is a flat seriously put down as a sea, and (certes!) looking out from camp just as day is breaking in red on the great expanse of waste lying at our feet, the outlook is reminiscent of a sullen sea. We, as it were, camped on the beach near by, while stretching far beyond lies the great sandy ocean shorn by the wind of anything that ever grew upon it. Tufts of sere grass the exception. You might carry the idea a little further,

and like ships away on the skyline, suspicion the faint
outline of one or two palm-like trees, mere pin-points in
the immensity. Into this desolation we plunge to-day,
our black guides warning us that we will be cheaply
out of it with four days' hard journeying, water the cruel
lack ahead. We are in for Zebulun's portion at last:
"They shall suck of treasures hid in the sand." Thus
spurred on, we cut off our first slice of desert in a five
hours' journey, lurching along over tiresome sand, the
joys of a flat-as-a-dining-table path quite lost in the
dragging, deterrent track. Towards the close of the journey
wells dug by former travellers begin to appear, and down
into these we anxiously peer for a sign of water. In vain.
Once and again, and yet again, we draw blank, all as dry
as a kiln. Not enough water to wash your teeth in, not
a drop. *N.B.* : Dig your well before you are thirsty.
Yet still we swelter on, more than a little hungry, more
than a little hot, more than a little dirty, seeking, ever
seeking the water we find not. Miles and miles of un-
mitigated desert—*voilà tout.*

At last our joyless, jaded men will no longer be
beguiled on by hopes of hypothetical water, so they declare they will dig. This they do, right nobly, under a
broiling sun, and although a solid hour of it sees no
result, still they dig on into the second hour with plucky
negro pugnacity and breathing as loud as a forge bellows.
That perspiration streaming from them in the sun, they
call "the salt melting out of the beef." All our superior
sagacity is scorned, the Bihean being quite sure that if

water appears at all it will be in spite of us. Finally he won't even answer our eager questions, but keeps a surly silence, thinking, no doubt, that the sound of our own nonsense will make us ashamed. Approaching one of these diggers, tongue hanging out of the head, I was alarmed to see the faddy old gentleman look up with terror—or a good imitation of it—and beseeching me with the sweat of honest toil on his brow to make myself scarce, or the boots would drive away the water. " Boots," quoth he, " are not for desert sands." But the darkest hour is before the dawn, and the great frosty chill in our soul is dissipated by a sharp pistol shot, " Water ! " his eloquent, unassisted noun scorning the aid of verb, adjective, or adverb.

Then a man's head peeps up above the top of the well, and again and again the old Greek " Eureka ! " rings out defiance to the desert. Anon comes a song centuries old, and sung in all Eastern lands, one song, many variants :—

"Spring up, O well !"

At first the stuff drunk is liquid mud, first cousin to dirtiest ditch-water of old England, but early visitors to the well find the sediment eliminated and a fairly clean drink the residuum. Besides, there is a real rift in this cloud, and barring colour and consistency this precious fluid is neither brackish nor bitter—why, sand is the finest filter going. Far better this than the many putrid African pools one must sample, brimful with tadpoles and insects as nameless as numberless.

But, as the natives put it, "there can be no birth without a pang," so the dawn of the 21st of October sees us stoically beginning a second day of the desert tramp, the absolute sameness of the chronicle being repeated with the certainty of a phonograph. The silent desert parching in the sun can now be seen to break away in weary waves of sandhills, and our caravan pace has degenerated into a crawl, the route really not as "the crow flies" but as the snail crawls. And sure, there is something of the infinite in the very monotony of this waste, the vast sweep of the horizon only deepening this sense of infinity. Our roasting English tweeds make us envy the negro who peels to the waist and wears the merest wisp of garment round his equatorial regions. Sun and sand rule the road, the sun smiting your head and the sand doing its exasperating worst for your feet. Then, ahead, like a lurking lion, there is the same old perpetual puzzle at sundown. To wit, how, where, and when to get the supposititious fire that will boil the supposititious water locked in the bosom of this desert?

Splitting the caravan into two, like an orange, the "water" section is left in camp to wring a few drops of drink from that dry desert, whilst the faggot-seekers scatter over the clean-swept sand for fuel. It soon comes out that, far from thinking this "fire and water" cleavage a mere accident of desert environment, our negro argues that these two elements have for centuries been owned as the great "Kings of Africa." Ask him to prove his case for the dual kingship of Fire and Water, and this is how he most quaintly works out at the Euclidean Q.E.D. "A king indeed is King Fire," says he, "for listen, oh listen. You pack all your treasures into your house, and ('*sweru!*') an advancing forest fire having licked up all the grass now leaps up at your thatch, and devours your all, licking up in flame even the last vestige of house and goods. But, look ye! down dips the sun, the cold night wind darts into your body, and you gladly kneel before that same King Fire (the destroyer of your earthly all), craving his cheering warmth. Yea, you beseech him to cook your food, so little dare you disdain King Fire.

"So, too, with King Water. The rushing water perchance swallows in death your loved first-born, drowned perhaps in a canoe or crossing a rickety bridge. Yea, he, King Water, is the murderer of your darling, but darest thou refuse to drink him? Contrariwise, at sundown you cringingly kneel with your cup and—and drink of your son's murderer! Hail, King Water! and hail, King Fire! though ye slay me, yet must I cling to you." Certain it is that, poetic ravings apart, this kingship of these elements is a dry old forensic dictum among negroes, and (arson excepted) damages from fire and water in Africa are disallowed on the plea that it is an "act of God."

More: next comes a choking simoom, every man lying prone on the earth, head butting the sand. Good it is to see the reign of Law even here, for your nude natives are a lawless lot, and the Lord thus gives them an excellent example of His eternal equipoise of law—these howling sandstorms, I mean, rushing like fiends across the miles of blistering sand. For, be it noted, this sun burns, and burns, and b-u-r-n-s until, at a certain point, it seems to have overreached itself. Thus having disturbed by rarefaction the atmospheric balance, out rush the sand-hounds of the desert, these whirling hurricanes that easily establish equilibrium as by royal command. They blind and choke mere man, no doubt, but nevertheless the perfect balance of Nature is restored by a perfect Creator. Nor dare a snug—and smug— Missionary claim exemption from a mouthful of dirt upon the plea that God's message has brought him to these wilds : are not " the winds His messengers " too ? You'll only get sand in your teeth if you open your mouth in objection. Moral : Rain or shine, do not tamper with God's government of His own Africa.

This is not all. Such real give and take is there in this desert panorama that we are not surprised when, by way of counterpoise, the pendulum swings from sand- storm to the old hoax of mirage. Curious policy of make- believe this, for here you have a dead desert that long ago has killed all the poetry out of the waste ; here, wonder of wonders, is a howling wilderness in a sham penitential way turning poet and cheating us with mirage. Stern and forbidding as the earth is about here, what is this if not the desert turning poet ? A mocking attempt, shall we call it, to produce an imaginary oasis in lieu of the real thing : else how can you square the undeniable fact

that the uglier the desert the more seductive the mirage?
(Granted, the said bewitching mirage is as much in you
as it is in the treacherous desert, yet is it not equally
certain that, given no desert, there can be no mirage?)
Be that as it may, here is the true tale of a mirage.   Back
came our faggot-searchers one by one, solemnly reporting
a lake to be seen away on the Southern skyline.   The
oldest Biheans with us stoutly refused to believe the thing,
until finally the wrangle came to an issue in my offering
to accompany four of our faithfuls to see for ourselves;
the *pro* lake and *pro* mirage factions being both represented.   (Rather reminiscent, this, of the *pro* water, *pro*
fire sections we left behind.)   So off we start, heading due
South and tramping for two solid hours; the *pro* lake
prophets developing a somewhat chastened optimism the
farther we penetrated into the void.   On and on we go,
hope finally sinking so low that it seems to ooze out of
our boots—no lake visible, or likely to be.   Only the same
old outlook on a limitless ocean of sand.   Yet here is a
blatant "*pro*-laker" at your elbow indoctrinating you
with his eloquent fiction of a man-in-the-moon oasis, the
earnest entreaty of the man almost winning you over to
his dream.   Certain it is, I have the black and white of
my note-book for it, that I too caught the same momentary mirage, and declared my own private and unalterable
conviction that the men were right, for—for there was a
lake!   But the Bihean who was our guide enjoyed my
greenness, and for many a day afterwards when we met,
his face wore a suspicious smile suggestive of the fact that

he was still chewing the cud of an exceedingly pleasant jest. As, however, we had the choice of either tramping on South at this rate for ten solid days of desert, or going back to camp, we preferred retreat. In all that weary counter-march we sighted only two living things, a jackal and a sad-faced gnu; our Biheans arguing that of the two the jackal was a peculiarly succulent morsel. Thus did we prove that a desert, so obviously a death-trap in many other particulars, caps all its sad shortcomings in this accomplished mendacity of mirage. For if water for the moment is not your pinch, then you are sure to dream of the far-away leeks and garlic of Egypt. And if perchance the Army and Navy Stores have cheated the wilderness by preserving Egyptian leeks and garlic, then some other dream is sure to appear as your "will-o'-the-wisp" of the night. Unfortunately, we had no animals with us: a horse or a donkey is never deceived by mirage. Smell, not sight, is their sure guide, and where an animal sniffs not moisture you may despise Africa's most seductive mirage. Away in the Western sky, lo! a dozen dark vultures hovering for the funeral of an antelope, the official mourners these, come to bury a denizen of the plains. More than mourners, they are the African grave-diggers; and, more than grave-diggers, they themselves are the grave, the spades their own beaks.

*   *   *

Not to mimic too much the guide-book style, let me write one word in retrospect on the configuration of the country. After crossing the Kwanza River heading East,

we encountered that curious switchback arrangement of
hills for the first week. Finally following this lively lot
of steeple-chasing it over the country, we are jolted down
into Luvaleland, literally "the Flats." Here the joys of
the future railroad surveyors begin, and long level miles
of country ahead will admit of a railway running like a
ramrod due East. Kavungu, afterwards the scene of the
sainted Cyril Bird's labours, was then only a dark den of
robbers, and a rendezvous for all the slave caravans of the
Interior. Here it is the muttering storm of revolt bursts
on us, and our craven carriers strike for higher wages.
After a five days' siege in our little forest zariba, the
enemy pulls down his flag, and all is in train for a start on
11th October for the last long stage of Eastward journey.
Struck the upper reaches of the far-flowing Zambezi on
the 18th, and on the 23rd swam across the Lukoleshe, its
last feeder intercepting our path. This means, of course,
that the rivers ahead all shed off to the Congo basin on
the North. You would have applauded the army of
youngsters struggling across the broad Lutikina where we
forded it hard by the rapids. With load on head they
pluckily fought the rushing sheet of water, now and then
making a grab at some big brother when the flow
threatened to swish them off their feet. By the 26th we
have, far on our right, the lonely Kaleñe Hill, on which
dark spot the lights of Dr. and Mrs. Fisher's house
will not begin to flicker for fourteen years to come. And
now we begin to pull ourselves together, for we have
passed the longitudinal centre of the continent and hope

wings onward. Then comes the crossing of the Lufupa and Lulua, two noble rivers in one day, with laborious bridging of the former. Camping on the off bank (oldest rule of the road : cross your last river for the day and camp!), the morrow sees us cutting across the "Zebra Plains"; no misnomer the name, for, superbly beautiful, there they are in troops sporting in the sun. A sort of safe postal address this, for Zebras, I fancy. Where are we now? Naïve nature already suspicions some impending change ahead, and the ground begins to echo a metallic sound. Pushing on, we pass within stone-throw of the great Miambo copper mines, a huge mass of mineral rock, riddled all over with marks of excavations, and all oxidised into green. Exactly like a great old fortress shaken by war and riddled with shell. Frowning buttresses and gaping gashes all over. At last comes the 1st of November and *dies memorabilis* of our venture. The path from our camp at Miambo is a gentle slope upwards for an hour, then along a level ridge boasting a stubborn growth of sharp cactus. We are not on the easy descent many minutes, however, when the hedging trees on all sides disappear, and here is the Garenganze at last! Across the laughing waters of the Lualaba, there we have the lovely vision of our blue Garenganze hills, and another (mental) vision of lively life ahead. Thus it happened that after thirty-two months of protracted endeavour *en route*, we pass through the Western door of Mushidi's empire at the Lualaba.

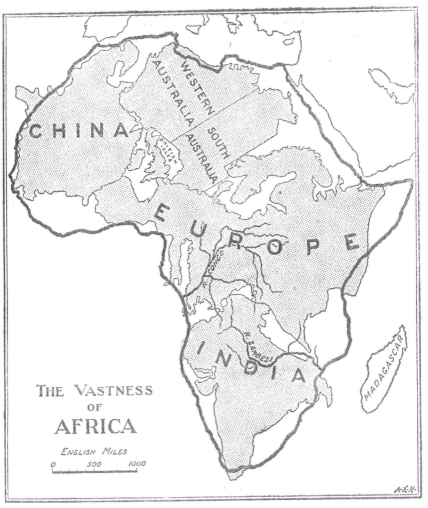

THE VASTNESS
OF
AFRICA

ENGLISH MILES

0   500   1000

THE vastness of Africa is vividly suggested by this map. India (1,574,450 sq. miles), China (1,300,000 sq. miles), Europe (3,700,000 sq. miles), Great Britain (122,500 sq. miles), and most of Australia (2,350,000 sq. miles) have all been laid (drawn to the same scale) on the face of Africa, and still there are many uncovered plots, equal to India in bulk. The total, 9,046,950 sq. miles against Africa's 12,000,000.

BOOK II

CHAPTER X

Farthest, but Shut In

"Solomon, where is thy glory?
It's gone in the wind!
Babylon! what of thy story?
It's gone in the wind!"

RÜCKERT (APPROX. FROM GERMAN).

*　　　*　　　*

"On crossing the Lualaba, I shall go direct S.W. to the copper mines of Katanga. Eight days south of Katanga the natives declare the fountains [of the Nile] to be. When I have found them I shall return by Katanga to the underground houses of Rua . . . travel in boat up the river Lufira."

LIVINGSTONE'S FAREWELL TO STANLEY.

*　　　*　　　*

"You know the hopelessness of such a task [as African Missions] till you find a St. Paul or a St. John. Their representatives nowadays want so much per year and a contract."

GENERAL GORDON TO SIR RICHARD BURTON.

CHAPTER X

Farthest, but Shut, In

WHEREAT the reader is glad, for at last, after thirty-two months' delay on the road, he arrives at Mushidi's great capital.

YOU think that this great negro London is a choice corner of the continent. Not a bit of it. By way of choosing a country Mushidi has blundered on a bare brown stretch of soil, flanked by two ribs of rocky hills, scarcely any timber for fuel and a scarcer supply of water. The city of Tantalus this Babylon should be called, for the water, as it were, is up to your chin, yet you can never get at it :

> "Water, water, everywhere,
> Nor any drop to drink."

The real rivers of the land, Lualaba and Lufira, just near enough on the map to make the teeth water, and just far enough to defy you to drink a drop. "Tantalising," we call it, but the "thinking black" metaphor for this same idea is the wild phrase, "the non-biteable elbow"! "Your elbow is near to your mouth, but can you bite it?" ask these thirsty ones. And the reason? The story runs that Mushidi was born out East in just such a barren type of land, the tribe all drinking from wells, and never seeing a fish. Far from being discontented with their lot, they made necessity a virtue and put the whole tribe under stern prohibition of fish, this taboo going down to endless generations. Here, then, you find Mushidi's reason for scorning the banks of such a noble river as the Lualaba—did not the despotism of custom doom thousands of souls to renounce a fish diet? The dead ancestors of Mushidi really rule the land from their graves in the Far East, and they alone are the supreme arbiters in morals. "Thou shalt not eat fish," say a thousand dead men, and Mushidi's millions quake "Amen." Let the living defy the voice of the dead: let them say, The times are changed and we change with them—say this in Africa and at once the door of the spirit-world is slammed in their faces, and their guardian spirits are turned to be their enemies. So here we are doomed to drink dirty water for many a day, the potion so putrid that it is impossible to drink any that has lain overnight.

It is at the Nkulu end of this capital that Mushidi has his headquarters, and here the Arabs have built him his Castle of Indolence in wattle and daub, a large but very shabby relation of Buckingham Palace. A cold, cheerless, mud barn, really, the grass roof forbidding a chimney. In Africa a room without a fireplace—and

there are too many such—is like a head without eyes
in it, a face without a smile. You shiver in it even
when the air is warm, and you wonder why you do
so. Not so the negro. The first Luban who saw a
fire on the hearth deplored such a wicked waste of
fuel, and on seeing the flame running up the chimney,
actually proposed to run up after it. If all the heat
goes out at the top, why not take the overland route,
why not climb the roof, squat on the chimney, and
catch it coming out?

In the days when I was the only white skin at
Bunkeya I got to size up my Mushidi rather closely.
Here the five hundred wives stream in on him with
well-cooked dainties, for do they not all vie with each
other to capture the Chief's citadel, his stomach? The
prose of this culinary combat, if converted into the poetry
of porridge, probably runs :—

> "The turnpike road to royal hearts, I find,
> Lies through their mouths, or I mistake mankind."

Thus it cometh to pass that, pampered with negro
luxury and softened by sloth, strength is forsaking
Mushidi's limbs as common sense his skull, and the old
tale is once again true that luxury is the conqueror
of conquerors. He never dreams what a great luxury
it is to dispense with luxury. Hungry as I often am
these days, Mushidi and I dine together on all manner
of messes, the only other invited guests being one or
two tiny negro tots who cannot aspire to be Mushidi's

rivals. I suppose it is on the principle of the smallest stars being nearest the sun that these doll-guests are allowed to join us, for even a group of elders is driven off and expected to eat our leavings. Mushidi's favourite name is that of a forest tree, and the loftier the tree, remember, the less shade there is at its foot. So Mushidi's very loftiness makes him lonely enough at these feasts. Even aristocrats like Talashio and Mumomeka are waved off. Of course, knives and forks are taboo, for why bring weapons of death to a feast, the emblem of life? Spurning, therefore, such new-fangled vulgarities of Europe, we follow the oldest track of the sons of men leading to the cooking-pot, and washing our fingers scrupulously, here we are in imagination sitting down with Abraham, Isaac, and Jacob, using Adam's knives and forks. Once, indeed, I produced a pocket-knife wherewith to aid mastication, but the startled king, alarmed at this lapse of decorum, seemed to imagine I was going to dine off, instead of with, him. There is sense, too, in this anti-knife idea, for surely we lose our good teeth for the similar reason as the savage has beauties. Our innovation of knives and forks has done it all; you cannot have your cake and eat it, and if a knife does the work of the teeth, then you lose the latter for the former.

It sounds very simple so to leap back a thousand years in table etiquette, but the fact is, to sup with primitive man you feel quite nervous about your first dinner-party. Only one dish is allowed, and you are even denied any liquid assistance to wash it down.   Having heard rumours of our "grace before meat" doings, Mushidi quite seriously wanted me to shut my eyes while he kept his open "to see how it was done."   Like the young heathen "Huck," it seems to him droll, so droll, this inability to proceed right off with our eating, without first of all mumbling something over the food—yet there is nothing wrong with it.   When he asked if he should "say grace" too, I gave him a nasty nag by answering, "No!   For it is written that God hath created meats to be received with thanksgiving *of them which believe and know the truth.*"   "Say something to God about the food" is a curious (and not bad) phrasing of the request for grace before meat.   Farther out East, where raiding is customary on the outskirts of some Christian native schools, the rumour runs that warriors reckon on the very devotions of the saints to swoop down and do cattle-lifting.   Like Mushidi, who asks me to pray while he keeps his eyes open and watches, these freebooters say : "Yes, let us wait till they shut their eyes and pray, then when their eyes are shut we will steal their cattle."   Thus the very phrase "to shut the eyes" ultimately works out at the very curious idea of "living for eternity," the thought being that the man who so prays is oblivious to the mere temporalities of life, for does he not shut his eyes and look off to the unseen ?

And so the royal meal goes forward with great decorum, our stony silence only broken by the dip of each sop ("a boat" they call it) into the sauce.   No spoon

allowed, so you, the possessor of a richly developed sense
of humour, must mop up the gravy with a sop of mush.
Talk about manners, some of the royal notions of *bon ton*
make you fancy you are dining in the moon. Yet how
can I laugh at him when I remember that our own Henry
the Eighth, with magnificent unconcern, did also eat with
his fingers ? And when hungry would he not take up his
victuals and swallow them in handfuls at a time ? Why,
Mushidi in comparison is as polite as a dancing-master.

Be it noted, this puzzling Mushidi is keen on writing,
and here in Bunkeya it is a sight to see every paltry
scrap of paper prized almost more than cloth. One man
after another treats a bit of old newspaper as tenderly as
a crisp bank-note, a rumour having come in from the far
Ocean that our race was really "ruled by paper." Even
calico is common, they say, but does not paper buy
calico ? So they seize on every scrap they can find, and
soon you see the Chief scrawling on it a rapid Pitman's
system of shorthand kind of writing. Since the days of
old when his ancestors scribbled with sepia on papyrus,
this is the first timid dip into the great ocean of Literature
by the mighty negro. With a dexterous sweep of your
borrowed pencil he flashes along the paper in a curious
switchback manner, the lines crossing and recrossing each
other in a hopeless tangle. Oh! ye who have seen a
spider crawl out of an inkstand and stroll across a sheet
of letter-paper; never since then have you seen the equal
in penmanship. And all this crooked calligraphy because
we as a white race are ruled by paper, forgetful of the

fact that although paper rules us, we at least rule our paper. What a black-and-white jumble of crooked lines! "Medicine," is what he calls it, and, truth to tell, so cryptic does it look that, in England, after vainly trying to decipher same, one would most naturally send it round to the local chemist to be made up as a prescription.

This "black-art" notion of letter-writing has got such a cunning grip of the negro brain that even your own black boy will recall you on urgent business by scrawling a few lines of zigzag nonsense on a bare sheet of paper. The real message, of course, is verbal, but these magic lines of criss-cross could not be omitted. Is there any significance in the fact that the negro word "to write" is only the word "to tattoo," and does he think that we tattoo on paper precisely as he does on his body? Even Mushidi, who does not believe in discretion being the better part of valour, has been known to scrawl one of these vainglorious cryptograms to his enemy in arms. I wonder, does he think that to have it out in black and white is better than settling scores in black and blue? Along with this funny stenography he (joyously scenting battle!) takes great good care to send the eloquent present of a hoe and bag of bullets, offering his enemy a this-or-that choice—peace or war, bullets or hoe? A sort of heathen Parcels Post arrangement this, I suppose, with accompanying communication per Letter Post.

No notion has he that in this writing of ours we catch the living thought as a word and imprison it on paper. The exact idea he seems to have of the business is akin to that of the little girl who thinks that by pressing the button she has thereby made the electric light. Pushing investigations, it leaks out that the Arabs have for long years juggled with the art of writing, this indeed being their greatest asset among raw natives. It is magic or nothing. Do they not believe that the most potent medicine is simply a written line of the Koran, swallowed by the sufferer? A literal use this of the prophet Jeremiah's saying : " Thy words were found, and I did eat them." The leaves of the Tree of Life are medicinal, but so, too, argues the Arab, are literal leaves of a book. Little wonder, then, the African clutches at the new idea of writing, for when he sees us reading he wakens as from a nightmare to discover that the whole heap of the past experiences of his race is lost to ken because of this lack of a literature. Yes, all the accumulated negro wisdom of centuries might have been his heritage if only somebody had dreamed of writing them down. But as it is, every black boy is thrown on the hard knocks of the world as though he were living in the year after Adam fell—no past treasure of written wisdom.

Probably, too, the negro vice of congenital lying flows from this same source of booklessness. For they have nothing down in black and white. Promises are merely verbal, not written, therefore the hardest-mouthed negro wins. Had he committed himself to writing, then, following the Arab idea of masticating paper, a hundred liars could be made literally to eat their written lies. Did not Christ meet all the Devil's lies with the one silencing

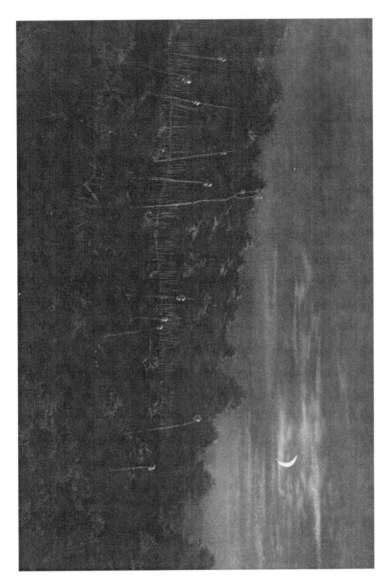

A Typical "Wipe out"

phrase : " It is written "?   Is this what Job means when
he cries : " Oh that mine enemy had written a book ! "?
Certainly the African has nothing in writing, hence flows
this flood of falsehood.   Hence, too, that proverb of
theirs, " When the rabbit was promised beans he produced a basket," the idea being that a verbal promise is only
valid when it is uttered, and not later.   Art thou promised
beans ?   Then produce thy basket and carry them off.

Exasperated at this lack of definite data, they (and
wouldn't you ?) have many a funny expedient to fix
facts in the mind.   When I saw the Prince Chamunda
he was almost buried in a great coil of knotted cord : his
perpetual calendar this, of the passing days.   Run on the
decimal system, every tenth knot is double, and as he
gazed on the increasing heap a sorry sigh escaped him.
Thinking me sadly lacking in scholastic culture, this man
laughed at my month of four weeks : he made it one
week = ten days, therefore thirty days = three weeks.   If
a month, says he, how can you divide it by four ?   But
this pioneer in time-tables was soon wiped out, for finally
the town rose against him and shrieked that this
" numbering of the days " was witchcraft : was he not
merely counting out the days of his neighbours unto
burial ?   Thus they strangled reform—a badly needed one
too, for quite an aged man will tell you blandly that he
is ten years of age.   Is this calculation correct after all ?
Does he mean that, sleeping away three-quarters of his life
as he does, it is fair only to count the meagre margin that
remains of non-slept time ?   Days they can count, but as

for mere hours! Not one clock or watch in the whole
land, and their mighty sun overhead is so very much the
national timepiece that whether you innovate a "Water-
bury" or an eight-day clock, "sun" (*nsaa*) is the only
name they can give such a tantalising ticker. And here
it is in this clockless life you find the real root of his
happy-go-lucky existence; never did that irritating tick-
tack tick-tack set the African nerves on edge; never did
that everlasting click-click of the terrible escapement of
a watch put him on his mettle as a man. This to a
negro—to put it mildly—would be equivalent to dying a
peculiarly unpleasant and unnecessary kind of death.
Time is passing, quickly passing; "but," objects the
negro, "why nag out the truth so brutally, why this
relentless repetition?"

If it be permissible to English the famous line of
Schiller, "The happy hear no clock," then, certes, all
Africa would arise and claim that great German as their
anti-timepiece champion. The pretensions, too, of this
preposterous little thing called a "sun," still at it after
sundown, still bustling on through the night with a tick
like a fever pulse! A "sun"? why, *the* sun, the genuine
article, has set long ago. Yet the commonest form of
treating the first few watches that came in from the
Atlantic was to keep them swaying to and fro—lest they
stopped. But they inconsistently object to the very
thing they encouraged. One old man solemnly resolved
to boil his ticker by way of curing it of this "bee-like
buzzing in the belly"; and another negro (younger,

therefore wiser) frankly solved the problem by eviscerating the inner wheels. With a kind of lofty obstinacy, these negroes would listen not at all to my short but masterly account of their delicate mechanism, and finally the poor palpitating watches were "killed" neatly and thoroughly, their tin cases becoming the smart snuff-boxes of such smart Africans.

Another attempt I saw at negro recording was in a little hut where I slept. Looking up to the beehive roof I spied a number of tiny white flags flying, mere ribbons of calico these, some grimed with soot, and one quite new. "Oh !" said the owner thereof, "these are receipts of debts I have paid." Commoner still is it to find little packets of twigs scrupulously tied together, the varying sizes all eloquent of some transaction represented by these vouchers—a long tusk of ivory, for instance, being memorised by a longish twig, and so on in ratio right round the various sorts and sizes of tusks.

*   *   *

The royal "sneeze," I find, is a solemn event here in Court life. For if this Mushidi can produce a successful sneeze in public, then the thousands of negroes acclaim such a sovereign act with a thunder of hand-clapping : "Long live the King ! Hail !" Therefore the oftener he so sneezes the longer is he supposed to live, the idea being that a sneeze is only a superabundance of life overflowing in friendly fizz. A paroxysm of sneezing only evokes a chorus of approval, and one almost suspects that the old man is addicted to the very snuffing that is taboo. As, therefore, all his oppressed subjects are presumably longing for Mushidi's death, this is the reason for his so theatrically brandishing this sneeze in their faces. A sort of health certificate it is, notifying all comers that there is life in "the old boy" yet, for has not the champagne of life still some fizz in it? Oh, that beaming smile of hope spreading across the monarch's countenance when he is waiting for his sneeze, notice of whose arrival has been telegraphed in advance. A-a-a-atchoo! comes the mighty deed, and the roar of response is so loud that you can almost understand what Xenophon means when he tells you of the famous sneeze that decided the fate of Athens. For is not this sneeze as historic as it is international? Compare in ancient Greece the greeting " Zeus preserve thee " after a sneeze. Or in ancient Italy the phrase, " Sit salutiferum," with its modern Italian equivalent, " Felicità." Or the German " Gesundheit," the French " Bonne santé," and the North of England " Bless the bairn," all after a solemn sneeze. The contrary, too, is also seen when His Majesty is indisposed, a mere royal headache or cold sending a shiver through the land. In Russia, one tear in the Czar's eye is said to cost a thousand pocket-handkerchiefs; but Mushidi, he goes farther, and resolves that if he cannot sleep he will let nobody else do so, saint or sinner. Many a midnight messenger does he send off to us to call the "men of God," and he gives his royal word with a royal oath that our medicines mean "Life Eternal." "*Kapalı Vali Okufa!*" he said as he gazed at the

bottles of physic : "There is no more death." The old
Napoleonic phrase, " As false as a bulletin," becomes quite
the common idea at Mushidi's Court.   " Eternal health "
is his dream—but remember the average eternity of a
negro lasts only six weeks.   A most nerve-racking ordeal
any such " treatment " ever is, because the native " witch-
doctors " are usually attacked for failure, and frictions
abound.   A favourite method of disposing of a nasty
drug is the common African device of taking the dose, not
in person, but by proxy, the real sick man believing that
if even his cousin drinks it for him, then the healing
virtue will be the same.   Have they not the same blood ?

Or smoke your medicine in a pipe, as one patient of
mine did.   Busy with something else, and mindful of the
dictum that the whole art of medicine consists in judicious
poisoning, I gave the lady three tabloids, leaving her to
dispose of them in the easy and elementary mode of such
a pampered form of dispensing.   Swallow them ? Not
she, my lady.   Meeting her an hour afterwards, the
only answer this negro sister gave was by pointing
silently to the huge gourd pipe she was then smoking.
Nor could I remotely guess what the solemn-faced
sacrifice meant by this pointing in such a scared way to
her pipe, until my eye caught the poor tabloids roasting
in the bowl like coffee-beans.   She cannot conceive how
decisive is a doctor's dose, but in a kindly way approves
all she can.   Put the clinical thermometer in her mouth
for a few seconds, and she sucks it solemnly for healing
virtue.   Remove now the said instrument and wave her

12

off—back she comes to-morrow for—for a second suck, the thermometer having worked mightily, yea mentally. She means, doubtless, to be cured by degrees. But Mr. Missionary, being a bit of a quack in his own quiet way, often finds his awkward and rather prickly professional pride humbled. He is nettled that the negro does not believe in him, and shivers even in the sunshine when he recalls Voltaire's biting phrase about pouring "drugs of which we know little into bodies of which we know less." A good treatment in Europe can be fatal in Africa. Mercury, for example, specific among Europeans, is, dose for dose, certain death to a negro. A proof this, of Voltaire's phrase.

The commoner pest is the malingerer who wants your healing balm. Balm, of course, in a bottle, the said bottle to possess a cork—for is she not in a sinking condition? Round the corner, in brisk business fashion, out goes the medicine and in goes the snuff, the bottle with the cork having seemingly saved this sinking sable sister. The same lady this who treats your Gospel in the same way, swallows the sermon and spits out the salvation. Contrast their treatment of one of their own old devil-doctors. He, oh, he is revered, and all because he makes them pay through the nose, even demanding an initial fee, *Chiteo*, before he stoops to take any case in hand. The real professional he. One such I found threatening a patient with sudden gunshot-death if he failed to find the fees—had cured his man and then proposed to kill him for the cure! He laughed at me for manifestly saving a dysentery case with lead and opium and getting nothing for it—he would have shot the very man he had cured. In other words, would have given him the lead without the opium.

*   *   *

But what is this Mushidi who thus drags his weary, wicked way through these pages?

Here is his history in a nutshell. Long ago, as a mere adventurer, he wriggled into the Lufira valley from the Far East, his followers numbering three men *plus* his wife, Kapapa—grand total, five souls. He is heading for Mpande, the Sanga Copper King, this chief having covenanted friendship with Mushidi's father, Kalasa. Here, then, you have the thin edge of the wedge of this future despotism, for this *Bulunda* covenant is of genuine sanctity among raw, unsophisticated natives. More than a mere chance acquaintance, he it is, this covenanted "friend," who must stick closer than a brother.

Now, the brother, or brothers, as in the case of this Copper King, had failed him at the crucial point, and is there not a Bantu proverb that declares a brother is born for adversity? Yet here was Mpande attacked from the North by Lubans, all his harem kidnapped, and no Sanga kinsman forthcoming to lend a fraternal hand—this, forsooth, in the teeth of the basic Bantu proverb-law that a brother is *born* for adversity. Who ever dared in Africa to fly in the face of a proverb? Is it not the smallest possible means of conveying the largest

amount of wisdom ?   But here in the nick of time succour
does arrive.   Look at this travel-stained band of four
men and a woman filing into the Sanga stockade at sundown : is not this Mushidi, son of the covenanted "friend,"
Kalasa ?   Truly, here *is* a friend that sticketh closer
than a brother.   And there the whole story begins, yea,
there also it ends, for there is nothing more to tell.
Mushidi said, " *J'y suis, j'y reste.*"   A born manipulator of
mankind, he made his dispositions accordingly, and with a
mere handful of men followed up the Lubans, attacked
by night, and rescued the kidnapped Sanga folks.   Watch
the momentous sequel.   There and then, in the double
heat of gratitude to the "friend" and rancour to the
deserting "brother," a solemn pact was sealed : punning
a variant on the old proverb, the grateful Copper King
in one historic precedent cut off all his blood kinsmen
"without a shilling" in the declaration : "A friend in
need is a brother indeed !   Thou, Mushidi, art my
Nswana, or heir apparent ; on thee only I bestow the
Omande shell !"   Now, here in this daring but dangerous
ignoring of sacred blood kinsmanship you have the
slumbering *casus belli* of the long-subsequent revolt of
the Sanga tribe.   Here, too, you have the mainsprings
of Mushidi's bloody policy in these later years—does he
not know that on the first sign of weakness the real
aboriginal lords of the Sanga soil will give his foreign
carcase to the fowls of the air ?   Here, too, you find
Mushidi's subtle reason for the building of a negro
cosmopolitan state—does he not know that in this

vast polyglot capital the aboriginal Sanga folks are outvoted?

Let it not be supposed, however, that to root out the aborigines is an easier thing to perform than to plan. These lords of the copper country, I have explained, are the Va Sanga, and a very poor sort of tribe of Judah, because their totem is "The Lion." Copying the lion, they alone boast a bearded manhood, and the longer the beard the more ideal the Sanga man. They spend years on the task of teaching this tribal beard to make a wonderful copy of *Felis leo*, and the Sanga man's heart-break is when he can only imitate a billygoat. The black Sanga showing his white teeth through the foliage of a long black beard, and rolling his "r's" like the Northumbrian burr—this is all the portrait you need of him. Yet *he* has the real title-deeds, and when Mushidi trained these Va Sanga as elephant-hunters he little guessed that one day, in revolt, they would draw a most careful bead on every Yeke man sighted in the bush.

(Later.)

This negro potentate is nothing if not superlative, and quite early in his curious career he resolves, in a blaze of tinsel glory, to wed a "white wife." So, with all his Eastern antipathies, he turns naturally to the West Coast, and in the pliant Portuguese sees the very men who will negotiate the dirty "deal." Are they not keen black slavers, and might they not return the compliment by selling him a white wife? He even presented his heathen compliments to His Excellency the Governor of St. Paul

de Loanda, requesting the hand of any of his young
daughters—the ivory dowry fixed at thirty tusks. Failing in this, his quest out along the Benguella road was
more successful. The stinging sarcasm of the proposal
was of course quite lost on the degraded Portuguese, and
one grim day, yes! "Madam Mushidi" actually arrived
from the far West. What a zenith hour for Bluebeard
when that daring item, so long down in his programme,
was marked off as fact stranger than fiction. Then it was
he proclaimed himself by the name "Telwatelwawatel-
wanekumwineputu"—the spelling is mine, reader, the
pronunciation thine. This means, "The always-spoken-
of-one, spoken-of-even-in-the-Courts-of-Europe," and the
title is a one-word unit rattled off breathlessly with no
pause.[1] But Mushidi was far too clever a person to see
anything exactly as it was, nor did he dream of those
domestic bickerings in store for His Majesty. A plain
man had married a brilliant woman, but what plain man
wants a blaze of fireworks at his fireside? Certainly not
this type of woman, for I once heard her call Mushidi "a
pig." Maria de Fonseca was her name, her father a
Portuguese officer; the proud brother being the famous
(or notorious) Senhor Coimbra, who lived west of
Bailundu. The same rogue this, Lourenço da Souza
Coimbra, who with his gang of fifty-two slaves tied in
lots of seventeen or eighteen, fell in with Lovett Cameron

---

[1] If you ask me how to pronounce this long-as-a-comet name, may I
parenthetically reply that it is done the way a great man said he pronounced
"Chicago"? "I never pronounce it," said he.

in Luba country. This man wrote a dying charge committing the guardianship of his empress-niece to me, and Maria de Fonseca was always very clannish to her own colour, calling them "brothers." "Queen Café-au-lait" is a happy description of her own pigment, but Mushidi always condescendingly calls her "our white sister." The sombre complacency of this degrading union is the dreariest part of it all, the Portuguese having merely sold the woman for a few hundred pounds. From the Mushidi standpoint, however, what he needed badly was an awe-inspiring prestige so great that the tribes lining his trade route out to the Atlantic will not dare to molest his caravans. For like the old Wagogo tricks on the road East to Zanzibar these Luvale live on the looting of passing caravans, and no sooner does a caravan pass into the Interior than these Luvale begin to plot its prospective plunder on the return journey. Thus even Mushidi's slave clientele run a risky game, for their road out west is bristling with Luvale "gas-pipe" guns. Sold by the stupid Biheans to the sly Luvale, the very guns they sold were pointed against them. This is why Kavungu is the great half-way point on which all homeward-bound Biheans concentrate; and only when they have massed in their thousands will they dare to sally out on the western road. Hence, then, the diplomacy of planning this Portuguese marriage, for with effusive flattery Mushidi was told it would link his capital with the Courts of Europe.

Infatuated with this daring link, he even resolved to

ape European ways, and one caravan he actually loaded up with ivory, the stringent instructions being to take it out to the thousand-miles-off ocean and receive as payment only English earthenware goods. Long months elapsed before the ambitious wanderers returned, the eloquent rattle-tattle of the loads of doomed earthenware being ominously metallic and tell-tale. When Homer at the dawn of history reminded the human race of the possibility of a slip between the cup and the lip, he little guessed what a vision of smashed cups would meet the eye of Mushidi as he gazed on those broken dreams of earthenware. Plates and cups, bowls and saucers, all broken to atoms, yet all solemnly taken out of the boxes with exasperating good humour. Each fragment judged to be a thing of beauty and a joy for ever. Even the smallest chips of china, with infantine gurgles of delight, were strung round the neck as ornaments, the handles of the cups innovating a new fashion in earrings. Such was Mushidi's attempt to take the kingdom of civilisation by force. And that fragile china is an eloquent enough symbol of the very civilisation he coveted, which smashed in his hands.

CHAPTER XI

Vice Versa

"With joyful enthusiasm they [the Britons] applauded this speech [of Galgacus], in their barbarian fashion, with songs and murmurs, and discordant exclamations."   TACITUS.

*   *   *

" Most of the inland inhabitants [of Britain] do not sow corn, but live on milk and flesh, and are clad in skins.   All the Britons, indeed, dye themselves with woad, which gives a bluish colour, and thus they are more alarming to look upon in battle.   They wear their hair long, and have every part of their body shaved except their head and upper lip."   CÆSAR.

*   *   *

"A group of ten and even twelve have wives in common, and particularly brothers among brothers, and parents among their children, but if there be any issue by these wives, they are reputed to be the children of those to whose house each respectively was first brought as a bride."   CÆSAR.

*   *   *

"Some people . . . may be Rooshans, and others may be Prooshans; they are born so, and will please themselves.   Them which is of other naturs thinks different."   (*Mrs. Gamp.*)   DICKENS.

CHAPTER XI

Vice Versa

WHEREIN the reader discovers that a tyrant is a man who finds his happiness in the misery of other people.

YET this kind of thing goes on and on, not the West Coast only but the East, not the East only but the South, a constant stream of these Mushidi caravans worming their way out to all the Coast settlements. There they gorge themselves with so-called civilisation; there, too, many are sucked into the whirlpool of gin-boozing, and dozens disappear from mortal ken, the probable prey of bandits paying them out in their own Mushidi coin. All along the East Coast you can find a Mushidite who, when he first sighted the Ocean, resolved never to leave it. And there he is to-day, a prosperous trader or the like, Arab skull-cap stuck impudently on his head, with all the old Hodge marks of his youth gone. "Absconded" is the English way of phrasing this runaway's action, but he had no compunction in charging Mushidi 100 per cent commission on the long Ocean journey, thus crying quits. Did not the king claim 100 per cent from the defaulter's own father?

At our end of the line, too, this identical thing is happening, many an Arab arriving at Mushidi's capital never again to leave it.   Mere packmen as such often are, Mushidi politely plunders the trader—with the man's own permission, the bargain being a dark affair in which the new-comer is presented with a wife and fields in exchange for the trade goods of some defrauded Coast merchant. Never will Mr. Packman sight the sea again, and never will the owner of the goods touch even a farthing in the pound.   Thus Mushidi squares accounts with his commercial foes.   Does the seductive Coast rob him of his caravans ? Then he will retaliate and pleasantly plunder a venturesome Arab of another man's money.   But by no manner of means are you to imagine that this tit-for-tat trickery is barren of result.   Truth demands the candid confession that this alone is the thing an African can understand. *Lex talionis* is written in his bones, and it is only when two rival factions are united in a common bond of horror of each other that they desist from crime.

*   *   *

But what about the Portuguese wife ?   Poor Queen Maria de Fonseca !   Some ladies realise that their fortune is invested in their face, and naturally expect to draw interest on the said capital.   Maria de Fonseca, alone of all her colour among a million blacks, found her capital invested not in her face but in her skin, and drew cent per cent interest accordingly.   Financial interest as well as social ditto ; for the lady who boasted—" My face is my fortune, sir !" she said—well knew that her boasted beauty, like wealth, is easily lost, whereas a white skin is a capital that is at par in Africa as long as life lasts. Her favourite affectation in dress these days is the wearing of loud velvet in voluptuous folds : blue, red, or yellow velvet one day, and brown or green the next. Arriving in the Interior, not by any means in the first blush of maidenhood, here she is frivolling about the capital, and hating the whole harem of rivals. Many an envenomed glance she shoots at an enemy, and many a plot she hatches for the downfall of some poor harmless soul. Talking Chiluba with a fierce flippancy, she it is who, Lady Macbeth-like, urges Mushidi on to his deeds of blood.[1]

(*20th December* 1890.)

One of the shrewdest revenue-raising tricks of Mushidi is the institution of a sort of Order of the Garter : the " Omande shell" decoration it is called. This amounts to the German status of Grand Duke : independent chiefs as far East as Ushiland (Mirambo, for instance) come West here to do fealty and receive the investiture. Revenue is Mushidi's idea in all this, and the fees are exorbitantly high, slaves paid away in gangs. And all this for the coveted boon of the " Omande shell " status. To particularise. Apart from the steady stream of payments made

---

[1] Aggressively self-conscious to the very end, her dying charge to me, her " uncle," was that her white skin should be buried in a white coffin ! Preached to, rain or shine, for many a weary day, she spurned the Christ, Whom she thought " a fool " for " dying like a sheep." Only once to my ken she patted Heaven on the back approvingly for having a toilet of " white robes," which she thought would suit her complexion ! One day, with tears in her eyes, she broke down and sobbed, " A slave ! yes ! They sold me like a mere chattel when I was a young girl."

by the aspirant from the very first day he sets foot in the capital, watch what happens during the last few minutes of the ceremony. Greedy all the way through, the officials now become vulpine, and instead of frankly placing the white shell on his head and finishing the business, they begin at his toes and propose to make six greedy ascending pauses before the crown of his head is reached. That is to say, each halt must pay toll for the Omande's upward progress, and the shell sullenly remains on the toes of the would-be Grand Duke until he pays a slave for its upward advance. The "toe" slave being paid down as currency, the shell may now gingerly ascend to the ankle, when another halt is declared and another slave paid away to trickery. The second toll having been thus paid, "ankle" slave his name, the shell now tardily ascends *via* the right side, and half-way up to the knee another ominous halt is declared for another slave to be paid away. And so on, to the tune of six slaves, these final fees are paid—a mere drop this in the ocean of greed.

*   *   *

To have a proper bird's-eye picture of our surroundings you must think of this black Babylon as a raging sea of slavery : Lubans from the North, Lamba people from the South, Lunda from the East, Ushi and Vemba from the South-East. The flotsam of negro humanity, here they are, so to speak, washed up on the shores of the capital, all jabbering out their own patois, and all daily taking on more local colour and simulating a sort of black cockney- ism. One of these, snatched from slavery, was the lad

Sankuru, and this is how it came about. His father and
kinsmen were killed off in the attack on their village, and
the little son was put down at Mushidi's feet in the same
row as his relatives' skulls. These skulls Mushidi formally
put his foot on, by way of "trampling on the necks of his
enemies," but the boy was spared and came to us. Picture
that little black boy sitting down with his hand on his
father's skull, like a young English schoolboy toying with
a football. Espousing the cause of the slave as we boast
of doing, Mushidi often twits us with our ignorance of
their wild ways.

Alas! it is true, they are a moral mass of putre-
faction; but the negro himself explains it all in his
luminous proverb: "Slave status causes slave state."
Body bondage means soul bondage. And so the days
pass, these polyglot slaves swarming round the king like
gadflies. Never before has such a mass weltered in Central
Africa, for a real black Babylon is his insane idea. A born
linguist, as I have said, Mushidi day by day pours out
cataracts of vituperation on the bowed heads of his
pudding-stone population. "Son of a dog!" and "Son
of the dust!" are the customary compliments he pays
even to his own elder brother, Likuku. Vaunting himself
to be not a man but a "wild beast," he roars more than
he speaks, and I suppose the Shakespearean comment on
it all would be the sarcasm in *A Midsummer Night's
Dream*—"Well roared, Lion!" This Mushidi roar,
though, is really the most hopeful part of his harangue.
The real danger is when he opens his mouth wide and

hen surprises his listeners with a shrill falsetto treble.
Then it is the death-warrant is shrieked : " Die ! son of
a dog, son of the dust." The mere torrential flow of
language is often an escape safety-valve, just as, on the
contrary, a silent Mushidi is an omen of his " nursing
his wrath to keep it warm." No mere figure of speech
this, for, night and day, it is a fatal fact that the fuse of
Mushidi's fury is always burning, and the mine may
explode at any moment. The Luban idiom for these
explosions of anger is the almost facetious expression,
" his kettle boiling over " (*Futuma*). Yet, doomed to
wrath as they are, some of the slaves are so precocious
that they can die without winking. With a strange
saturnine humour, they even crack a joke within an inch
of death. A sort of lull between the lava showers is the
idea. Literally " in the jaws of death," as an audience
of Mushidi is called, there they are, cracking their joke
even when the said jaws are in the act of crunching them.
And why ? Only the pure nonchalance of fatalism. Some
are erratically quite lively when " the hour " has come ;
hence their own negro death-ditty :—

> " Oh ! when the tortoise in the fire is dying,
> 'Tis then he sends the fire-brands flying."

Into this stubborn slave element, then, Mushidi, with
great, and it must be admitted almost justified severity,
carries death with derision. He merely reckons it all so
much rank growth that has to be cut down. Many a
time I plead for a doomed man's life, and many a time

Mushidi retorts that "Slave blood is bad blood." On the surface, certainly, he is right, for all who have worked among slaves know that bondage of body induces also bondage of brain. That is to say, as the slave has been valued only as a current coin in commerce, he fatalistically accepts the valuation and really becomes as dead and metallic to all human susceptibilities as a literal coin. Why then be surprised? Men who have no rights cannot justifiably be complained of for having any wrongs. Yet hundreds of African travellers have ignored this negro truism and slandered the slave because his degrading status has degraded likewise his state. It is ridiculous for a man to go and treat a negro as though he were a demon, and then express surprise that he is not an angel. Even we Missionaries are reaping the harvest of this oppression, for the worst type of convert is a redeemed slave. The man is still in a fog, and has not yet shaken off the chattel idea even in the glorious idea of the Gospel. Is this the reason why Gordon of Khartoum was betrayed by the two men he had recently released from captivity? Who threw the bomb that killed the Czar Alexander? Who, if not a liberated slave? And if you breed slavery in the bone for centuries, how can you annul it all by the cash payment of an hour? There is a magic key even for this lock, however, and it is found in the fact that the only way to open another man's heart is by opening yours to him. I find that the message that comes from the heart will contrive to reach other hearts. So literally is he a mere captive coin that,

on the exchange value of two sixpences for a shilling,
I have seen two boys bartered for one man. One such
boy I have already referred to, and only do so again to
remind you that his name is "Sikispence," representing
his exact market value in Lubaland, one coloured handkerchief at 6d.

(10*th February.*)

From the East many emigrants have trickled in, the
trans-Luapula Vemba people preponderating. They it is
who have advised the king to substitute the punishment
of "hand-lopping" for theft, instead of the death penalty,
and this has been the source of much uproarious debate at
Court. The cadaverous native logic is so elucidatory of
"thinking black" that I repeat it. When Mushidi
twitted them with the absurdity of the thing, these
Eastern folks argued the point at great length, and with
much frothing at the mouth. "We cut off the hand,"
said they, "because the hand steals." "I," laughed Mushidi,
"stab them in the heart, because the hand never stole
anything yet, it is the heart who is the thief." This, too,
is Mushidi's argument against tearing out the eyes with
fish-hooks as a punishment for adultery. "Eyes?" says
he, "the real eyes are in the heart, and death is the only
true blindness." They laugh, but Mushidi has both law
and logic with him. Clever at repartee as he is, the
twinkling old tyrant fairly routed them with his "summing
up" on this mutilation subject. The king *loquitur* : "I
dreamed a dream, and lo ! I saw that the human Heart
and the human Face had a quarrel. Objected the Heart to

the Face : ' Why did you not groan just now ? Why laugh ? '
Retorted the Face : 'The cheeks only do what the Heart
commands.' Yea, further, I dreamed a dream, and lo,
I, Mushidi, heard a loud racking cough, most painful to
the cougher. Said the Heart to the cough : ' Oh, you bad,
you cruel cough, to rack me so with your coughing.'
Said the cough to the Heart : ' Bad and cruel ? How can
I be bad, coming up as I do from the depths of such a good
Heart as you ? ' "

Not these Vemba folks only but many another droll
emigrant tried to trek in towards Bunkeya to seek his
fortune. For when this Mushidi leapt into the light of
history in the Interior, the good news spread, and many
a young man out East, catching the spirit of the thing,
resolved to go West and win to wealth and lands of his
own. But Mushidi, so to speak, like the dog he was,
snarled, stuck to his bone and showed his malevolent
teeth. He would none of them. Scared off some of the
adventurers would not be, however, and to this day in
the North, Luñungwa, Ñwena, Kaseva, are still in posses-
sion of lands won by their own prowess. Lands, mark
you, that gracefully avoid Mushidi's boundary on the
Lualaba East.

One famous failure there was, however, and he resolved
to go down to history as " a bad 'un "—Katigile his name.
Ostensibly a copper trader like all the Yeke band, he was
only one more pirate ship out on the Central African
ocean of commerce. But K., dismally defeated as he was,
went away back East with hate in his heart and a soul

13

baked hard in the fire of adversity. If he could not die famous he would end infamous, so he planned a devilish deed. Yonder far East, and tucked away in between the Wanyamwezi Hills, was his natal village, where the pest of chigoes had never yet come; well, here is his chance: why not import a plague and die infamous? This would ease his endless pressure of penury, this, the mad idea that his name, as a grey monument in history, would ever be linked with the introduction of such a deadly plague. So he dared the deed and cursed his native land. The collecting of "seed" chigoes was too easy not to succeed, and he safely let them loose on their bad business of hate. Years after, when the townsfolk out East fought in a frenzy of determination to eradicate that chigoe pest, many a curse was linked with Katigile's name. Yet some people say the Devil has no Missionaries, and no propaganda! The heart of man never showed more truly the bad stuff of which it is made than just here in this baneful deed. Even Katigile himself died with his toes eaten by chigoes, cursed with his own cruel curse.

*　　　　　*　　　　　*

So the days drag past, seemingly a mere hyphen and connecting link. Mushidi holds on to us, and we hold on to the country. "If you are tied in ropes," says the proverb, "the more you tug the tighter the knots become," so even here we learn to bide God's time. (Is it not in the Captivity Epistles that Paul writes of the Church's heavenly calling? Seated in a dark Roman prison, was it not just then he claimed to be seated in the heavenlies?)

The sorest thorn in our side these days is the resident Arabs at the capital. They make a dead set against us, buttering up "The Sultan" for hours and plotting darkly. Every time we pass their camp going on to Mushidi's they curse Christ with bitter blasphemy. The revengeful relish in their invectives is the darkest smudge in all our experience; verily, the poison of asps is under their tongue. Yet they pray for hours and by clockwork from the highest to the lowest—pray to God and curse His Anointed. No wonder the arm-chair Englishman misunderstands it all. "On one occasion," says Augustus Hare, "I was present at a garden party given by Lady Salisbury in honour of the Sultan of Zanzibar. In the middle of it the Sultan came up to the hostess and said, 'Now, please, it is time for me to say my prayers. I should like to go to your room and be alone for ten minutes. I always do this four times a day.' The Archbishop of Dublin was so delighted with this, that on being presented to the Sultan he said, 'I am glad to have the honour of being presented to a man who has made a promise and kept it.'" But contrast the same sort of Zanzibar Arab here with us in the African bush, not in an English flower garden. *Kuomba Muungu* is the great Arab phrase, "praying to God," but locally this formula has become the term for murder, *Tu na kwenda kuomba Muungu* being the double equivalent for "Let us be off to prayers," or (save the mark) "Let us be off to kill." It does not often happen that staid old English can hit off such gruesome drolleries, but you have

the identical idea when you misspell "pray" as "prey"—
these devout Arabs do nothing but prey.   Theirs it is, at
any rate, to explain why *Kuomba Muungu* doubly denotes
prayer and plunder, worship and war—only another proof
this, that we are the poles asunder.

When the thermometer goes up the barometer generally goes down.   Even so Mr. Arab and Mr. Missionary :
your A is his Z; your beginning, his end—literally so,
I mean, for the whole A B C of this Arab problem is
only a mere matter of his own actual Arabic A B C.
There, in that Semitic alphabet of his, beginning like
Hebrew at the right and working across to the left side
of the paper, there, I say, you have the whole typical
story of Arab and Englishman.   Always missing each
other and never meeting, we work the page of life from
left to right, and he glories in doing the diametric
opposite.   Muruturutu laughed at me in disdainful Board
School fashion for reading out the Bible from left to
right : it obviously offended his academical susceptibilities
as much as seeing a native pretending to read a book
upside down.   "The blind man has bought a looking-
glass!" is their high-flown hint that all such pretence of
reading is of no value.   Can you eat your dinner standing
on your head ?   The which is a parable, I repeat, for the
difference between us is one of standpoint, but stand-
points so mutually antagonistic that blood would flow in
rivers, as in the old days of the Saracen conquest, but for
the English preponderance in quick-firers.   The Arab
himself sees worlds of meaning in this sharp contrast of

the two adverse races beginning to write at the opposite sides of a sheet of paper, and certain it is, that the gulf cutting off the Arab from the European is "as far as the East is from the West."

Take the Gospel. "Believe or die," says he—"Believe and live," say we. Take polygamy. We proclaim Christ born of a woman, and the dignity of her sex: last at the cross, first at the tomb—they glory in polygamy as the only true code of marital morals. We crusade against the bondage of the slave—they are the notorious slavers of Central Africa. We quote the Golden Rule, "Do unto others," etc., as the Christ's incipient abolition of slavery —they retort with the Devil's golden rule of £ s. d. We prove that to barter human beings is to deny that man was made in the image of God — they quote Mohammed who enjoins the selling of a slave. Now precisely as with this sharp cleavage of slavery, so too with much more. Take the Arab doctrine of force, as against the Christian doctrine of persuasion: here you have the most thrilling contrast of all. We point to Christ inculcating a crusade of love and peace in His very *last* commandment: "Go ye into all the world." They point to Mohammed among his *last* acts planning a bloody war of extermination.

(Later.)

One incident I recall, a tragedy that burnt on my mind indelibly this Arab *versus* Englishman contrast. It was after the smash-up. A great Arab, Kasokota his *nom de guerre*, is condemned to death by court martial

—crime, the usual charge of high treason. The Belgian Commandant quaintly notifies me, as Missionary, that up to twelve noon I can see to the Arab's soul, and after that, by the clock, he will deal with his body. So there, sitting under the acacia tree, "this side of the portal," we talk for eternity. Not many minutes now, and his despairing, dying cry will go ringing up to God. But I soon discover that the convict chain round his neck is only a type of that other Koran chain binding this dignified Arab, soul and body. Rubbing shoulders as we are, the old gulf of East and West yawns between us a thousand miles. At the outset, he clutches at me as a drowning man will clutch at anything, and beseeches me to plead for his life. Urges eloquently, that here he is "dying like a sheep," and not a member of the Court knew one word of his language. With alacrity and in spite of official umbrage, once, twice, thrice I go to the Commandant with the doomed Arab's plea, only to be told with a civil stiffness that my business is to save him from his eternal doom. When, however, I get back to the prisoner under the acacia and tell him how sadly sealed is his fate, the door of Mr. Arab's heart slams on my Gospel. He starts to preach to me, if you please. Repentant? No. He dies like Lord Mohammed, wishing for bloody war. Here is a man quite certain that we English never can perform the Arab acrobatic feat of crossing the narrow bridge of Sirat into Paradise. This bridge of vast length, as narrow as a hair, the edge thereof as sharp as a scimitar, spans the abyss of hell, but all impenitent Englishmen will fall headlong before a puff of wind sent by Allah. There, in that one Blondin boast of the Arab acrobats, you have the volume of their self-righteous ideas : to the right, Jehennam, or hell ; to the left, Jenneh, or Paradise ; and every mortal must walk the razor-edged Sirat barefoot, eternal destiny the issue of this religious tight-rope venture. The Gospel of the Christ Who saves His own murderers and makes a Paul out of a Saul, His diamonds out of soot, is nonsense to them. What Mr. Arab preaches is a message full of all the old elemental passions of the race : an eye-for-eye, tooth-for-tooth recrimination. Two hours later, I saw that proud Arab's dripping, newly washed garments hanging out to dry, each doleful drip telling the sinister tale that the executioner had claimed them as his fee for the dark deed accomplished. Drip ! drip ! from the dead man's clothes came the echo of their own awful Arab warning : " *There are no fans in hell.*" He lived hard, worked hard, died hard, and then how hard to go to hell after all !

(12*th March.*)

These roaming Arabs bring in rumours of far-off Missionaries, which reminds me that this chronicle is not an autobiography, and my narrative has run on too much in the "nasty nominative." Let us think of others now. Farthest in geographically as we are, it is also our privilege to be farthest in ecclesiastically—sort of Scouts of the Church of God, if you please. Take our bearings. In 1890 the Missionary Map runs thus : Out in the Far

West, our nearest [1] ecclesiastical neighbours in the Garenganze are those splendid American Board men, distant roughly 800 miles in Bihe. Often when lonely, the very thought of noble Currie trimming God's lamp at Chisamba comes in on us like a whiff of ozone from the far Atlantic. Then, turning South, our nearest Christian neighbour is the sainted Coillard far down in the Barotse Valley, 600 miles away. Looking North towards the Equator, and a good thousand miles off, are the graves of the Combers on the Congo. Nearer still, our good friends on Tanganyika Plateau, the L.M.S. of historic renown : my beloved friend John May was one of their noble men. But the best wine comes last, and the crowning boon of all is Livingstonia on the far Eastern skyline. Four hundred miles distant, there you have "the Bishop of Central Africa," Dr. Robert Laws. Interdenominational in the best sense, this good man's sunny, hospitable heart has a place for all of us, and the only furlough I ever had was a happy year's sojourn out East at Livingstonia. Thus, having viewed the place in its deep penetralia, I know whereof I affirm : there you learn how true it is that the seemingly cold Scotch are only icebergs with volcanoes underneath ; thaw the northern ice and you get to the Scottish fire. Dr. Laws it was, who cut into the lazy lotus life of the Nyassaland negro, and made him honour hard work. A glance at a Livingstonia Report reveals a sturdy type of service that taboos a mere mist of fine words, and clings to sane statistics. The

[1] See p. 138, *ante.*

Industrial Department, particularly, turns out a robust type of pick-and-shovel Christian, and this healthy thing has no doubt saved the land from a great reactionary apostasy. Thanks to Livingstonia, the Garenganze got its New Testament[1] and teachers, and centred in Dr. Laws' great enterprise are the hopes of wide Central Africa. In a quaint old map of Africa, published in the guess-work days of 1815, the only brilliant bit of work therein was a true prophecy of Livingstonia. After creeping cautiously round the African coast-line, the daring carto-graphist put down his prophetic pen near Lake Nyassa, or " Maravi " as it was then called, and wrote : " Mountains of Lupata, or the Spine of the World." Now, all this was delightful, because authentic prophecy, for in the long-subsequent Livingstonia that appeared in those very latitudes, the word " backbone " is the keynote of it all.

[1] Through the instrumentality of Dr. Laws, our Luban translation of the New Testament was published by the National Bible Society of Scotland.

CHAPTER XII

Shut In, but Almost Out

"On that hard Pagan world disgust
   And secret loathing fell:
Deep weariness and sated lust
   Made human life a hell."

*   *   *

"Can the Ethiopian change his skin or the leopard
his spots?"   JEREMIAH.

*   *   *

"Ye must be born again."   JOHN.

*   *   *

"The sun can mirror his glorious face
   In the dewdrop on the sod;
And the humblest negro heart reflect
   The life and love of God."

CHAPTER XII

Shut in, but Almost Out

*I*N *which the reader, being removed one thousand miles from his nearest shop, learns life's greatest lesson, that the Infinite God is the God of the Infinitesimal.*

HERE it is, on the spurs of the Bunkeya Hills, Mr. Arnot first built his Mission hut-house, a solid but not too ambitious structure. And here too we salute those of "our own company," Messrs. Swan and Faulknor. Cut off from the outside world as they are, no doubt "the banner over them is love"; but so, too, there is sadly waving over their little far-away cabin the yellow flag of quarantine. Faulknor, a shining saint, has found Africa to be one long hospital of pain. Two men all alone in the lonely Interior seem a poor, inadequate sort of testimony, yet so normally necessary is it to be mighty in word and deed that the sick man prayed while the strong man preached, and thus he also serves who only stands and waits. Certainly in the mouth of two witnesses, word and deed, every word was established, for while able Mr. Swan preached Calvary his good friend Faulknor carried the cross of pain. Bedridden though he was for many a day, he soon found that when God permits you to take a back seat you can have a very good time. Besides, as the average African can look through your body like glass, Faulknor's "living epistle" was eloquent the whole day long, and ever answering the challenge of the relentless negro stare. In Africa our faces are our coats of arms. For all of us the great danger in African mission work is, that often our preacher's bow is not so tightly strung in private as in public life, and the native puzzles his head over this. But there was many a song of triumph even under that drooping yellow flag of quarantine, and Richter perfectly describes the gains this good Canadian got out of his pains. The burden of Faulknor's suffering may have only looked to outsiders like a tombstone hung round his neck, whereas in reality it was only a weight necessary to keep down the diver while he was collecting pearls. God in all lands must cross His Church before He can crown it, and it is the late George Müller of Bristol who tells of one of the pearls brought up from these depths of suffering. One day his vast enterprise on the Ashley Downs was down to zero for the orphans' "daily bread," but the dinner-bell rang in heaven and a much-needed gift arrived. Where did it come from? Mr. Müller says a *sick* missionary from the wilds of Africa was the donor—*this* man who had been shut up in the Interior, grievously, almost permanently, disabled. Yet so grateful was this bodily wreck for a safe return to England that he struck his slender balance of resources, and poured it all at his Master's feet.

Shunted off thus into a sort of siding, the tide of roaring life sweeps past us down in the valley of the Capital, an all-day stream of visitors trickling in to us among the rocks. Arriving, as we do, almost empty-handed, Mushidi despises us for our own impecuniosity.   In harsh and unembellished terms he insists that we are no " whites " at all.[1]

Rooming, as we utter strangers to each other do, in mud African houses, then, oh ! then is love's crucible, for often incipient fever makes a good man carp at rough fare —a good man, that is to say, with a bad body.   How many people in England quote the text about brethren " dwelling in unity " who only see them in the busy street, or at a week-end meeting ?   Let them come out to Africa and learn the trials (and triumphs) of so literally dwelling in unity in a hot " station."   Never out of each other's sight.   In moderation I am bold to suspect my friend might find me passably or even mildly entertaining, but in such frequent and overwhelming doses one must pall on one's poor brother.   The trouble is, that one is tempted far too often to speak one's mind, forgetful of the fact that in speaking your mind you must also mind how you speak.   Even the most genial of souls soon surprises himself more than his friend by a snap of irritation quite foreign to his temperament.   This is Africa at its old trick of fastening on its victim, and tightening the tropical grip on his soul.

[1] So, too, Dr. Moloney ; in his book he pities us and cannot "help think-ing that a profound mistake was committed when the Missionaries were dispatched into this barbarous country hundreds of miles from a European post."

Memo. for Missionaries : The closer any two bodies act together, the more oil they need. Even when Mr. A. is a mere echo of Mr. B., the result is that Mr. B. deplores his own echo and refuses to father it. A well-balanced Mission is like a well-balanced world : it is only kept right by two tendencies working in opposite directions—one throwing out and the other pulling in. Brother Centrifugal is only right as he is seconded by Brother Centripetal, and either dare not lack the other. I know two good men who had a rare royal time together for years, yet Brother A.'s favourite tune was, " In the sweet by and by," and Brother B.'s, " In the sweet Now and Now." When Brother A. saw the rain, he would unerringly surmise, " This will make mud," then Brother B. would chime in, " This will lay the dust." Saith Brother A., " I am sorry it is no better." Quoth Brother B., " I'm glad it is no worse." Yet these two saints (oh yes) get along happily together, because soaked deep into their souls was the divine doctrine that God's Church is a complete unity of various temperaments and methods. What kind of music would you have without sharps and flats ? The wheels of a watch, remember, move contrary to each other, and thereby alone can you get a good time-keeper.

Yet show I unto you a more excellent way. Better, better far the Missionary (dear, dead-and-gone Cobbe, for instance) who had a happy soul balanced in equal ratio by the same two laws that make the planet earth such a well-balanced sphere, the one pulling him into God's presence, the other driving him out in service.

Remember, as the days pass, our Western road is blocked and no supplies can cross the Lualaba, but the malefactors who have done it all are really benefactors. Well spake Hudson Taylor, when he affectionately bade us farewell, "The Devil can wall you round, but he cannot roof you in." We always can reckon on the bit of blue overhead. What to outsiders may seem the hateful exigencies of poverty, is to us merely God removing the clogging weights to make good our motto : The maximum of power with the minimum of machinery. Granted, I say, many solid considerations against this idea of our meagre Missionary pioneer outfit, but granted also many obvious gains for all our pains. Mr. Lane on leaving me here in the Interior after some months of the bread of affliction, wrote of all his privations : "Trying as things were, I would not have forgone that blessed season of trial for all the luxuries of civilisation. As I take a backward look my heart rejoices, and I am increasingly realising the blessedness of having come forth looking to the Lord alone for my supplies." Paul fondly boasted of his "manner of entering in" among them, and in some severe sense your initial choice of the manner of entering in among an African tribe will wholly determine your subsequent line of action. The effervescent negro will easily fall down and worship a caravan that parades as much of the Lord Mayor's Show element about it as possible. What he wants is something violently spectacular and "striking," as he names his own word for "glory." Thus out of sheer desire for your African's welfare, you must needs strip yourself of impedimenta in order to outwit the cupidity of the black man.

The highest compliment I have been paid in my bush African wanderings was when a snob chief gave me a dole of forty yards of calico as a pitying alms, because I was " out at the elbows." Of course I have since paid him his own with usury, but the link binding us in friendship is all the more real because the initial bounty was on his part. There is nothing to be ashamed of in poverty except being ashamed of it. The best pair of boots I had for many a day were a Portuguese convict's, bought from a negro. So, too, with a mysterious suit of clothes which I rescued from a slaver— the fit was faultless. Far too faultless, for it clung to me as tight as a wall-paper. So, too, with much more. This famine and fever land in a special and extraordinary way clears the field for a full display of the power of His might, for man is often brought low with all his shrewd contrivances, and only God can avail. The last and nearest commercial banking-house in the world was just one thousand miles distant on the seashore. Your deposit account might be *ad libitum*, but your powers of cashing same in the long grass were at zero. Certainly the pampered civilisation of Great Britain is all on the side of unbelief, for everything is too cut-and-dried, and runs in a fixed groove, comes as a matter of course, not as a wonder. Here, in the bush, it is delightful again and again to watch how God hears you scrape the bottom of the meal-barrel. Again and again, with "dramatic neatness of Divine method," the dinner-bell has gone in Heaven for my "surprise meal."

It was hinted to-day quite blandly that we must be runaways rom justice. We are nobodies: where are our belongings? Yet here again we have gains for pains.[1] After all, we dare not ignore the fact that the mere temporalities of the Missionary, with his creaking boots, do bulk far too largely in the greedy gaze of our bush negro. A Missionary without God—not without supplies —is like a rabbit against the Russian Empire. Oh, the abysmal and abominable chasm between Mr. White and Mr. Black! The mediocre Englishman with his mass of belongings is, by the negro, literally and repellently called *Leza Mukulu* ("O great God"). The same thing this, as when some raw natives looking over a Mission fence at a simple wattle-and-daub house said, "Ye are the people of God: look at the size of your houses."

Even our endless praising of God before the raw native is misunderstood, and certainly twice I have heard a negro grunt, "Yes, well you might praise God, He has been good to you." But aback of all this, there is a blacker subtlety still, I mean the endless negro suspicion that God is an Englishman: the bare-footed Christ of rocky roads in Palestine they cannot conceive. They are sure that we are the spoilt and petted children of a pampered civilisation, and as they

---

[1] Dr. Moloney's statement that not only did Mushidi call us "white slaves," but that he also despoiled us of our. goods, errs in the important particular that we had no goods to despoil.

look at the vault of the sky curving down to meet the horizon in the direction of Europe, they actually believe that Heaven meets earth among the white men. No wonder Malemba once interrupted a sermon of mine on the murder of Christ at Golgotha with the stinging retort : " Ay, you white men were a bad lot to go away and kill The Best One like that : we blacks only kill criminals." " And then," said he, " far from being ashamed of what you have done, you come across the seas to tell us you did it." That this idea is deeply embedded in the negro mind can be proved by re- membering that the revolting blacks of San Domingo shouted out the same dread war-cry. Devastating the plantations with murder and fire and led by a fanatic, their bloodthirsty cries rent the air, " The whites killed the Christ, let us slay all whites ! " How different the fawning attitude of a sleek, well-fed " Mission " native who listens to even a corrosive rebuke with a beaming smile ! The fact is, these obsequious, beaming blacks who make an avenue for you to pass through into their country, propose to treat the Missionary precisely as you in England treat the postman—that is to say, they acclaim him not for what he is in himself, but for what he brings. And this would be delightfully all right pro- vided the negro welcomed us as a letter postman—God's postman bringing God's letter. Alas ! he thinks we are parcels postmen, and any of the humblest ameliorations of civilisation about us develop in the negro that avarice known locally as " the big eye." Thus, even when we have drained our last drop of tea, and all the meaner facilities of life have departed from our mud hut, we still see Divine intent in it all.   For God had only removed the gilt from the gingerbread of our "white" prestige in order to proclaim the poverty of the Cross.   And this mollified all our soreness.   Christ's cause in Africa is too often wounded in the house of its friends, but never so grievously and gratuitously as when a Missionary of the Cross beats easily all his fellow-Europeans in this matter of first-class get up.   The best houses, best furniture, best eating, all at "The Mission."

Out towards the Atlantic Ocean our nearest shop is just one thousand miles off.

One sacred calendar of mine contains the following categoric and genuine gifts, "nick of time" succour we call this :—

One woman—35 baskets of flour.

Another—25 baskets of flour, 4 baskets of green vegetables.

Another—22 baskets of green vegetables, i.e. green corn, cucumbers, pumpkins, etc.

Another—15 baskets of flour, etc.

Fifteen others might be added with totals of ten, nine, eight, six and less baskets of flour, corn, etc.

> "His methods are sublime,
>   His ways supremely kind ;
> God never is before His time,
>   And never is behind."

And where is the man longing for apostolic precedents who would exchange these glad trials of faith for a king's ransom? Weary in the wilderness trail, you listen, and lo there is the bubbling brook by the way, and drinking you do lift the head. These are mercies from God's right hand. The provocative policy of our entering Africa loaded up with impedimenta does not give the raw African a chance really to help the Missionary: he cannot conceive of such a rich Missionary being honestly pinched. Give him the chance and you will marvel: it will be the story of Ebed-melech the black man over again. His own colour had abandoned Jeremiah, and there you have the Hebrew prophet down a hole, no water and sunk in the mire. The accurate analogy this of an African Missionary cut off from his ocean base and, humanly speaking, in a hole. His own colour, I say, abandoned this white prophet, and then it was a black man came to the rescue. What saith the Scripture? "So Ebed-melech the Ethiopian took the men with him, and went into the house of the king under the treasury, and took thence old cast clouts and old rotten rags, and let them down by cords into the dungeon to Jeremiah. And Ebed-melech the Ethiopian said unto Jeremiah, Put now these cast clouts and rotten rags under thine arm-holes under the cords. . . . So they drew up Jeremiah and took him out of the dungeon." A widow's mite and a negro's rotten rags and cast-off clothes—how like God to honour them with such a royal recognition.

Well it is we have no Society guaranteeing us a salary, for the said Society would be politely and cleverly baffled how to get at us with £ *s. d.*   Shut off from our nearest bank one thousand miles, surely here is a true test of faith.

(1*st July.*)

In our little mud Mission House we have a number of redeemed slaves around us, but they are nearly all a bad lot.   Studying slavery as I am daily doing here at its fountainhead in the Far Interior, this is the honest deduction of it all : rug up a man from the roots of his being—home, kinsmen and liberty—then transplant him as captive chattel, and verily, not even the warm fostering care of a rescuing Missionary can soften the grudge out of him.   Here, for instance, is a case in point.   A band of slave-children, recaptured from the Arabs, is domesticated in a model Mission known to me.   The years pass, the ex-slaves are trained and fostered so painstakingly that the good Lady Missionary has literally turned the tables, and become the slave of the ex-slaves.   Yet these jet-black beauties have their growling grudge still. Wondering what it all means, you push investigations, and after a few exploring remarks, you find—can you take it in ?—that these rescue Missionaries are only reckoned *the-last-therefore-the-worst* link in the long chain of captivity.   For, remember, after all, Home is sweet Home to the tiniest baby negro, and the smallest of them, far away in captivity, sings a song of his fatherland :—

> "Can Vemba's land be old?   Never!
> Yes, old it may be
> And cease to be free,
> But Vemba is Vemba for ever."

Thus each gang of slaves is really a nest of hornets, and patriotism is throbbing in every black breast. Try to bribe this exiled slave with a sugar sop and he sniffs with suspicion at the very sugar. *Kwetu!* is his magic word for "Home," and there is clannish courtesy in the very grammar of the plural: you dare not say "My Home" in broad Africa. "Our Home" is the compound family formula. In fact, there is no such word as "Home" apart from plural usage, which proves that enshrined within the one word "Our Home" there is locked up the vision of all his kinsmen dear. This astounding attempt of a slave race to coin and copyright a speciality in such a word as "Home" even beats its famous English rival: beats it, I say, because at least we can use "Home" with or without any pronoun we like, but the African has so tricked the tongue that no word for "Home" exists apart from a pronoun—"Our Home" or "Your Home." To say mere "Home" is not merely bad form, but no form at all. There is no such usage. Now, lest peradventure this be thought mere "Exeter Hall," you must stand with me, and listen to a slave crooning his "logical" rhyme against the very idea of human bondage. Literally there are both rhyme and reason in the words :—

> "As a bird in the course of its flight,
>   On some branch will not choose to alight,
>   For it likes not the tree,
>   So man's heart doth resemble a bird,
>   To coerce it would be as absurd,
>   For the heart must be free."

Surely this doggerel proves that the old phrase "as free as a bird" is a world-wide metaphor.   Thus you see that even in grinding slavery your despised negro chattel gets poetry out of his prose of life by thinking of the old home in the Luban marsh where "*mama*" (yes, the same old English word) is longing for her lost bairn.   One such mother I redeemed from her fifth term of slavery, the story all being told in that inconsequential tone that makes one proud to live and die for old Africa.   For there was a haggard woman explaining nonchalantly that five times she had sold herself into slavery because her little boy who changed bondmasters was a slave; each time she followed up her son, gladly enduring bondage under five slave-owners, in order to be near her boy.   This was time number five when I broke her chains!   And all for maternal love.   That lad grew up to be one of our earliest converts on Lake Mweru, many of his best natural qualities coming from that slave mother.   Somebody was right, surely, when he said so sagely: "I think it must be somewhere written that the virtues of the mothers shall occasionally be visited on their children as well as the sins of their fathers."

*   *   *

Probably, the most striking thing to be seen at the Bunkeya capital is the roaring function of a "Triumph" when a returning general is acclaimed as victor by the assembled multitude.   Never did Roman general thundering down the *Via Appia* with his victorious legions at his heels feel more inflated with feat of arms.   This is the

day when negro festivities reach their zenith and even
deep-dyed enemies agree to sink their grudge and run
with the full tide of good cheer. The Lunda man who,
otherwise and elsewhere, would avoid his Luban enemy as
though he were a pestilence, is to-day in high glee feast-
ing on the common bounty. Thousands and thousands
of slaves are here drinking themselves tipsy, the very
drink being the famous "barley wine" of Xenophon and
Tacitus. With all the sympathies and animosities of
cats and dogs, here you have them for one brief day
deceiving each other into a false fraternity as frothy as
their gallons of beer.

Twisting into the capital since daybreak, and from
all points of the compass, you might have seen the beer
caravans arrive, drums roaring, goats and sheep piping
a shrill treble to swell the noise of festivity. Every rag
of coloured calico is to-day sported in the sunshine, the
essential bit of the rig-out being a turban of some sort.
Meanwhile the great Mushidi, who is bent on besting his
imaginary rival, is in the hands of his satraps, who are
dressing him up for the show, the distinctive feature of
his purple and fine linen being a vesture, twenty or
thirty yards long, to which they finally add his regalia
of "Omande" shells. Certainly he takes the shine out
of everybody, for hanging round his neck, like a walking Christmas tree, they have dangled scissors, looking-
glasses, and curious sundries.

But where, you ask, is the victorious general all the
while? Denied entry, he, be it noted, has been hanging

round impatiently for weeks on the remote outskirts of the city, Mushidi simulating a yawn at every mention of his name, and petulantly refusing " to vote" the said Triumph. So true to the Roman analogy is it all, that the river Lunsala has been marked off as this General's Rubicon, across which he dare not come unless officially notified to do so. Runners, however, are daily pouring in from his camp to jog the king's memory with the acts of valour of his shrewd and restless warriors, until finally, out of sheer exasperation, the great "Tomboka" day is named. Virtually, of course, this is the old admission wrung from the Cæsars by the Prætorian Guard, that the King is only King because of their swords.

Mushidi's simile is better when he grudgingly agrees that his army and he are related to each other as the one blade of the scissors is to the other—you can only cut the political cloth as they snip together. And now all is open-mouthed expectancy, for Mushidi is borne aloft on a zebra-skin palanquin by more than a hundred men, and a far-off war-song tells of the approaching general and his army. Then the royal drums answer the distant call, the hoarse advancing cries quickly becoming louder and louder. Here they are at last coming sprinting round the corner, the advance guard flourishing their arms with mimic menace, every man of them sporting one or several putrid skulls with a trophy-taunt. Then comes Mukanda-vantu, the general, flushed with victory, and, following him, the long string of slaves captured in war. How reminiscent all this of Paul glorying in the fact that he was Christ's bondslave and led about in triumph as Christ the Conqueror's trophy.

Swollen with pride and satisfaction, the generalissimo advances with a strut into the centre of this vast sea of brilliantly clad negroes, followed by the captured chiefs, or prisoners of high status, hard in his wake, this line of the captured tailing off in the broken-kneed dregs of slavery. They are nearly all women, however, a proof this that the men they fought were really masculine enough to die rather than be captured—hence these heaps of heads hidden in clouds of flies. One brute, you notice, has three skulls tied together dangling from his mouth, and Mushidi claims all these heads by formally descending from his throne and putting his foot on each one : a sort of trampling on the necks of his enemies, I suppose. Meanwhile, the army has fired a deafening *feu de joie* point blank in our faces, and then begins a show of sham fighting during which different detachments are seen in attack and retreat, now simulating a clever ambush and anon springing like panthers from the grass. There is an end to all this, and a facetious one. Like Nero, who was vain of his music, Mushidi has the vanity to think that he can—dance. Dull, dazed, and dumbfounded you, a spectator, can scarcely believe your eyes when the old man is seen to descend and begin his rheumatic shuffles, a dancing bear indeed ! Nearly tripped by his own bunched-up vesture, these contortions are a speciality, and called the R.A.A. dance—Royal August Antics, that is to say Could you not more truthfully translate this R.A.A.

" *Reductio ad absurdum*" performance? Have you caught the picture? An old man trying to dance with a thirty-yards-long loin-cloth artistically bunched out in flounces round him, and worn just as the planet Saturn wears his rings.

Nevertheless, in spite of all these fireworks and army antics, you can see at a glance that this mass of men without drill is only a poor decentralised mob run on the go-as-you-please idea. The only apology you can make for it is when you rub up your history a bit, and remember that this feudal system of every sub-chief collecting the men of his district and mobilising around the king is the only thing the world knew, from the days of Moses up to the time when Cromwell raised the first standing army.

CHAPTER XIII

Black Suffragettes

"Shrine of the Mighty! can it be
That this is all remains of thee?"

*　　　　　*　　　　　*

"I have seen the wicked in great power, and
spreading himself like a green bay tree. Yet he
passed away, and, lo, he was not; yea, I sought him,
but he could not be found."　　PSALM xxxvii. 35, 36.

*　　　　　*　　　　　*

"I am the green bay tree [Chitavatava] who first
sprouted in Sanga land."　　THE EMPEROR MUSHIDI.

*　　　　　*　　　　　*

"And so they've voted the Devil out,
And of course the Devil's gone;
But simple people would like to know,
Who carries his business on?"

CHAPTER XIII

Black Suffragettes

*WHEREIN it is clearly and con-
sistently demonstrated that even
a worm will turn.*

(10*th July.*)

MORE executions of women, which means more
putrefying skulls and clouds of blue-bottle flies.
Skulls heaped on long rustic tables, skulls hanging
up on trees like hat-pegs, skulls with yawning mouths that
would not shut even in death. This Bluebeard business,
remember, means hard detective work, and the Emperor
spends sleepless nights raiding his own harems. Five
hundred (and a fraction) wives and not a padlock in the
land. It is on this sorry score blood runs in torrents,
for the paramours are legion, and often the true, because
prior, husbands of the stolen women. Mushidi knows all
this and more, knows he must keep running to the red,
reckless expedient of killing even on suspicion. For owing
to the ramifications of this polygamic mob of wives and
concubines, it is now easily evident that even Mushidi has
outwitted Mushidi. It has become his nightmare this,
for how is he to order his house in the severe sense

demanded by his status? Are not his most trusty
Kalamas all equally suspect? A *Kalama* is a chamber-
lain, but the very watchmen are the thieves, and the
Arabs are right when they say of these traitors, that
Mushidi had given "the cat the duty of keeping the key
of the pigeon-house"! Exasperated as he is, it is just
here Bluebeard yawns and resigns all pretensions to dealing judicially and fairly with his victims. Baulked in
a systematic scheme of spying, he has resorted to
"dreaming" his victim, ignoring the fact that even in
upside-down Africa dreams go by the contrary. Did he
not himself tell me the other day that having dreamed a
banquet, there must be a famine? Poor Mushidi! This
endless round of harem marriages is a bad, black business
for the country. Killing his wronged victim as he does,
he only comes off second best. For at least the doomed
slave has relief from his bondsman's groan in a sharp,
short death, but how can Mushidi escape the thraldom of his
own heart? He has brute power enough to kill them in
heaps, but how much more horrible if Mushidi had the
power to compel them to live. From what I am learning
these days, seemingly the true definition of "tyrant" is a
man who finds his happiness in the unhappiness of others.
Little does the merciless old brute guess that judgment
has a rod in pickle for himself even now. He forgets that
to refuse to forgive is to cut down the bridge you yourself
must one day cross. His is the old thick-headed idea
that it is possible by digging far enough into the human
body with a spear to arrive at the real living man. But

even now the reflex revenge is speeding on its way to keep the sure law that a tyrant is best embalmed in his own blood. Here he is day by day despising our glorious Gospel; flattery, sickly flattery, is his mode of attempting to spike our Gospel guns, and the glib tongue reveals a hard old heart seared to it all. Preach on Love with a capital letter, and by a wriggle he is out of the whole subject in a moment—what does he, a polygamist, want with the Love that passeth the love of women? King or slave, this glibness of tongue is Africa's endless horror. Wherever you move the wise old saw perfectly expresses our longing: Rather a negro heart without words, than negro words without heart.

(Later.)

Now let me try to tackle in cold ink this horror of polygamy—a subject, alas, almost certain to incur the vitiating touch of coarseness. We have already seen all the Mushidi institutions built on the bedrock of Nature's precedents among the animals. (Precedent, not principle, remember, is the only law in Africa.) Here, then, in his colossal system of polygamy, you see only another instance of the Bantu curriculum in the University of the Beasts. A sociologist far away in England can work up a whole bookcase of plausible data on such an ancient subject, toying with his pet-doll theory before the study fire. But here, on the edge of Lufira Valley, you frankly see polygamy cradled amongst the zebras and antelopes. Thence, anon (and quite as frankly), you see the same polygamy invade the native

town from the plains. Who, for instance, does this
Bluebeard chief pretend to be, if not "the bull of the
herd"? Again and again I hear beast-precedents quoted
in support of native customs, and all in the gruesome
formula: "So hath the Lord commanded us." Thus
this old Emperor with his mob of five hundred wives is
merely an attempt to live à la the Lufira quadrupeds. At
Munema I heard some Court gossip about an exceptional
Amazon who was numbered among these "hen-cooped"
wives. This woman—no slattern she!—dared to preach
in a dark, hinting way the far-off dream of women's
rights, but King Bluebeard got wind of it through her
rival. With regrettable vulgarity, Mushidi called the
propagandist "a goat" for such silly speech. "Yea, my
lord," Mrs. Amazon pouted, "even the goats are a
model marriage, for the female has as good a pair of
horns as the Billy."

＊   ＊   ＊

Have just had a long talk with our Mrs. Amazon,
and a strange story this Shila woman tells. A real
Suffragette, she is the member of a woman's secret
society that boasts of big deeds in days gone by.
Listen to this eye-opening history of such an incredible
woman's movement in Far Central Africa.

"Why is it," she asks, "that the foreign Lunda tribe
is now in the ascendant around Lake Mweru?" Well,
a family dynastic brawl did it all, and a woman (again!)
"was in the transgression." Nkuva, the lord paramount,
was her own brother, but did he not dare to slay and

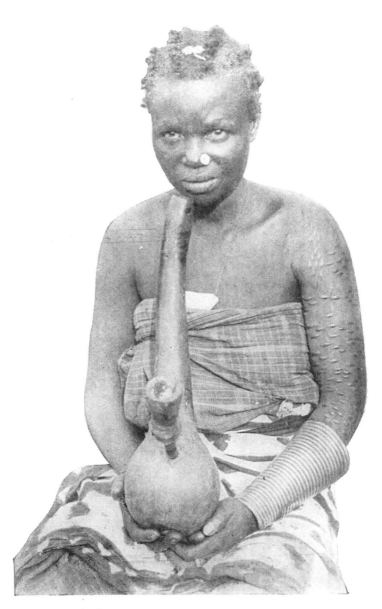

ONE OF MUSHIDI'S 500 WIVES.

skin her son, his nephew, to make a kingly carpet of
the human cuticle? To have her son thus so literally
"trampled upon" in both life and death was too
exasperating for the Princess, and in hot revenge she
called in the foreign Lunda tribe from the Far West.
This, then, is the real beginning of the famous Kazembe
rule in the Luapula Valley, and by a woman's invitation,
and not conquest, are they there. So typical is it all,
that when you try to unravel the tangled tale of any
African tribe's history, a few exploring remarks reveal
that some silly daughter of Eve robbed them of their
Eden—yes, box the African compass, and one key will
unlock all the dynastic locks: *Cherchez la femme.* That
Princess, though, had to pay a big bill for this the sweet-
ness and terror of her revenge. For when the avenging
Lunda arrived from the West, the leader ominously
struck his spear into a tall sycamore tree, thus arrogating
to himself dominion over all these Luapula lands. In
other words, having entered by the Western doorway,
he forthwith locked the door, putting the imaginary key
in his imaginary pocket. Thus, even thus, were the
Shila folk driven forth from their Eden, just as, not
John Milton, but a woman, was the real authoress of
Paradise Lost. But watch the Suffragette sequel.

Far from degrading the cause of woman in the Far
Interior, this very feminine treachery stiffened the back
of her sex, and really conduced to the amelioration of
her lot as the degraded chattel of her black partner.
This, in fact, is the true genesis of that "Zenobia" class

15

of women chiefs to be found in the land. To this day the common ruse of a crushed wife is to make a gracefully turned allusion to that revolutionary deed of a negress long ago, the covert threat in her hint being that what woman has done, woman can and will do. And the husband brute has the sense to wince truculently at the very memory of that woman's treachery long ago, his sheepish, discomfited look revealing that the woman has struck home. Certes, there is nothing can move a drowsy old African like a jag from past history. Having no literature, the African as a consequence clings tenaciously to the past precedents of his race, the antiquity of a fact being its sanctity.

But there is more to follow. Far more interesting than this ascent of woman to the status of a Zenobia queenship is her daring to combine, and form this great secret society of theirs into which no man dare penetrate. All pivoted on that one woman's wrong long ago when her son was skinned to make a human carpet. These black women let their unfettered fancies roam over the vast sphere of their sex's wrongs, and this black Club of theirs is the sacred confessional. Often a husband goes foodless if Mrs. Amazon is attending a Club meeting, and oftener the happy and harmless wife becomes, after initiation, "a new woman" indeed.

"*Budindu*" is the name of this female freemasonry, and many a feminine titter can be overheard at the expense of the men. The rites of initiation are nameless, but the general idea is that of a Benefit Society, whose supreme function is to scrutinise the cause of death of any of its members. As African men often play their women the scurviest of tricks, it is absolutely necessary that these women combine in some sort to beat the tom-tom of their sex. This secret society it was that decreed a "Married Women's Property Act" long before the belated English Act of 1883, and on the death of one of their guild they pounce down on her moveable estate "to the uttermost farthing." Some of these female Club decisions have indeed assumed portentous proportions in the high politics of Central Africa, a notorious instance being the ceding of the whole north shore of Lake Mweru to satiate a *Budindu* Club claim. For they fastened on the Lake King with the almost trifling plea that one of their princess (*Inamfumu*) members of the guild had been delivered of a still-born child, and for this " crime " the King of all Mweru (her husband) was forced to pay a large slice of territory. Beginning at the Muntemune River on the north-west corner of the Lake, and sweeping right round the map as far as Kalembwe's on the east, this poor henpecked King solemnly expropriated himself of all that land to appease the " lioness robbed of her whelp," *i.e.* the princess who bore him the still-born child. This, in fact, was the biggest legal fish the Club ever fried, and these Suffragette Lake ladies clothe themselves with impressiveness as they tell the twice-told tale of this, the Waterloo of their Club. Yet, so binding and final was this territorial decision that to this day, if an elephant dies in the waters of the Muntemune with its head pointing to the north bank, then the ivory is claimed by Mpweto at the Lualaba crossing.

(Later.)

As farther West, so too here in the Interior, there is the usual African massacre of the innocents ; "dentition deaths" these are called. Read this Luban episode. Here is a bonnie baby doomed to die because its little milk teeth "sprouted" on the wrong—*i.e.* the upper—gum first. Far from being the usual little black bundle of screams, behold, a dear little, queer little morsel who *must* be murdered. This dental abnormity is the tribal terror, for every negro must go the way of his blood, must wear the blinkers, so to say, must follow his father's lead. Here, then, is a baby who dares so early to break normal precedent in the fashion of teeth, and the cherub must die as a monster. No Rachel ever weeps for such a child, and when the mother detects the first tooth on the wrong gum she flees from the innocent, frozen with fright. For does not the proverb say that the babe that breaks the normal law of dentition must be broken ? *Lutala* is the child's name, and the idea is that there is a fiend taking ambush inside such an abnormal baby, therefore death is the doom. For if a demon be inside baby, and baby be inside the town stockade, then woe to that town, and woe to that baby. The chief Nkuva is a case in point. He was the father of three bouncing boys all of whom he murdered in succession, the appearance of the upper teeth doing it all. When dentition drew near the poor mother spent three agonising days in suspense, each baby being spurned like a serpent when he revealed his terrible upper teeth first. But No. 3 settled matters, and the chief having spurned his babies, finally spurned their mother as the latent cause of it all. Instead, however, of this disgraceful divorce dislocating her whole life as in England, she married a negro friend of mine ; their first baby had normal dentition, and now the lady flourishes this fact in the face of her ex-spouse with withering scorn. The Kingdom of God, however, is not for goody-goodies, and this very murderer of babies broke with it all and yielded to the Christ Who loved little ones. " Suffer the little children to come unto Me," said He—yea, and let their murderers come also. Was not Christ's first offer of pardon to His own murderers ?

But in Africa it never rains but it pours, and here, while the ink is still wet, my boy Mirambo comes fluttering in with devastating tidings. Just back home from the South, he finds his baby-boy has disappeared. Query, Where is baby ? Then ekes out the tale of another " dentition death," this story being quite a speciality, for baby was so hearty that he had sprouted both an upper and a lower tooth at the same time. What must be done ? A fisherman took baby away out into mid-Lake, and baby even laughed with glee as the bad man tied a rope round his waist and on that rope a stone. Baby even crowed when the fisherman took him up in his arms, but splash went bonnie baby into blue Mweru. And all because he was a neutral and had teeth on both gums on the same day !

A tremendous business this teething institution. Farther North, a Chief with quite a dandified air produced a royal babe who had passed the curious ceremony of "the justification of the child." He certified the youngster as his very own, the scion of a Royal House, with the real Kalamata nose as flat as a button and the real Kalamata pugnacious bawl. Or to speak in the language of printers and publishers, an exact edition in duodecimo of the larger work in folio, both bound in best brown leather. Baby was beplastered with white chalk, and feeling so uncomfortable that he bawled as loudly as though he were twins. For to-day his delighted mother could scarcely believe her eyes when she beheld her off-spring had really sprouted a tooth normally—and bang! went an old flintlock to herald the great news. A long swing of the pendulum this, for up to this point the child has been looked at askance, and reckoned only a mere "*It*"—won't somebody invent a new pronoun?—a mere mushroom pretender to babyhood, your toothless child being a nonentity. Right on from birth, the Spartan mother has made him rough it, all injudicious coddling being considered detrimental. No rag of calico is bare baby allowed to wear, even out in the cold night air, the elastic functions of the body thus getting a chance to be exercised. Malnutrition they do object to, however, and the cherub is nearly choked by the purely mechanical manner a coarse porridge is rammed down his little throat. The youngster's mouth is opened so wide that it mono-polises nearly five-sixths of his face, and through this huge aperture the porridge is pushed home, baby the while nearly kicking his little feet off as the alarming alternative to howling. This ventral distension is finally so alarming that they must leave off on the plea of incapacity, the trouble being not too much porridge but too little baby-boy. Yet all this is mere dessert, for, to the cannibal, nothing can compensate for "God's own sacred way of giving milk"—his mother's breast. Of course, they bathe the rogue, but the bath is not such an affair of immense and intricate pomp as in petted England : with cold water in the cold air they tone up the small black body to play the Luban tune.

Now, however, that the little one has toed the tribal line and produced this terrible tooth, the father feels as tall as the Eiffel Tower, and he declares his son " justified." The technical term for this justification is the old Bible one, " I will give him the white stone," and this *Lupemba* is the same word for the squaring of any outstanding account—not a bad idea of justification for a man-eater. The ridiculous Mama now runs with the tide and insists that the tooth is a prize sample : in fact, she so hugs Master Tom Thumb that when I last saw him he was in a state of suspended animation. This, then, is the sort of christening of a young cannibal, the tribal test being one of tuskers. Yet they sell their bonnie bairns for a mere song, that father with cold glittering eyes coveting calico in exchange for his own flesh and blood—fancy a being wearing a warm human skin bartering his own blood and bone ! You can cudgel your brains for a reason,

but will only find it after you have settled that other
poser of why he can eat both human beef and bone.
The selling is surely minor in comparison.

(10*th August.*)

But what about preaching all this time ?   Day by day,
at his lordly banquet of local politics one is itching to get
in a word of wisdom edgeways.   True, our evangel is the
very last thing Rex wants, but as even roast beef however
well cooked makes bad dessert, I proposed that he should
give me an opening for my creature-humbling, Christ-
exalting Gospel.   To delay to do right is to decide to do
wrong—then why delay ?   Told him that even a pagan
like Aristotle rounded off his great book *De Mundo* by
saying that it would be impious not to mention the
Creator thereof.   This sharp shunting on to another line
he thought a bit too intrusive, and was annoyed that I did
not take his petty polemics much more seriously.   Why
not keep to the easy-souled paths of diplomatic agreement ?
What mad moonshine was this our persistently pointing
up to God's sky and calling *Him* true King of Katanga ?
Was not he, the black one, Lord of the land, and when
every cock in the land crowed did it not crow " Mushidi " ?
Every man in the country, too, did he not make the pre-
scribed prostrations and call him " O Lord God " ?   He
thinks we are fools for disdaining his negro politics, pretty
much, I suppose, as in Paul's day the Greek's meaning for
the word "idiot" was "a person who refused to meddle
in politics."   Little he knows that to the very end of the

age God represents its rulers as "wild beasts," the one immediately preceding the coming of the " King of kings " being the biggest beast of all—*The* Beast.

Only once can I recall his ever sitting out a formal meeting. The Chief seemed superbly indifferent during the whole sermon on "Blind Bartimæus," nevertheless he had his innings after me, preaching a counter gospel for the Devil.

" We are blind, are we ? Well, then, O man of God, so be it, and please note (1) that a blind man only knows what he touches with his fingers : *i.e.*, let us grip your Gospel in our fists, and then we will believe it.

" (2) Remember, also, that a blind man must be careful of what he eats : *i.e.*, give us time to consider your Gospel for a century or two.

" Finally, no blind man ever forgot the road to his mouth : *i.e.*, if we find this Gospel of yours to be beneficial, then we will take it without pressure." Yet people think of these folks as dull-witted, ox-eyed blacks. Only another instance of the old truth that " not many wise, not many noble," care a straw for salvation. The smallest streams hold the biggest trout, and our happiest times are, not with the Chief, but with outcasts in Sychar ministry. Depend upon it, the publicans and harlots will go into the banquet of Life before King Hoity-toity. Ah, if sin were only better known, Christ would be held in higher esteem.

*   *   *

But do not imagine that our Mushidi will have nothing to do with religion. Did we but encourage him in the

idea, this is the mad monarch who would build a cathedral
as high as the pyramids, cementing every brick with
blood.   Yes,

> " a huge temple, decked by Herod's pride,
> Who fain would bribe a God he ne'er believed."

Anything colossal appeals to his small mind, and indeed
the proper noun "God" is in daily use for surpassing
bulk or greatness.   He would dearly love to send out a
"search warrant" for a congregation, driving in hundreds
to this Devil's fold by sjambok.   He, too, would negotiate
baptisms of the "King Menelik" order, "baptism by
capture" as it is called.   Do you know that hundreds
of Africans in the North are pounced down on by royal
command, and *en masse* driven like silly sheep into the
river?   There they are divided into bands, the Wolda
Gabriel and Wolda Jesus, and thus they sin the bad old
sin of making Jesus Christ King by force.   Truly the
Kingdom of Heaven suffereth violence.   Was it not the
Church's worst day when it was able to shout "Victory!"
on a successor of the Cæsars holding the stirrup for a
Christian bishop to mount his horse?   But all this
"Defender of the Faith" rôle is denied him : it would
be about as appropriate to allow Mushidi to "run the
Mission" as it is to see Bishops in the House of Lords
or a lady in a smoking compartment.   Yet he has his
affectations of morality.   Oh yes!   This is the old show-
man who poses as an angel on a mud-heap.   By way of
wrapping the robe of the Pharisee round about him he

A LEARNED LAKE MWERU CHIEF

daily preaches against tobacco as either snuff or smoke.
Pipes of wood or pipes of gourd are all taboo, and the old
definition of this vain thing pleases him hugely : "A tube
with fire at one end of it, and a fool at the other." Only
by stealth can a smoker puff his cloud, and no snuff is
allowed under severe penalty. One poor fellow who forgot
himself into the indiscretion of a pinch of snuff in the
royal presence was maimed for life. The punishment
farther North for this nasal inhalation is the cutting off
of the lips. Mushidi's axiomatic definition of tobacco is
"death," and he gets leverage for this idea in the local
etymology of the word *Fwaka* = tobacco, *i.e.* the death-
dealer. Is this the true genesis of the old Raleigh story
of his servant suspecting he was "on fire at the mouth"
and pouring cold water on the pioneer smoker ?

*   *   *

Mushidi, I find, is really an Emperor, because all the
aboriginal kings for hundreds of miles stream in and do
fealty. No fussy genuflexion this, but the simple and
solitary shout "Conqueror!" (*Kashinde*), with one
clap of the hands. If you quiz one of these chiefs as to
his rights of kingship, at first he shivers at the im-
pertinence of the thing. Pushing investigations, however,
you find that very rarely has he real title-deeds, and not
even the red spear of Rob Roy, to prove his rights. The
fact is, many of these lesser chiefs have won territory in
lawsuits ; not hard muscles but hard mouths doing it all.
Take some data. Lokona has ancestral rights to his
territory, because the first of his dynasty ate a dog at a

neighbouring king's court. Behold that first Lokona
forced to eat his first dog, yet even as he digests this
new sort of canine mutton he meditates a lawsuit, the
plea running : " Why should I, a salt-of-the-earth Sera
man, be so insulted in being invited to break taboo by
eating the dog of a barbarian ? " So to prove great
moral wrong inflicted by such gastronomical exertions
over an unclean pug, this founder of a dynasty turned
sick as a Bay of Biscay voyager, the end of that victorious
vomit being the ceding of large tracts of territory, flowing
streams, and a good larder of antelopes in the plains.
Quite a brisk bit of business that " beware of the dog "
lawsuit, for to this day, far from railway train and
teeming city, a Lokona still reigns in the sylvan quiet
of his forest. Yea, if ever in the far future one of the
dynasty boasts of note-paper and a coat of arms, it is
conceivable that he will have worked in somewhere a
victorious dog in the family crest.

The adjacent fisher chief Muvanga, who owns the
Bethsaida of Lake Mweru, has likewise lawsuit title-
deeds to his bit of foreshore. What was the forensic fight
about ? For many a year these Muvanga chiefs were
poor highlanders forced to till the sour soil of the
plateau, getting only a glance of blue Mweru through
the trees. Down below, the fisher-folk had struck it
strong in an endless harvest of fish, being thus fat and
filthy in obverse ratio to the leanness and cleanness of
the hill-men. With the acumen of an old campaigner,
however, the chief on the hill knew that his day was

IT'S NOT THE HANDS THAT STEAL,
BUT THE HEART.

drawing near—a mere chance ultimately changing the colour of the map—country, I mean, for the negro knows nothing but the real map of nature drawn to the scale of eight furlongs to one mile. Well, the happy day came when one of the hill-men, prowling down in the plains, spied a crowd of Lake dwellers huzzahing over some find they had made—iron-ore it turned out to be. But shall we not rather call this an unhappy find, for did they not seize the wandering highlander and slay him as a sacrifice on the opening of the mine? Remember, in Africa, without the shedding of blood there is no—no anything, so how could they dare exploit this new mine without the traditional human sacrifice? Indeed, these nude capitalists of long ago are rather reminiscent of modern Steel Trusts in the fact that they believed strongly in sacrifice, but only to the extent of making some scapegoat outsider the sufferer. So they slew this man and sprinkled his blood down the open mine, "cleansing by blood" the mineral deposit. And thus it was the clock of destiny struck for those hungry hill-men, their vengeance not taking the form of a shrill warcry but rather a long nagging lawsuit. For days and months they doggedly pushed their claim for compensation, the fisher chief Ñongwe temporising like a shrewd old lawyer. A tangled tale that lawsuit, a tale of loops and ties, loose threads and entanglements, inconsistencies and nebulous nothings. But fine words even in Africa butter no parsnips, and finally the highlander snatched a legal victory—verdict: That the said Muvanga receive a slice of foreshore for dry season corn and a share in the fisheries of Lake Mweru. Thus the meekest of all the Muvangas climbed to the twin-summits of his ancestral ambitions, and red blood did it all. Then it is the nude negro makes you rub up your English etymology, for do not "blood," "bloom," and "blossom" all come from the same root? And here, in the mud-marshes of Africa, do not the tribesmen say, "No blood, no blossom"? Quite an amusing side-light all this on Mr. Stanley's boast that in founding the Congo Free State he had made "treaties with four hundred and fifty independent chiefs whose rights would have been conceded by all to have been indisputable, since they held their lands by undisturbed occupation by long ages of succession by real divine gift."

But "'tis always morning somewhere in the world," and our Lord Jesus Christ Himself has added a happy postscript to this history—I mean, the conversion of this aboriginal chief whose dynasty it was that shed the sacrificial blood. Ñongwe is his name, and his predecessor crossed over to Kilwa Island one night to rescue a prisoner, but was murdered by the Arabs just as he was putting out to sea for the return journey. This meant a stampede back upon us at Luanza, leaving the lands of his ancestors to elephants and game. But those Arab curses again were merely a sort of upside-down benediction. Certainly God made the wrath of Islam to praise Him, one vivid, electrifying flash of faith saving Ñongwe's soul to eternity. Thus, by a long roundabout route, Christ the Sacrifice redeemed this chief from all the troubles

brought upon him by that first human sacrifice long ago
—by blood cometh sorrow, therefore by blood cometh joy.
Yea, I might almost say that all things in poor old Africa
are sprinkled by blood, and without the shedding of
blood there is no—no anything. Little did these old negro
miners guess how symbolic it all was, that spilling of
human blood to celebrate their find of minerals—a Transvaal War, and many another wrangle, all so symbolised in
that shedding of blood over ore.

(Later.)

Hurrah! here they come. With the breaking of the
south-west monsoon here come the royal rains at last—rains
that, at first blush, seem as the angels of God, converting
bare brown Africa into a paradise of green. Let a month
rush past, however, and you begin to take back all your
compliments, for this grass gets out of hand, becomes
erratic and unreliable. For the traveller, too, it is often
one long dismal succession of drip, drizzle, and drench;
then, as the rank tangle shoots 12 feet high, the early
ducal-park aspect of the meadows is lost in a wild pro-
fusion of stubborn cane-grass and scrub. And thus, in a
flash, you see the real reason in so logically legislating
for Africa such a clean-cut system of half-and-half weather,
the summer seemingly as absurdly wet as the winter is
absurdly dry. For owing to the great rivers only being
so many mere canals with inadequate banks, the end of
the rains sees them leaping over into the plains where for
months they wallow in merciless marshes. (The truest
snapshot of all this was taken by Isaiah, the Prophet,

long before the days of "Kodaks," when he described
Africa as the continent "*whose land the rivers have
spoiled.*") The sleeping-sickness fly, malarial mosquito,
and endless etceteras are all cradled there in these
squelching bogs of despair. In plain English, these
marshes mean that this Africa of ours is really rotting for
four months yearly, and all to the tune of millions of
malarial mosquitoes humming their sweet tenor.

Then cometh climax. For sun, stink, and sickness get
so bad that the God Who sitteth o'er all waterfloods calls
an imperative halt to Nature in its mad career. And lo!
from mid-April to mid-October, the land swings back,
like a pendulum, to the exciting extreme of a season
of sun, only sun with not a dream of a drop of rain.
Monotonous months though they seem, what is really
happening is that this scorching sun is most surely and
solidly drying up the awful fecundity of the marshes.
The meteorological objective, in fact, of all this is a
working out at that great "spring cleaning" of Africa
called "the smokes": now it is our dark green land is a
weary expanse of sere yellow waste, even the murderous
marshes cracked solid and dry as a kiln. "The sickness
of the land," they call it, and now it is any irresponsible
nobody can, with one lighted firebrand, send broad Central
Africa up in a blaze. Then, too, it is this irresponsible
nobody is overruled by a responsible Somebody, who
uses this beneficent antiseptic blaze to purge out of
His own Africa everything that doth offend, from sea
to sea.

(1st December.)

To-day I tumbled headlong down one of the pitfalls of Court etiquette by daring to wear a pair of glasses. An old Mutoni lectured me that on approaching such a King of Timbuctoo a strong point of etiquette is to doff, not your hat but your spectacles, for such a man is called "Mr. Four-eyes" and is a horror. So, in spite of any little visual defect, you must climb down to the normal use of two eyes, not four. Nor may you even screw a monocle into your eye, for then your name is "Mr. One Eye" (why not "Mr. Three"?). The method in this madness is a real peep into the dark chamber of the negro brain, for he detests eye-glasses with a reason. And thus it runs. In Africa you must not only set a watch upon the door of your lips, but must also be inscrutably careful as to your tell-tale face, for with the wary eye of an experienced angler the African can easily fish news out of the two deep liquid pools of your eye-balls. To him eyes speak all languages under the sun, yea, they talk better than tongues; for if the eye says one thing and the tongue another, then will he plump for the verdict of the eye. Hence this antipathy to "Mr. Four-eyes." To don these glasses before a chief is a traitor's act, for are you not thereby putting yourself as far away from his ferret eyes as you are bringing him nearer to your own? The insinuating logic of the thing is so convincing that you frankly own up to having been un-pardonably rude in wearing spectacles. What could be more crushing than the ancient African rule, "Distrust a

16

man that cannot look you in the face, and distrust a woman who can "?

Instead of a field-glass or eye-glass firing his fancy, he will lecture you on your poor eyesight, and rather ingeniously argues that our tallow candles and oil are the cause of it all. God, says the negro, has made the human eye on the recuperative system of a long dark night as offset to the hard white glare of the blazing sun, and every sunset God draws down the blinds of darkness. That balmy night is life's surest because methodic eye-salve. Thus it is that for centuries the negro has scored in having no lucifer matches but the stars, no lamp but the moon, his reward being that, matched against a white man in the woods, the spoilt child of candles and lamps can only see yards for the African's miles. Call this the law of compensation or anything you like, but do not miss the point that here is a compensation that really compensates. The enforced darkness nurses the eye, thus preserving the keen edge of vision. If I remember rightly, did not Benjamin Franklin calculate that we could pay off the national debt with the cost of candles and lamps that would be saved if we went to bed at sunset and got up at sunrise?

Nor is this all. Our sense of hearing is weakened likewise. For, seemingly, we Europeans cannot have our omelette of civilisation without breaking quite a number of eggs, and our handy box of matches and our candles are merely two more broken eggs for the omelette. That is to say, they are quickly killing out of us all the old savage sense of quick hearing. True, we still talk about "cocking our ears," but in the dark we stupidly scratch a match to find out what made the noise, whereas *the negro having no matches must, in the dark, make his ears tell him all.* The drum of his ear is both match and candle, and in the broad racial sense the negro verily has his reward. For the hundreds of night sounds—rustlings, twitterings, raspings, tinglings, and roarings—are all known to even Africa's tot, the ears being called his "eyes of darkness."

But matches *are* a boon, notwithstanding, and there often comes the painful pinch when you find yourself benighted without a kindly lucifer match. In these wilds the philanthropic beam of a farthing candle is too high an aspiration, but, other things being equal, the native can always produce light by rubbing his fire-stick. Often your most urgent need is a match for a midnight alarm. True, we have plenty of electric light, when the Lord switches it on in the sky ; and many a good turn it has done me. I was in a tight corner in the Sera plains when a humble lucifer would have been the simple solution. Black clouds had rolled up from the far Kundelungu range, and the heavens rang with the loud artillery of thunder. Then the lightning began to fork and flash. Driven into a deserted hamlet before the advancing deluge, a random choice of a hut was made— too random, alas! for the thing was many sizes too small for one. Only just in the nick of time, for growl went the bursting thunder, and the torrential downpour was upon us. Doubled up there in a leaky outhouse with an odd flash of lightning for your only candle—oh for one of Messrs. Bryant & May's best! (Why is it that the African says, "Think snake, sight snake"?) A sudden thought came. What if——. Just then, hiss, went the notorious noise of an unseen "mamba" from a corner of the dark den, and it's oh, indeed, for a kindly match now, just now. My heart seemed to stop for repairs. As though this longing for a lucifer had actually pressed the invisible button of an electric-light current, flash! came another single steel-blue streak of lightning, and there, plain as a pikestaff, a long green snake showed in the flash of fire. Atrociously, maddeningly, for one flashing moment, I sighted my co-occupant of the den, then, back both man and snake were hurled into the blackness of that pestiferous gloom. Oh for a kindly lucifer! thought I. For who does not know that a snake never really attacks a man, only bites out of fear, and only because you have stumbled over him in error. Need I say that, as that mamba blocked the doorway, I had to tear down the grass wall for escape, preferring my sheets of rain to a snake under the other sheets. The blackness makes you a baby in helplessness, therefore a baby's fancies and fears flood the brain. Small wonder the negro has such a sharp sense of hearing, the slightest sound being telltale: "the sharpers," he calls the ears, and surely the reason is found just here in his negro life, lacking utterly the adjunct of match or candle. For if we played-out Europeans hear a noise, then straightway must we blunt the edge of our sharp ears by striking a light to decide the cause. Whereas the African's ears are his "darkness-eyes," and they must play the part of both match and candle. This auricular sharpness is also called "spiked ears," and seemingly our so-called spike of acute hearing has become blunt, because it thus depends on sight to solve the problems of sound. This, he says, is the reason why God, Who divided the twenty-four hours into darkness and light, also divided man into ears and eyes, the correlatives with twelve hours apiece. The Faraday who made the world ring with his *Chemical History of a Candle* would most surely have enjoyed this negro's lecture on "The Philosophy of a Candle."

CHAPTER XIV

Thus Far and no Farther

"When they were but few men in number; yea, very few, and strangers in it. When they went from one nation to another . . . He suffered no man to do them wrong; yea, He reproved kings for their sakes, saying, Touch not Mine anointed, and do My prophets no harm."   PSALM CV. 12-15.

*   *   *

"Beneath the cross of Jesus
    I fain would take my stand—
The shadow of a mighty rock
    Within a weary land:
A home within the wilderness,
    A rest upon the way,
From the burning of the noontide heat
    And the burden of the day."

CHAPTER XIV

Thus Far and no Farther

WHEREIN the reader painfully learns that a tyrant is only a slave turned inside out.

(*2nd December.*)

THE King disdained my salute this morning; turned his back on me and muttered murder. I warrant you, this Mushidi in the sulks is quite a dangerous item in our programme. Then it is his crafty look reveals potential blood, your blood and nothing short of it. "White men?" said King Cut-Throat the other ominous day with disdain: "Oh, out East near Unyanyembe we killed several." No thought pursues me so persistently as this: nag, naggingly does it try to gain admittance into the soul, the old David-in-the-dumps whine: "I shall one day perish by the hand of Saul." Those murdered whites he boasts of were, of course, poor Carter and Cadenhead—a touching tale that, if all were known. Carter, an Englishman of great ability and British Consul at Bagdad, one day burst on astonished Central Africa with four Indian elephants. The tale of his triumphant entry is a thing still told with bated breath far into the heart of Africa. Livingstone and Stanley are as nobodies compared with this "Lord of Tuskers" who made the Rugarugas marvel at the subjugation of such monsters. On the 20th of October, behold! the triumphal entry of these four white men riding their pilot elephant, the natives all amaze and wondering whether they are mad or dreaming. Never was advance guard of travelling circus acclaimed by English rustics as on the great day when these swarming negroes saw such a passing strange prodigy—a whole tribe struck all of a heap and stupefied! Were not elephants the local terror and did they not kill many a native? Yet it is one of the ironies of contemporary history, that there, stuck high on that elephant's back, you have four white men who symbolise the coming struggle for supremacy—two Belgians and two Englishmen! A prophecy of history you can certainly call it, for who is the second Englishman if not the poor ill-fated Stokes? There they are, rubbing shoulders on the back of an elephant, Carter and Stokes (English) with Popelin and Van den Huvel (Belgians). Who would have dared the thought that one day a Belgian would hang that same Stokes on a forest tree in the wilds of Africa? With pleasing ignorance and charming stupidity, the negroes never dared to dream that those four whites were not one in nationality and fraternity, and had they guessed the coming rivalry their joy would have known no bounds. But long before Stokes died at the hands of a Belgian, Carter and Cadenhead fell unwept victims to the Rugarugas. Hurrah! was the shout of these bandits on the 20th of October, and the following 25th of June saw the very same negroes shrieking death. Yet Carter in his death is even more famous than the Carter who petrified Central Africa with his marvellous Indian elephants. Attacked at Pimbwe on the 23rd June, Cadenhead fell dead to the first bullet. Seeing one white man dead, their 150 Zanzibaris fled, leaving Carter alone to face the murderers—no, not wholly abandoned, for his faithful mahouts and servant Mahomed—honour the brave!—stuck to their master. Far into the marshes of Africa they still tell the tale of that brave British Consul who sold his life so dearly, and even the Belgians call it "une scène terrible, un combat digne des anciens heros." Seventeen times his Winchester speaks, and seventeen men lie dead. But this is not all. The carbine cartridges are now finished, but with a defiance born of desperation he falls back on his revolver, the circle of fire narrowing in on him—a pack of howling wild beasts. Of course, they too could shoot, and indeed, quite early in the fight, a bullet had pinned poor Carter to the ground, the warning this, that escape is now impossible. Seeing death ahead, he coolly and carefully pulled out his watch, wrote a farewell note, and begged Mahomed to make off with his papers to Karema. Then, after making good practice with his revolver for some time, "death and he lay down together," as the murderers say. Nor do they blush to tell me how they mutilated the poor body with revolting cruelty.

So there you have the meaning of Mushidi's dark hint to us: "Whites? Oh, we killed several."

(Later.)

I thought I knew my Mushidi fairly intimately, but to-day he quite nonplussed me by spitting in my face. In a flash, I thought that here was a chance to share in the sufferings of Christ: did they not spit in That Face from Which one day the heavens and the earth shall flee away? But a tardy explanation of this foolery was so suave and conciliating that I soon saw that I had lost martyrdom. That spit was not a mere expectoration but a compliment; not a spit, in fact, but a spout, for his mouth was full of beer, not holy water but holy beer. Well, it seems that I had caught him in the spirit of worship which in Africa also means the worship of spirits by the drinking of beer. This worshipping (*Kupara*) literally means a spitting or spouting, and when they have spouted consecrated beer down into the ground, they then start and link up the living and the dead by spouting beer all around the place. This arrangement harmonises exactly with the negro's ideas of fellowship in dirty doings, and an Englishman would need to wear a waterproof and an umbrella at such a function. It really rains beer. Moreover, this curious custom of worshipping the spirits with a drink called "spirits" is very subtle, the hint seeming to be in the fact that a fainting, half-dead man can be vivified by such a drink. But the river of time is indeed brackish with the salt of human tears, and here is Mushidi crouching to the spirits and pleading their aid at the very moment when he is surrounded by the accusing bleached skulls of his victims. Yet, "nobody

really dies" is the negro saying, so to him that white
skull is merely the last surviving wind-swept room of a
wrecked tenement.   Now only a warrior's punch-bowl, the
very skull that

> " was once ambition's airy hall,
> The dome of thought, the palace of the soul."

Nevertheless, if you want to guess even faintly at the
curious convolutions of the black brain, you must seize
upon this great system of spirit-worship, which is one and
indivisible across Africa.   The whole theory is merely the
solemn result of the negro as a race looking steadfastly
into the continents of death and eternity.   What is this
fiction but a farrago of sense and nonsense?   The ardent
spirits of the living and the dead linked with these ardent
spirits—of beer.   Worshipping by fits and starts and
sometimes only once per annum, the negro can only
cordially dispense with worship after he has dispensed
cordials.   Do not they accuse us of the same thing when
we place wine on the Lord's Table?

*   *   *

But there is more in it than mere tipple—tragedy, call
it.   Watch this African's definition of spirit-worship, a
sorry enough solution of the problem.   Here it is.   Shut
up into one sentence the kernel idea is the negro attempt
to rob the awful and unknown spirit-world of its double
sting of loneliness and frowning distance.   Does it not
envelop him, and out from the unseen depths thereof are
not daily darts showered against him?   Hence his solution in this bridging process, *i.e.* the boast that a de-

ceased mother is still linked with her living children
by the very blood she has bequeathed them. That is to
say, yonder in that frowning lonely spirit-world, menacing
his life at every turn, he *has actually* a blood kinsman as
daysman and representative. She, too, was once hungry,
once weary, once jagged with earthly pains and penalties.
To prove this link as both intimate and dear I have
heard a man murmur in spirit-worship, "Oh, mother,
behold this blood now coursing in my body, thou didst
not merely bequeath it unto me, but it *is* thee!" Here,
then, you find the tenacity of belief that he, the living
being, can bridge the awful gulf because the dead did
not entirely die—did they not leave some of their own
literal blood on this earthly side of the gulf as an in-
tentional link? There, then, is his bridge across the
chasm, and if you urge that it is not real, but merely his
own mad conjecture, he will retort that the bridging
initiative was not his at all, but rather that of his own
guardian spirit, who will not (*because cannot*) sever the
link between the living and the dead. Instance, even
a tiny boy, who, long ago in war, was swooped down
on in his natal village—query: How can he worship a
mother he never knew? The boy's retort is that, albeit
he was so torn away at birth from his unknown mother,
yet surely he, too, was born as much as everybody else.
That he never knew her is less than nothing at all to
him, for he has only to pinch his flesh to remind himself
that *she* gave him this body. So there he is, working
away at the building of his little temple to the " unknown

god "—his nameless mother's spirit. For although unknown yet is she well-known, yea, here is her own blood flowing in his own veins. Hence the double deduction he makes that, even in the spirit-world, throb for throb of his earthly joy is hers, even as stab for stab of his pain is hers too. It is all "mother," "mother," mark you, and no mention of his father, for often he does not know his name, and just as often—hush! the mother knows it not either.

And so he "bridges the gulf." For does he not believe that in every pang that rends his heart his guardian spirit has a part? The victim of many a cruel and ungenerous blow in life, does he not still reckon on the dear old maternal solicitude for his welfare? God, he thinks, is too busy up among the stars to bother about him, but not so his "mama." Watch the subtlety of all this, for like a dam of rocks relentlessly solid, here is a barrier ever blocking the advance of the Gospel. To preach Christ as kinsman-advocate before God is to the negro only, in other words, a branch of the same spirit-worship. Wearied by the well of Sychar, thirsty on life's road, and pained with the pangs of suffering, does He not now sorrow with us in our sorrow? Poor old African, groping after, if haply he may find. The only way he hopes to capture the stronghold of The Unseen is by this flank movement of kinsmanship—to him the line of least resistance, being the warm, cherishing heart of his defunct mother. O for ten thousand Christians to advance in the Lord's name and shout to-night above all the wintry

winds of Africa : "I am the way." It is easy to talk
loosely of the Gospel of Nature softening men's hearts,
but Paul agrees with Tennyson's "Nature red in tooth
and claw" when he says that "the whole creation
groaneth and travaileth together in pain until now."
And it is precisely this moan pouring into the negro ear
that makes him think of God as a malignant demon,
mocking at his pain, and pouring contempt upon his
life. The impassive serenity of Nature in all the struggles
and anguish of life maddens him into open revolt, for
do not the serene stars rise and set with callous calmness
over the storm and stress of his life ? There is the Gospel
of Nature for you ! Moral : Herein is love : not that we
get to love God by looking out on cruel Nature, but that
He loved us and gave His Son a Victim of the same
cruelty.

(3rd December.)

Have just had a "borderland" talk with an old devil-
doctor, and he tells me much about his professional
headquarters. Away down the Lualaba the natives
have located their "Cathedral of the Congregated Dead"
in a dark, umbrageous ravine. Their idea is that for
hundreds of miles around the spirits all concentrate into
this weird amphitheatre of the dead : "Chivawa," they
call the mysterious place, and dead bodies scattered far
over hill and dale in their graves—or no grave at all—
have each a representative spirit here in their Parliament
of the Dead. "The spot where spirits blend" is their
phrase, but the blending is in loud debate when the

demons shriek out invectives. In this Assembly there is
no President or Mr. Speaker, and the logic of these demon
utterances is so illogical that the Lubans have seemingly
broken into the spirit-world at the lunatic asylum end.
Distinctly Dantesque is this gulf of theirs, the very look
of the place suggesting uncanny, supernatural notions.
Reluctant daylight only trickles in here and there through
the mountain fissures, and as Nature has such a very
definite voice to the negro, why wonder that they all
seem to hear her proclaim the special sanctity of this wild,
woeful region? "Dim religious light" with a caution.
The acoustics of the place are so wonderful that a mere
whisper is caught up and goes echoing on and on through
the galleries and corridors of the mountain. When I
passed down there a wet wind was blowing bleak, and the
noise came groaning out from the Cathedral entrance like
a huge organ. Far from being a mere thing of contemporary gossip, this Chivawa (like its sister-
cathedral Songa farther South) is the High Court of
Appeal in all tough lawsuits—its yea utterly yea, and its
nay, nay. After wrangling out hot legal puzzles in their
hot little hamlets, the final word cannot be said until
Messrs. Pro and Con go off on their hundred miles
tramp to throw themselves for adjudication at the feet of
these mighty dead. "The plunge into darkness" is what
this sort of legal gambling is called. The old vein of
incipient flippancy is now gone utterly, and there these
negroes lie prostrate in suspense. He who awakes out of
his swoon to find himself beplastered with white chalk—

let the welkin ring, for he is justified. He who, *per contra*, finds himself covered with charcoal must himself die the death by fire and become charcoal. With all this rival-religion idea of theirs, how hard it is to persuade such a superstitious people that the best way to see Divine Light is to put out their own farthing candle! Yet these negroes laugh when you tell them of the prisoner into whose cell the light came through a little crack in the wall. And one day, when they came to destroy the wall, he bitterly lamented because it would destroy the crack through which his daylight came. Our message rings out one note, and one only: "See thy Sin, but behold thy Saviour."

One rarely seen old man has a great say here: Kavoto, they call him, a weird old magic-magnate who has made the whole land hum with his dark doings among the lions. But how can we distinguish the bones of fact from the drapery of invention? The *cum grano* story runs that from far and near he summons his lions to receive their fetish orders; no doors locked in his forest hamlet, and they trot in and out like friendly mastiffs. At sundown, he sends out this "lion-call," a rumbling roar simulating their cry, and in they bowl to supper. Then it is they are commissioned N., S., E., and W. to raid villages and pick off the various victims of his hate, "orders" being received at this Lion Depôt and carefully executed. That is to say, A. deposits a sum in Kavoto's hand for the murdering of B. by lions, and the specialist guarantees results. The old map-makers were right when, in lieu of any known name to print over this spot in Africa, they put down the eloquent prophecy : *Hic sunt Leones*. Who told them of this Lion Bureau? The two mild-mannered chiefs who to-day vouched for these strange doings seemed greatly pained when I hinted that this sort of thing could not be accepted without a certain amount of intellectual jugglery. They repelled my insinuations with real Luban scorn, and to convince me, one of them flew off like a rocket extolling the Lion King's occult powers : proof after proof[2] he brought into his oration ; grand words to express poor ideas, a racehorse drawing a donkey-cart. Yet very sure am I, Herodotus would have filled pages with just such trash.

What does it all mean? Is not all the world under one's waistcoat? Well, deducting adequate discount only leaves a little balance—but much in that little. For all Africa believes in the transmigration of a living man into a living lion, believes that lions lend their bodies to human beings for the inhuman purpose of grabbing their fellows. This Kavoto knows, and this he capitalises. Hence this opening of a Lion Shop— Transmigration Specialist, wonders while you wait. Pay your money and pick your victim, for does not the name Kavoto mean, the Lurker-to-kill? Even far-off white men, white dabblers in the black art, have been reported to pay eagerly for the death of a victim ; Arabs, of course, being regular customers. Worse and higher still, it is said—well, never mind what is said.

[2] ???????

(*3rd December.*)

I have just had a big brawl with M. over refusing to write out to the Ocean for more powder and guns. The old days of the poisoned arrow are passing, and something with a big bang is the substitute. The lion pulls down the zebra in the moonlight, the leopard springs on the antelope, and, says Mushidi, why not the big man *versus* the little man in the war of extermination? "These were my claws," said he to-day, pointing to some old bows and poisoned arrows of the early days. With the innovation of "Waterloo" flint-locks and "Crimea" cap-guns, of course, the execution has become more drastic and decisive. When Mushidi got his first guns of the "gas-pipe" genus, then it was he really conceived his "God" pretensions; was not that flash in the pan of his flint-locks followed by the roar from the barrel a true copy of the Almighty's thunder and lightning? But he bemoaned the paucity of these "God-firers." His nucleal armoury indeed only boasted the grand total of five flint-locks, and—like the small boy's five loaves of life—what were these five guns of death among so many negroes to be slain? Thus Mushidi moaned, and the moaning climaxed in a midnight council, with the hatching of a famous miracle-lie. And thus "the gun-lie" ran. Out among the unsophisticated negroes the heresy was preached that Mushidi had not merely omnipotent guns but omniscient bullets. In other words, they were stuffed with nonsense that he or his delegate, by merely drawing a gun-trigger at random could thereby send the said omniscient bullet, sure as the scent of a blood-hound, zigzagging through the land, dealing death to all desirable victims. More : they made a double lie out of double bullets ; two bullets like two pills being a double dose of death, the said bullets separating to find different victims *ad infinitum.* Superstition dies hard, but here in Bunkeya it doesn't die at all. So well does this idea of " God-firing " soak into the negro brain, that when I was down in the Lufira Valley the King's brother corroborated this idea. He had gone out into the savannah to try his *Bwanga* or luck at hunting a herd of red-buck round the ant-hills ; but when he had hoped to draw upon one of these decisively, flash ! came a vivid fork of lightning, half blinding him for the moment. A second passed, and then he saw nearly the whole heap of buck lying stone dead from the forked flash. Then it was, rubbing his hands with glee, the noble hunter naïvely said, " Fancy ! God beating me at gun-firing ! "

It was with this blasphemous idea he pushed his " God " pretensions in Lubaland on going North to Kayumba's. The legend of Kara ya Rova found all over the Garenganze took Mushidi's fancy. This Kara ya Rova is the legendary Creator of the Human Race, called literally the Captain of Humanity, and he it was who headed for the North with the long Indian file of human nations in his wake. We, the whites, were there with our federal ancestor, and they, the blacks, were there too. But spying on the march, day by day, a changing panorama of bewitching vales watered by noble rivers, they one by one dropped out and turned aside to a lazy lotus life in Africa. We, the hardier whites, held on our Northern way until we were dropped in our respective habitats. Pointing to the mountains, they show you solemnly his alleged "footprints" in the rocks, for in those days, say our good black geologists, "the rocks were soft." These footprints, of course, are a fraud and merely the "pot-holes" common to all the world's river-beds, erosive in character; nevertheless, it was appropriate that this "footprints-graven-in-the-rocks" idea should catch Mushidi's imagination. Deceiving and being deceived, humbugging and being humbugged his whole life, it was in the essential irony of things that he, The Fraud, should believe such a fraud. The conscious grower of a metaphoric mushroom empire, he vainly longed to go down to posterity at least "written in the rocks," if not with the iron pen of history : was not he, too, "God" as much as Kara ya Rova? Did not he, too, daily and hourly mould the fates and fortunes of men? So the fiat went forth, and Mushidi, standing as solemnly as though he were being measured by a shoemaker, got his footprints carved out of the rocks. More than that, he had a backgammon board cut out in the rocks—a memorial to all generations.

Here it was at Kayumba's he, resolving to make a water-bottle never before made by man, flayed a human being to make a water-bottle of the skin. Hence the catch has gone down to posterity, "*Mushidi wa funda mu ku funda muntu*," the horrible play on the word *funda* being that it means doubly " to teach " and " to take the skin off," just as, in a weaker sense, a master beating his slave will pun on the same word to say, " I will teach you," *i.e.* I will beat you till some skin comes off. This skin of a human being is most touchingly called " the seamless robe," the idea being that when God created man He clothed him with a seamless robe of skin. Little wonder that the memory of the other sacred seamless robe of Calvary came to me very vividly in almost an exactly similar connection as the story of the Roman soldiers gambling for Christ's robe. There, too, in Mushidi's capital were four cut-throats, with red turkey-twill turbans, who had returned from a fight in the North. Swooping down on the town, they had killed off most of the men, dragging South the women and boys as slaves, and here you have four soldiers with only one slave between them. Moot-point : What is to be done ? Why, of course, *Teya Buvale*, or throw the dice, for ultimate ownership. So there, behold them gambling for a slave, and now it is in the excited gabble of the gamblers you can overhear the snatch-phrases, " Let us gamble for our *seamless robe*," *i.e.* a human being. But on pushing investigations you find that while this is literally a metaphor for the actual skin, yet as a " whole skin " even in English means a live body, even so there is a double innuendo in Bantu. For the seamless robe of skin is to the negro a type of the unity of that slave's body who could not be cut up into four portions to accommodate the four warriors, hence this gambling : " Let us not rend it, but cast lots for it, whose it shall be." As not even a bone of Christ's body was broken, how suggestive the fate of both His robe of cloth and robe of flesh!

But there is a glimmer in all this gloom. In the darkest den of Africa, the doctrine of the Immortality of the Soul is flaming like a fire, and the deeper you dig the higher it flares. *Bipeds only*, too, the door being slammed on quadrupeds. Bird or beast, do not dare suggest to the Luban that animals are immortal. Here is a whole town actually gone off its food and solidly refusing to eat until *nem. con.* they come to a decision on a question of—of metaphysics. 'Tis passing strange. When I came on the scene they had been at it for four hours, the debate a wild thing: Has a dog a spirit?

The judges were in the blues when I arrived, and insisted on my umpiring their hard-mouthed wrangle. The older folks stamp with indignation at the insolent idea, and the Freethinker who set this ball a-rolling is having it hot, the heretic! At last they have nonplussed him, for he lamely confesses that, of course, dogs as a rule are—well—only dogs, a species of local canine mutton, that is to say, but this dreadful dog was—w-a-s, a wonder. The whole debate, it seems, masks the mouth of a trap, a lawyer's trap, and a law-suit is lurking in the background all the time. For if he can successfully insinuate that an exceptional dog may (ahem!) exceptionally have a spirit, then he is going to have the law on them, for he avers a dead dog is haunting him to his undoing. This dog, be it keenly noted, was not only a hunter's dog but really a greater hunter than his master. Day by day, it would go off on its own, lurk on the edge of the plain and, with the spring of a panther, drag down an antelope, a devoted gift to his master. This *entente cordiale*, between man and dog, went on and on, until the neighbours envied both man and dog; so one day—dark *dies memorabilis*—they pounced on the hunter, claiming damages for a slight indiscretion on the animal's part—breach of dog-etiquette, I mean, not man's. Stealing eggs, nothing less, was the accusation. Result: the culprit pug was condemned to have his ears cropped, and with the disappearance of the devoted dog's ears there also disappeared utterly any devoted gifts of game. Knotty point: When he lost his ears, did he lose his scent for game? Answer: No, not at all; he went still at it, was still successful in the chase, but—but snubbed his master for permitting them to crop ears. Did he eat his captured game then? Certainly not; how could a dog with such a prohibition bred in the bone, how could it dare such a deed?

This, then, is what it did do—and here it is we tumble plump into mystery. Adjacent to the townlet is a wild bog into which the Lualaba lavishes its waters, the dense tangle being hopeless and shutting in the water from view. Here it is the dog discovers a hole for hiding his trophies. Day by day (it all came out afterwards) he revengefully rammed down that hole his spoils of the chase, a real case —if you but change one word—of " a dog in the manger "; he didn't eat the meat himself out of canine honour, and he slyly saw to it that nobody else would. Then came

(what should have been) the end, but the end is not yet.
Poor Bow-wow died, died of chagrin, some said; died of
disdain, said others.   And now trouble begins to fall thick
and fast among the hunter's friends.   You remember that
hole in the dark bog and you recall how the dog frequented
the spot; well, that hole, the folks say, is an endless shaft
that leads down to the bottomless pit of the demons.
This man's brother, at any rate, went there one day, broke
through the thick papyrus down to the water, a huge
crocodile snapped up at him and down he went with a
shriek—yes, down the dead dog's hole.   At home, too, in
the village, it is the same thing, death after death; illness
after illness, and all dogging the hunter's kinsfolk who
betrayed the dog.   So here you have the whole story of
this wrangle, but the town stops its ears and denies that
a dog with no spirit can haunt the living.   The only
haunting a dog does locally is a slight canine indigestion
after they have swallowed him.

So here once more the old idea is proved that immortality is not a mere doctrine but an *instinct*, a much
more serious thing.   Grotesque and diversified in its
million manifestations, no doubt, but a notorious instinct,
and as such sure, yes, surer than the instinct of the bird
of passage never deceived in its migrations.   Sure as the
bee when it elaborates the cell for the future honey.
Sure, yes, surer far than that instinct of the butterfly and
beetle when they prepare the cradle and the food for the
offspring they will never see.   Even Darwin was forced
to own the vast ramifications of this instinct of Immor-

tality among degraded races of men, but curiously argued
that "if the human mind was developed from the lowest
form of creatures, then how could that mind—human
though it was—be trusted in its *instincts*?" Of course,
the bewildering part of all this is that the speaker is the
same Darwin who sees elsewhere instinct as a mighty
guiding law ruling the creation like clockwork, and unerringly causing the swallow, for instance, to shoot South
overseas for the sure sunshine and the flowers. Not by
whim or caprice, but by law—the law of instinct—does
that swallow dart South to the sun. Then, Mr. Darwin,
why deny to the mighty soul what you grant to the
small swallow? Are ye not of more value than many
swallows? Moral: The thirst for the Infinite proves the
Infinite. "Sir, I hold," said Emerson—and well spake
he—"I hold that God Who keeps His Word with the
birds and fishes in all their migratory instincts will keep
His word with man."

(Later.)

Mushidi was very meek and mild to-day as he
received some bold blacksmiths from the South-East.
They have him wholly in the hollow of their hand: no
smith, no soldier—no Tubal Cain, no sword or ploughshare!

The best because busiest bees in the hive of Central
Africa are these tough old blacksmiths who turn out the
iron ore. Long bony hands they have on which the
muscles stand out like whipcords. Made not of flesh
and blood, but of asbestos, these funny fingers of theirs

can juggle with live coals of fire and scarcely be burned, hence the common conceit is to call their fingers " Fire-tongs" (*Fimanto*). There is poetry in these brawny blacks, but they live their poetry like men instead of singing it like birds, and far and near they surely have their reward. All eyes look East, Kishinga way, when the roar of the rains is near. Are not those hundreds of miles of smiling African tillage all traceable to this man who digs the ore from the hillside and manufactures hoes, spears and axes ? Although their ideas are the crudest of the crude, still they combine in a solemn cult the caste of Tubal Cain, let us call it. Bound by a code of stringent laws, these " thou-shalt-nots" are a pathetic mix-up of soul and matter, faith and works, mud and stars. They are sworn to temporal celibacy and severely dieted ; can only eat out of certain pots, and cannot, dare not, eat certain animals—*e.g.* the hare. Their furnaces make quite a show of hard enterprise, and the function of filling these is the occasion of a solemn fast when no soul of man other than these sons of Tubal Cain can be about. Then it is all the folks shut themselves indoors while this " furnace-feeding " process is going on, the men of the cult calling out menacingly the while. But as most things in Africa are a mad mixture of mind and mud, the fetish, *i.e.* religious element, is of primary importance in it all. For it is " God's ore," they say, and this Spirit-mediation theory of theirs is only a frank refusal of these blacks to admit that mere stout arms and tough muscles have all the say in God's own world. " Who first drinks, first thanks," say they. And this African of ours and his "other-worldliness" is deeply touching—wouldn't even condescend to argue with an Atheist. "How do I know there is a God?" he asks. "How do I know my goat passed over that wet ground if not by the footprints she left in the mud?" Thus any such phrase as "laws of Nature" is unknown to him, for an act postulates an agent, and what is Nature but God's mere minion? No Atheist could hoodwink a black man with the notion that mere laws explain everything, for your negro retorts, "As if a law does not require construction as well as a world." Another of these men proved the existence of God by the quiet query: "Who ever forgot there was a Sun?" A proof this that he reads his Book of Nature so well that in every rock and tree God is staring him in the eyes and shouting in his ears. Yet in the teeth of this, such an expert as Burton could insist that "the necessity of a Creator, so familiar to our minds, is generally strange to savages. In the present day, the African races generally have never been able to comprehend the existence or the necessity of a One God." Fie, Sir Richard! Even Cicero long ago could declare that "there is no nation so brutish as not to be imbued with the conviction that there is a God." So, too, Plutarch: "We may search the world throughout, and in no region where man has lived can we find a city without the knowledge of a God or the practice of a religion." And the whole continent of Africa choruses an eager "Yes!" to these ancients.

*   *   *

Some more eye-opening "thinking black." This pug-nosed negro of ours has really a brain of phenomenal range. This you can best believe by wiping off the old slander that he is poor in numeration, for his unit is the "terrible-ten"—another pinprick this, I know, into the bubble of tradition. Terrible ten, indeed, for starting so ominously with a round number he soon soars into the blue of arithmetic. Thus, leaving hundred (*Chitōta*) and "thousand" (*Chihumbi*) far behind, he reaches the figure for a million (*Mudinda*). Then with this as a jumping-ground, he leaps forward into planetary arithmetic in the word *Diita*, a million times a million. Here, however, his mind calls a halt, for man's empire is lost in the numeration of immensity, nevertheless he tricks the tongue into coining a word—*Diŏna*—the "all" things, that is to say. The panther spring of the black brain is now baffled, but not beaten, and far up in those giddy heights he starts to dare classify grades of immensity. For this *Diŏna* is (1) the speechless; (2) the voice-stifling; (3) the measure-defying; (4) the unthinkable. A daring "grand total" idea this, of locking up all expanse in the universe into one word. Asked, however, to be concrete, and not abstract, he says, with an apologetic flourish of metaphor: The grand total of all immensity may be stated in terms of—ashes: *id est*, all things viewed as separate units must be conceived as the finest powdered ashes ever known to man. For unthinkably fine though they be, they are yet only a mass of granular units! Thus quaintly and unquestionably the

African can philosophically say, " Praise is silent before
Thee, O God, in Zion." Very inflated all this, to be sure,
and very much like mere man soaring up to the blue in
a toy balloon ; yet, nevertheless, here is proof of grey
matter in the black brain. Certainly here is a man who
deserves better than the Government dog-bark of autocracy ; even as here is the real reason of many a black
bark answering white bark in revolt. Depend upon it, ye
rulers with the Rod, this black man is as strong in brain
as in biceps.

(Later.)

We Missionaries are accused of making big bouncing
assertions about our African's mental ability, and even
many a good friend of the negro claims to be forgiven if
he cannot hear of this without impatience. Living as the
black man does at the very bottom of Life's hill, the
inference is surely a very fair one, that the African is
mentally incapable of seeing anything in the light of an
abstract principle. Hence that weary and too confident
assertion that this African of ours cannot possibly be
strong in abstract ideas. The late Dean Farrar may be
isolated as a serious type of such friendly academic critics,
and what I propose to do is to quote Farrar as a heavy
philologist against the negro and then proceed forthwith
to hand him over to the tender mercies of the two great
African grammarians. That is to say, Dean Farrar, a
good negrophile, is to be viewed impersonally as a very
fair type of the average Oxford Don critic who subjectively
decides on a question really not in his sphere. Appleyard

and the late Clement Scott will on the negro side be quoted as representing the two extremes of a long line of Bantu study. Of course, as nothing short of philosophy is our pro-negro claim, we will be slavishly literal, and cling hard to this one test-word: The Abstract. Philosophy is the Abstract. If, therefore, the African can be authoritatively proved to be strong in the Abstract, then the African, *ipso facto*, is proved to be a philosopher.

"The vaunted wealth of Bantu turns out to be a concealment of their poverty. It is due to that *utter deficiency in abstract.*"

FARRAR.

"Bantu is highly systematic and *truly philosophical.*"

APPLEYARD.

"The (Bantu) language has the *fullest expression of the abstract* one has met with; broad and delicate in its conception, essentially *suaviter in modo, fortiter in re!*" CLEMENT SCOTT.

Here, then, we behold in sharp juxtaposition the oldest story of *pro* and *con* cross-swearing in the world: Farrar's loose subjective vagaries confronted with hard, stubborn, objective data. What a swing of the pendulum from zero to hundred! Is black white, or crooked straight? This is the thing honest men yawn over—arm-chair dogmatism in England breaking a lance with "the man on the spot"—our venerable friend Quod Erat Demonstrandum Esquire smiling down so condescendingly on plain Mr. Quod Erat Faciendum. The former correct and subjective to his finger-tips; the latter with his jacket off sweating over objective data, filling dozens of note-books. For Dr. Clement Scott is surely a good example of being very, oh! very much Mr. Faciendum. If his above-quoted words seem to be exaggerated and sweeping ("the fullest expression of the abstract one has met with"!), does he not substantiate them all in his 737 pages of genuine Bantu idiom? Tortuous and tricky, and to the tune of hundreds of instances, he it is who has followed the marvellous negro far into the *penetralia* of "thinking black." Emerging from it all, in a wonder that is almost dismay, Dr. Scott gasps—for "gasp" is the word—that Bantu has "*the fullest expression of the abstract* one has yet met with." And philosophy is the Abstract, remember; *ergo* the African is proved to be both brainy and beefy—in fact, has brain as well as biceps. Contrast Farrar's serious assertion as to the African's "*utter deficiency in abstract*"!

CHAPTER XV

Red Sunsets

"Ah, the land of the rustling of wings, which is beyond the rivers of Ethiopia."   Isaiah.

*   *   *

"In that time [from beyond the rivers of Ethiopia] shall a present be brought unto the Lord of hosts of a people scattered and peeled, and from a people terrible from their beginning hitherto: a nation meted out and trodden under foot, whose land the rivers have spoiled, to the place of the name of the Lord of hosts, the mount Zion."   Isaiah.

*   *   *

"Oh the generations old
 Over whom no church-bell tolled,
 Christless, lifting up blind eyes
 To the silence of the skies!
 For the innumerable dead
 My soul is disquieted."

CHAPTER XV

Red Sunsets

WHEREAT the reader is sad, for the adjective is found to enter the superlative degree—black, blacker, blackest.

(7th December.)

ONE for Mushidi! He tells me that he has never yet suffered living sacrifices in the capital here, whereas all around every little H.R.H. Nobody cannot be buried without them. These terrible tales— "red sunsets," they are called—are hardly tellable, for here it is we reach the part of this diary that should really be written in red ink. The sun (*i.e.* the Chief) is sinking, and he must sink in red—a real scarlet sunset, and no mistake. It is quite certain that every poor chieflet demands his regal right to drag down with him to the nether world at least one or two splendid specimens of the human kind. *Mpaki* is the dread technical term for this institution, and these are mostly women-folk, the demand being that the living sacrifice must have no blemish. No wonder when an

18

African hears that line of the Bible he shudders:
"The rich man died, and was *buried.*" Instinctively
they think of a holocaust with its stream of blood;
and then it is Jeremiah's famous "weepers" put in an
appearance, professional tear-manufacturers these, who
produce—for a consideration—"tortoise-tears" (*sic*) by
the jar-ful. "Consider ye, and call for the mourning women, that they may come; and send for cunning
women, that they may come: and let them make haste,
and take up a wailing for us, that our eyes may run
down with tears, and our eyelids gush out with waters"
(Jer. ix. 17)—how often have these words been uttered
in Lubaland! Two of the prettiest wives are gloriously
dressed and anointed with oil to accompany the corpse
to the "west coast of Africa," *i.e.* the spirit-world
(*Kumbonshi*), and never, never to come back again.[1]
They always say that these and the like go to their
own death with alacrity; and when I protest later,
they remind me of a case very well known to me by
a personal link. That is the Mbogo Senior incident
down in the Sera plain. At the *Mpaki* ceremony,
and against all entreaty to the contrary, the infirm old
wife of his youth insists upon accompanying her own
consort down into the tomb of suffocation. She brushes
aside the younger folks, and orders the catching and
cooking of her best barn-yard fowl for her own last
supper. She assists in her own "death toilet," her own

[1] That is to say, the setting sun symbolises the advent of dark night,
i.e. death.

A LUBAN LADY.

cleansing, and her own anointing unto her own burial. "Nay, who should go with my lord but me?" said she in response to the "death-orchestra" of the wailing cunning women who were raining down "tortoise-tears." And then, in the evening, when the sough of the first night-wind passes over the great fen-bog, behold this old living sacrifice hobbling along with her gourd tobacco pipe in its little basket to attend her own funeral—no wail : nothing ! and the dark eternal sets in. There, in a death of suffocation, she received her "John Anderson, my Jo !" in death's embrace, in life and death one. Surely, here in a pathetic sense we see them sleeping together at the foot of life's hill, after many "a cantie day" together. On the surface, here is the kind of incident claimed as a feather in the cap of polygamy, and a mad Mormon would challenge monogamy to produce in like environment a like demonstration of conjugal affection. But such conjugal love of two souls only proves monogamy. Only a week before their twin-death and burial, who should come up from the plains to pay us a most punctilious visit but precisely this dear old lady, Mrs. John Anderson, and her Jo, of course ! They hobbled over the hill together, a true instance of negro man and wife who had projected their last visit to "town," as they call our Luanza. A brief week thence saw the tragedy.

(Later.)

By far the most exasperating "red sunset" known to me was the death of my old friend of years, the great

Chona. As Lord Paramount, he was the owner of broad
lands, and what could you expect? Still, that is just
the sore point, for we had lofty hopes that the Chona
—"Destroyer," the translation—in his peaceful death
would create a clean and bloodless precedent for the
young generation. Now it ekes out that one of his
strongest reasons for not becoming a Christian was his
fear that he would lose the divine honours of a vermilion
sunset. What a poor King Jesus Christ was (he argued)
to die in darkness as a felon ! How, then, did this Chona
holocaust eventuate ? After all, it is only another proof
that the African at home is lord of his own soil, and
can outwit a white man any day. Even your Sherlock
Holmes would soon find mere fertility of brain handi-
capped by the fact that he was only one against a million.
For, when this great Chona fell ominously sick, I saw to
it that several lynx-eyed negroes were hanging around,
their plea for loitering being the medicine I had sent.
Nevertheless, long ago the old councillors, who sniffed
treason in the very appearance of these Mission negroes,
have plotted their being outwitted—and remember, for
Reynard to outwit Reynard, the subtlety must be a
marvel. "As false as a bulletin," became a proverb
in the days of Napoleon ; so these old "death-doctors"
copied France, and resolved to create a strong diversion
to the North. Thus at daybreak the news (as first bulletin
for the day) was on everybody's lips that the sick King
had been removed by night to the North—the heat, the
marsh, the billions of mosquitoes, the ostensible plea for

the change of hospital. (*Entre nous*, the King is really dead in his house, but no "red sunset" can take place while the enemy, in the form of my messengers, is ambushed within the sacred atmosphere of death.) But they have been outwitted, sure enough; and when all is in train for a start, out they spring like panthers from the dead King's hut, blood having already begun to flow in the death of the weary old nurse who got sudden death as her nursing fee. Silently as suddenly they now slam the door of the harem, wherein a dozen wives are cooped up like animals for the sacrifice; and the slam of that door is answered by their moan. The "red sunset" begins. As, however, it is all ceremonial in character, this "charnel-house" work has a "method in its madness." There is, first of all, we have seen, that sacrifice of the old nurse; then comes another human sacrifice before the royal corpse can cross the threshold. Then the whole Via Dolorosa to the tomb is "painted red"—another human life has perforce to pay toll for the corpse to pass the town gate; then, *en route*, by a sort of "minute-gun" arrangement, death follows death till the tomb is reached. Of course, old scores are wiped out in blood along that "path of thorns" (*sic*), and the man or woman who on that day has no brothers or cousins among the wire-pullers is in peril of his carcass being given to the fowls of the air. But these things are only the beginning of sorrows and the end is not yet—the end, in fact, is indescribable. For the tomb itself is the climax in a double sense. Down in

the huge pit there are the deaths from suffocation; and
up in the sunlight, on the new-made mound of earth, there
is a thing called "the blood-plaster" (*Kushinga ne milopa*).
A mere plebeian negro can only boast of a mud-and-water
plaster, but old King Coal claims a blood-and-mud one.

*   *   *

Here is the reddest "sunset" of them all. From red
we have gone to redder, and now let us round it all off
with reddest. For the adjective has surely entered the
sad superlative degree: the groans on the crescendo;
deaths amounting sweepingly and authentically to the
"wipe out" of *a whole town*. Note the italics, for there
is nothing visionary or elusive here. The mother and the
babe unborn, the family of six or seven strapping sons,
the boisterous band of precocious negro youngsters, the
grandfathers and the grandmothers—all, cent per cent,
dead in a heap, *plus* King, *plus* Queen, *plus* satellite
concubines. Did I know the man? Yes, very familiarly.
Could I authenticate such a sweeping "wipe-out" of
human beings? Yes, to the satisfaction of every reader
of this book. Am I talking in tens or in hundreds?
Hundreds certainly, and not tens. And that is where
the story begins, the whole tale hinging on the sweeping
character of this annihilation of a solid town. Figures,
I know too well, are tricky things in Africa—witness
the modern tentative census papers. But, granted they
all entered a trap; granted, likewise, this death-trap had
no vestige of a back door; granted, further, only three
souls emerged therefrom, more dead than alive—and then

surely the deduction is inexorable that the whole town
was wiped out of existence.   I seem to see that old friend
of mine now while I write.   A brave chief, he added to
his prowess in war the exceptional merit of being a
laborious hunter.   Big-game hunter all his life, hundreds
of animals had fallen to his old flint-lock; but in
his youth he had been soured by a dastardly act of
mutilation, an enemy having cropped his ears.   When
we met, he was a dreaded "Black Flag" in revolt who
had taken to the Likurwe Hills, pouncing down on passing
caravans, and demanding all their powder, lest it should
pass on into his enemy's country and be used ultimately
against him.   One such caravan so tied up was our own
Mission's, a band of Biheans probably two hundred strong.
Resident as I was in his enemy's country, it was a
precarious business to cross the lines and enter his
stronghold; the Black Flag, remember, does not know
the Red Cross.   That visit, however, was a success; and
having struck a bargain which acknowledged his right
to the plundering us of all powder, we bade the last
farewell.   As we were parting for ever, he slyly un-
coiled his turban, revealing the Royal cropped ears,
much as Cæsar might have done with the wreath he
wore to hide his baldness.   "Look," said he, "I am
fighting for my lost ears."   Poor Rob Roy, he had only
a few years of life, and then came his Turneresque
sunset, when he dragged the whole town with him down
to the grave.   The story is a cave-tale, and would literally
be entitled "The Last of the Troglodytes."   The trap in

which they all died was a limestone cave, and so utterly
did they disappear from mortal ken that natives will be
wary of all such subterranean holes in future.   Briefly, it
came fearfully and finally to this.   When this chief made
his last stand, he retreated back on this huge cave,
resolved to die grandly, impressively, and magnificently
—die with all his people round him like a winding-sheet—
a common cave-coffin for the lot.   Long ago he had made
his dispositions for such a startling " sunset "; so with a rush,
and under cover of night, the whole town stampeded into
the trap, a cave seductively large, provisions in abundance,
and firewood.   But alas! unlike many of its spacious
sister-caves with as many tunnels as a burrow, this was
only a long deceptive " blind-alley "—blind the cave, and
doubly blind the hunted-down negroes who entered it.
For with a salvo of applause the enemy now rushes up
to the cave's mouth and seals the entombed doom of
all that horde of foolish fugitives.   There is no shriek,
meanwhile, from these runaways.   Oh no, only the
beginning of the long, lingering end.   With a refinement
of cruelty, the enemy now sits down at the cave mouth
and starts to " plug the leak," a process this involving
the blocking of the cave's mouth with rocks; then, over
the rocks, a banking of earth—thus pathetically and
literally making it a colossal tomb with the old orthodox
mound of earth on the top.   And so autumn wanes.
The long days pass, days in which, with sinister significance, the great blue-bottle flies hum in and out of the
chinks of the rocks to tell the tale of corruption.

But what about those three women who escaped? Listen! Some weeks elapse; then out through one of the limestone chinks you can hear a gentle moan—telltale moan of a human being. There it is again, and this time, out through the same chink, comes a wail of the moribund: "We are all dead. Oh, let me out!" She is a woman moaning, none other than Nanga, who used to live over at Munema village. Outside the bully warriors are shaking with fear at this voice from the tomb. Then they summon up courage to challenge her that she is lying, and that she has only returned from the dead to be their undoing. But the answer they get is her sepulchral offer that if they will only disentomb her, she will gladly permit her two hands and feet to be cut off, if she is found to have lied to them: "O ye out in the sunlight, sitting down to the banquet of life, let me out from this Lake of Fire." So at long last here she comes, extricated from the cruel debris to the light of day—she and two poor half-dead mortals. Yes, they bring a gruesome tale from that "land of the dead," a tale of slow, lingering emaciation and dissolution. First the food failed, then the faggots, and then came the exasperated expedients for firewood—all the old gun-stocks and spear-shafts burned off first. Then—good-night!—the great gleaming tusks of ivory. This tomb-cave, be it noted, was also the chief's treasure-trove, and there lay the accumulated ivory of years. Thus he died in his glory, heated at a funeral blaze of burning ivory, "Emperor's Fuel," they call it. It beggars all description.

Just one gleam of glory shoots up before darkness descends. Not long before, I found myself in that doomed town preaching in the moonlight with a tragic intensity. Surely in a glad, good way this was a silent, secret factor in their eternal destiny.

(*9th December.*)

Notwithstanding all his mad mob of cut-throats, I opine that Mushidi will not be able to reckon on even one solid band of braves when the day of doom draws near. Here they are in thousands, all armed with "Tower" guns, but nothing even faintly approaching the idea of a Tenth Legion of Cæsar or an Old Guard of Napoleon. True, he can count on many a strong individual, nearly all the satraps round the throne being linked by marriage to the despot: Kasamina and Mumoneka, with many more, are as brave as loyal. But mere personal prowess can never be equivalent to the discipline of the machine. Besides, this free-lance idea only means that every leader is playing for his own hand; and when that works out (as it often does) at one courtier against another, then the foundations are shaky. Really a kingdom within a kingdom is the idea, and the concentric waves make rings within rings of plot and counterplot.

Still, there is no man in the whole land who cringes so submissively as just one of these great ministers, and Mushidi persistently repels them with a pelting storm of abuse. Not once but several times he has sized up a too ambitious type of Joab minister, and got rid of

him in the polite old way of sending him off to kill
or be killed in war. Even his own princes he treats
in the same "go-to-shear-and-be-shorn" way, the
recent case of his son Chamunda being notorious. Too
enamoured of his father's own wife, Mushidi at once
ordered him up to the North to fight Chona; and after
a year's hard struggle the poor prince came back, broken
in two bones, a cripple for life.

And this, remember, is the regular treatment meted
out to any black son of Zeruiah who is too strong for
him. With the ladies, however, it is drastically different,
and even a dame of high status is coolly executed in
the capital as an advertisement in harem discipline.
Who will ever forget the great death of Queen Matayu?
Here was a lady of lineage, brought in from the Far
East by the Arabs as an offset to the Maria de Fonseca
marriage of the Portuguese, the two Oceans bidding for
Mushidi's commerce with the debasing bribe of rival
queens. Poor Mushidi, he has had to pay for it in
blood, this Eastern marriage; for does not the native
proverb say, "Eat the bait, and you are on the hook"?
Certainly, this Arab bait was seductive; but as the
days passed the news began to spread round the capital
that the "Eastern Lady" (*Mukodi Wa Kavanga*) was
a Jezebel of no ordinary sort. Death after death by
poisoning was brought to her door, the climax being an
attempt on her own son. "Oh!" said Mushidi, "we
will soon settle that"; and forthwith he convened a
council of elders, who doomed her to die. So there and

then, with no dawdle, and ignoring all political complications of the future, Tete and Kavalo, two generals,
went across to Munema, and were received of this
Jezebel with her usual smirk of coquetry. Invited into
her own house on a plea of privacy, she was strangled
on the spot as a witch, the mob in the capital declaring
that Mushidi was perfection in so scorning the high
status of such a grand dame. Cast out on the Lunsala
Flats, that distinguished witch's body was despised by
every passer-by, and speedily became carrion for the
scavenger hyenas ever on the prowl. Jezebel, I have
called her, because that name in her last moments
became awfully and literally appropriate. For as these
executioners entered her courtyard, the good-as-dead
woman cried out the most ancient greeting in Africa :
"Is it peace?" (*Mutende?*) And in that subsequent
hurried strangling of their victim they could be heard
literally answering the old Jehu taunt : "What peace
so long as your whoredoms and witchcrafts are so
many?" But Mushidi has not had long to wait before
he learns that here is only another annoying illustration
of the fact that women are the source of all his woes.
The roar for revenge can now be heard on his Eastern
boundary, the Rugarugas taking the field as champions
of the dead Jezebel. Thus it comes to pass that the
dead Masengo is the *casus belli* of his Sanga civil war,
just as in the East another wild war is waging over the
death of Queen Matayu. Does this justify the Spanish
saying, "Where woman is, there trouble is"?

BOOK III

CHAPTER XVI

"Nemesis, Daughter of Night"

"Though the mills of God grind slowly,
    Yet they grind exceeding small;
Though with patience He sits waiting,
    With exactness grinds He all."

*   *   *

"Instead of enquiring why the Roman Empire was destroyed, we should rather be surprised that it subsisted so long."   GIBBON.

*   *   *

"Down they come these ancient nations— down they come one after another, for lack of righteous-ness."   MATTHEW ARNOLD.

CHAPTER XVI

"Nemesis, Daughter of Night"

WHEREIN the reader ponders the profound difference between eating what you like and liking what you eat.

THE end is not far off now, for here in this large rambling metropolis you see Mushidi fiddling while his Rome is burning. If ever the clock of destiny struck with decision it is just now, the final simultaneous smash of such varied and conflicting elements all falling like one well-aimed blow. (By the way, see here, once again, how God can rule by His over-ruling.) For now, when these Rugarugas begin to drive in the Eastern end of the Empire, now it is the Sanga civil war has broken out right in the capital. And precisely as though these propitious events have all been elaborately telegraphed across the seas, now it is that Europe gets excited about Katanga. This year 1890 is, indeed, a climax date in the high politics of "the scramble for Central Africa." For, if to be first in time is to be first in dignity, then the English claim the country. As far back even as 1875 Lovett Cameron's great journey across Africa had revealed the Katanga country as a highly mineralised territory, and ever since then Cecil Rhodes and his disciples had mentally annexed it for South Africa. The British argument for annexation, if not logical, is at least geographical, for is not Katanga a true dependency of South Africa? Moreover, the Congo is far too unwieldy; and has not Belgium bitten off more than it can chew? Would Katanga have ever had sleeping sickness if linked up with the Cape and not with Boma? Thus it was that while four ponderous Belgian expeditions are slowly concentrating on Katanga, an Englishman forestalls them all. Much to King Leopold's chagrin, and before his elaborate caravans are above the horizon, Mr. Alfred Sharpe (now, of course, Sir Alfred) wins his spurs by walking right into Mushidi's den with a mere handful of boys: proposal, Annexation by Great Britain. At first it was all too exasperating, this blunt diplomacy, a plenipotentiary with scarcely a shirt on his back. Repelled by Mushidi, and indeed almost murdered had he known it, Mr. Sharpe went back East, never dreaming that the grim chief was so struck by his honesty that he was soon to relent and recall him. For relent he did. If you will allow me to be slightly autobiographical, probably this tale can best be told in the first person singular. It was on this wise. One morning when I turned up at Court to salute, the King startled me out of all my company manners by appearing in hat, coat, and trousers, and, wearing his tie under the left ear, insisted that English, and English only, was his Court language. Then he roared loud and long, and this was the kind of thing :—The King was pleased to say that he had slept well and—to a purpose. The King (invention again!) was glad to greet one more of the many thousands of Englishmen known to him. The King was pleased to order that the Union Jack of red, white, and blue was the only pleasing political combination of colours in the world. That English likewise was the only true speech of man, and he would make all speak it. This command he followed up with a rigmarole dream of "London Town," curious impressionist sketch of that great capital compounded of Arab fables and our narratives, the only sure thing being the blinking lamps down all the London streets. He had been there last night per dream chariot, and was just back: "Goody morning! goody morning! all of you." Next he springs a surprise on me, a Missionary trapped into politics. For, having thus personally visited England—by moonshine—and verified "London Town" as the world's greatest village—"The King's Kraal"—he now desires me to recall *Kadindo* (Sir Alfred Sharpe), and he will give him his gold, give him his land—or more, if he stickles for it. No mere passing whim this of Mushidi's, as Dr. Moloney proves later in his pro-Belgium book. "Captain Stairs," writes Moloney, "for close on four hours plied Mushidi with argument upon argument to induce him to take the Belgian flag—he was willing to receive the Ingereza (English) flag, but not that of the Free State."

This, mind you, from a member of the Belgian expedition, and proof positive that I did not engineer the

Anglo-Mushidi *entente cordiale.* Well aware am I how puerile all this must seem to my Belgian friends—I, a Britisher, puffing my own race in the third person. Nevertheless, there you have the naked truth of the matter, and history owes to Mushidi the attestation that he did shout: "Sons of the dust, we know the English to be the true people!" No amount of arguing, explaining, and smoothing down could convince a Belgian that this writing East to bring in the English was on Mushidi's genuine initiative. All the appearances are against us, and they naturally only see in all this one more instance of the unplumbed depths of English subtlety. Yet the fact is, with these good Belgians pressing down so belligerently from the North, Mushidi proposed the oldest and simplest of black tactics—namely, the exploiting of one white nation against the other. *Memo.* for Missionaries: Do not dabble in "high politics," so called; our politics are higher than the high.

So time goes on until one eventful day a roar from the North tells of the advent of the Belgians, and here comes brave Paul Le Marinel first. He has been following up the Sankuru from Lusambo, and, escalading the Mitumba Range, arrives at the capital only to be repelled by the Emperor. The founder of the first Congo State *poste* in Katanga, his arrival was desolated by a cruel fire, the huge caravan of supplies going up in smoke, and jeopardising the future occupancy of the country. Poor Legat and Verdickt, who remained, have many a hard day's fare in store for them, yet to these able men the

Congo State in Katanga owes all. After this first
expedition, a pause; then comes Delcommune, a late
second. He has followed up the Lomami, and striking
Lake Kissale on the 27th August, 1891, arrives at the
capital 6th October. *Item:* Lost Lieutenant Hankansson
at Kinkondia, killed by the Lubans. *Item:* Makes overtures to Mushidi, and is repelled. No. 3 Expedition is
still from the North, and led by a charming gentleman,
Captain Bia of the Guides—the same explorer this who,
in the following May, died in my arms away South at
Ntenke's. (The same Bia this who executed the murderer
of Major Barttelot, leader of Stanley's rear column.) But
none of these men struck a blow, and it was reserved for
an Englishman to hoist the Congo flag. This was
Stanley's friend Stairs, who was then slowly advancing
from Zanzibar; a poor man he, daily embarrassed with the
stabbing idea that he, an officer holding the Queen's
commission, was called upon to repel the advance of his
own Union Jack. He it was who intercepted Mushidi's
written command by my hand to recall Sir Alfred Sharpe.
Fancy an officer with a delicate and scrupulous sense of
honour waking up to the piercing realisation that he had
become the tool of a foreigner, drawing Belgian money
to combat English pretensions! The truth is, this poor
fellow was trapped into a very delicate position, not of his
own seeking; and as the days advanced, the monstrous
enigma of his anti-English duties became a nightmare to
him. Dying as he did before leaving Africa, I have sad
reason for believing that this brooding over the dilemma

hastened his untimely end. Nicholas I. of Russia died of bronchitis : so the bulletin said. But did he? Did he not rather die of Alma and Inkermann? "His was," wrote Mr. Stanley of Stairs, "one of those rare personalities oftener visible among military men than among civilians, who could obey orders without argument, and without ado or fuss execute them religiously : courageous, careful, watchful, diligent, and faithful."

And now for the ending of an epoch, for the capital is at last giving unmistakable signs of that process known as "breaking up." From the East came Mushidi long ago, and here comes Nemesis from the same quarter. Sitting talking with an Arab one day in his verandah— the 28th November—behold, five Zanzibaris march in from the East, turbaned, and armed with breech-loaders. The sentimental if not substantial element in this advance guard is that their leader is Stanley's own Masoudi, and he bears a letter from Stairs, who is advancing slowly from the Lualaba expedition, 300 strong, and armed to the teeth. This historic letter is one of the usual charming *billets-doux* in which Captain Stairs and his four companions formally presented their "salaams" preliminary to presenting their arms. They, says the epistle, are coming to clothe the naked land and are only bent on acting peaceably. Finally, after much groping about for Mushidi's weak spot, the letter cleverly finds it in rounding off with the lucky phrase : "I am the Englishman 'Lord of Artillery' (*Bwana Mzinga*), W. E. Stairs." Finds it, in all conscience, Mushidi's weak spot, for although all his instincts are up in arms against these intruders, yet this happy tag of Stairs as to nationality quite makes Mushidi's heart "white," as he terms it. "They are English, do you hear, sons of the dust?" shouts Mushidi to the crowd of people, "and we know the English to be true people." Then he blows a heavy blast through his nostrils and orders me to write out his royal reply. Not a philippic this, but a chat on paper in which Stairs, with wave of royal hand, is invited to come on and put these Belgians in their proper place. Once or twice I was just reaching for a metaphoric bucket of cold water to dash on Mushidi's political plans, when he struck in again and again with his favourite and favourable description of the English people — too favourite and too favourable, as time would tell.

Now comes the great Lord Mayor's Show day—14th December—when I am delegated by H.R.H. Mushidi to push out to the suburbs and meet the advancing expedition, orders being stringent that I must lead them to a stipulated camping-ground in the capital—there or nowhere. Lean and travel-stained, here they come at last out of the grass with flags flying, Captain Bodson, the Marquis de Bonchamps, Dr. Moloney and Robinson, led by Stairs, who headed the Indian file. Fresh and trig from Europe, how they stare at me in my bush rags and shaggy, unmanageable whiskers! We greet each other in French and English—French, I mean, as far as the irregular verbs and no farther. But this wayside pause is soon broken, and on we surge for Mushidi's in a cloud of dust—dust in our eyes, dust in our teeth, and dust all over. And now we are approaching the exciting goal. The distant roar of the capital grows louder and louder, and soon the curse of Babel is upon us, Bunkeya's polyglot negroes roaring out their rival jargons of welcome. But scarcely has Captain Stairs set foot in the capital when Mushidi illogically recoils from his own theory that the name of an Englishman equates the *summum bonum*. He who knows how many beans make five has more than half surmised the truth when it is too late. A wolf has come in sheep's clothing. What elegant fiction is this? Why does this Englishman fly a Congo Star? Why has he Belgians with him? Why did he intercept the Mushidi missive recalling Sir Alfred Sharpe? No wonder from that hour of disillusionment Mushidi's shrivelled face became an impenetrable mask, the old brain plotting deeply and darkly. But it cannot last long. Four days of skirmishing—diplomatic skirmishing I mean—and then the end. Is it a grim joke this petulant idea of Mushidi's that he wants Stairs to be his "blood" brother? On the 17th the same proposal, "I want you for 'blood' brother." The 18th ditto—same "blood" brother petulance. The 19th—still he invokes the phantom of "blood" brother. Finally comes the 20th and crack of doom, real red blood this time—and without the brother. It was like this. On the 19th, Stairs had hoisted the Congo Star on the high sugar-loaf hill adjoining Nkulu, the same peak this that had challenged Mushidi's fancy to put an ivory house on the summit:

then came the Belgian proclamation in which he was de-
barred from ever again shedding blood. But the King
has given them the slip, for under cover of night he has
gone to Munema, one of his first towns in the country.
The Munema where he is soon to die ; the Munema where
his first wife, Kapapa, is—a weedy, depressed-looking
woman ; the Munema where he began, and where he
will end. So Stairs follows the King up. Directing
operations from his fortified camp, Captain Bodson and
the Marquis de Bonchamps cut across the valley in
pursuit, a halt being called at the Munema gate. Four
head-men are sent in with an ultimatum, but an hour
passes and they return not. Are they dead or are they
prisoners ? This brings matters to a head. After parley
it is agreed that Captain Bodson enter alone, the body
of troops remaining outside with the prearranged signal
that they rush in on the first sound of firing. The same
Bodson this, remember, prize revolver shot, whose every
aim is a hit. So in the bold Captain goes—yes, in, never
to come out again. Advancing on to the royal palisade,
behold ! Mushidi surrounded by a body-guard of his
ghillies, and in the centre the four emissaries—prisoners.
Bodson, nothing dismayed, comes slowly on, and Mushidi,
King to the end, lurches at the intruder with a long
sword, then falls stone dead to the Captain's revolver.
Now for reprisal. Bang ! bang ! go the "Tower" guns
of Mushidi's body-guard, and poor Bodson falls, mortally
wounded, with the dying shout, "I have killed a tiger !
Long live the King !" The Zanzibaris who rushed in

were so maddened by what had taken place that they cut Mushidi's head from its trunk and carried it on a pole back to the camp.

"Every bullet has its billet," and the death that stiffens kings and slaves alike had gripped him. "There's no pocket in a shroud," says the proverb, but Mushidi didn't get a shroud, much less a pocket in it. Thus it came to pass, as so often happens in this old world's history, that the man who had spent a lifetime laying violent hands on hundreds of innocents must himself make exit by the identical doorway of a violent death. "I happened," says Dr. Moloney, "to glance at the dead man's face. It seemed to wear a mocking smile which somehow wasn't easily forgotten." Even in death the last look he left on his face was a perfect picture of that curious career of his, the wolf and the pig still struggling together in the dead features — Satan's signature, indeed. Better for him had God's witnesses never come to his country than that, having come, he should have turned a deaf ear to them, and closed his eyes against the light. This Mushidi was emphatically a man "wrapped in the solitude of his own originality." His head—and he was proud of it—was shaped as I have seen no other man's, the bumps towering away like Alps on Alps marking him off as one capable of doing wild, wicked things. Ever since I have known him, a look of cunning craftiness clung to his shrivelled features, his general demeanour overbearing and haughty. With him it was emphatically *Aut Cæsar aut nullus*, every one in his country laid under tribute to serve him. "He used," says Dr. Moloney, "to call these worthy men, the Missionaries, his 'white slaves,' insult them before the public, and despoil them of their goods."

Across the Eastern doorway of his empire on the Lualaba, Mushidi had figuratively written the prophecy, "My death will come from the East." All travellers entering from the East were suspect, and the most able diplomatist had a hopeless task before him. Nor did the wily old warrior draw blank here in this death-prophecy of his. Yes, die he did, and from the suspected East the mortal bullet came. All his life he dreaded that East Coast and resented with extreme asperity the advance of any stranger along his old route. Does not the thief who burgles through the pantry window suspect that the policeman will follow by the same aperture? Little did Mushidi imagine that his own curiously shaped head was destined to make the long journey out to the Ocean preserved in a petroleum tin. A mere instance of the curio craze writ large, the Central African negro thinks that preserved head of Mushidi the cap and climax of it all. For was not this the Mushidi who made his Babylon a vast museum of skulls? Skulls piled up in pyramids on long tables; skulls used as drinking-cups for warriors; skulls hung up like hats on pegs on the lifeless spokes of withered trees. Such a "dramatic neatness" do they see in God's methods that they speak of the dead despot's skull ever "dripping, dripping blood all the long journey to the Ocean." This curious idea of the "blood that never dries" sends its roots down into the belief that kingly blood never washes out. Of course, such a wonderful head performed miracles. I remember travelling in the wake of the famous skull of Mushidi, camping at the same spot as the victors. It was here Mushidi's skull performed a supposed miracle, for under the very tree where it was placed for the night, the artful ants worked hard, and simulating a skull they made a perfect mould of the "sacred skull" in the form of an ant-hill!

But we are doomed to black, blacker, blackest. Hard on the heels of the Sanga guerilla warfare comes dark famine, just as in the Apocalypse the red horse of the second seal—war—is followed by the black horse of famine. Galloping through the stricken land, like a sort of third seal, "I saw, and behold a black horse—*but he that sat thereon had a balance in his hand.*" Thus, even in sore trial, our God does not leave us desolate, for we see also divine balance where dying natives only see the rushing black horse. (Ay, beyond and above famine, balance, and seals, we see the Loving Lamb Who alone is worthy to open any such seals. And are not we counted worthy to suffer?) The binder of the Bible, seemingly, is as important a personage as its translator, for my little pocket edition opens automatically at Genesis and Romans. Surely not the binder but the Author does this good thing for me when in trouble, my Bible opening simultaneously at the black side in Genesis xlii. and the bright side in Romans viii. :—

"All these things are against me" (Gen. xlii. 36).

"All things work together for good" (Rom. viii. 28). This benighted famine experience is called by the Arabs "seeing the stars in the day-time." Even before Captain Stairs' arrival from the East with his large caravan, the country had been steadily sinking under the indirect pressure the Va Sanga were bringing to bear upon Bunkeya. So much so, that when the new-comers arrived, the tide had gone far, far out in the hemmed-in capital. Food could not be had for the buying, and the natives everywhere, hollow as a drum, were eking out an existence on roots, while they watched their corn ripening with loaded guns. Every thief was shot at sight, and even soldiers were bulleted. Thus matters stood, I say, even before Stairs came with his Arabs, and now begins a struggle for existence such as never before happened in these parts. His soldiers turn out to be (what alas, Koran chanters often are) an unscrupulous lot, and loot cruel and wholesale seems to be the order of the day. The strong come off better than the weak, but the victors fare badly enough; eighty of their number have died in the capital, *plus* seventy dead or missing. As for the poor natives, they are wiped out in hundreds, specially all the old folks, who, hollow eyes unnaturally large and bright with the weird lustre of famine fever, are forced to the wall. Thus Africa reads us the old lesson that having no imports, it can only as a vast continent live one year at a time. The least tampering with the agricultural year means blighting famine : explorers, beware !

And how do we live? Here is a subject the very

mention of which, I regret to say, is calculated to disturb
the gastric functions of the stomach.   Even the Marquis
de Bonchamps, from many of whose opinions I disassociate
myself, is quite correct here.   Escaping for his life to
Europe, he arrived August 1892, and declared that for
twenty-seven days their expedition had nothing better
to live on than locusts, ants, and even grass.   This witness
is true.   In these gnawing days of famine I can tackle
grass with famished gusto ; grass seeds boiled to an emerald
gruel is a famous food—*Musunga wa Chifufia*, or sulphate of copper porridge, the name of this green gruel.

As an anxious alternative I also eat and enjoy thousands
of white ants with ravenous content.   The said ants with
a good supply of salt make an excellent repast, for being
obese little insects they frizzle finely in their own fat.
Don't forget that one pinch of salt, though, or you have
spoilt it all.   One pinch only ?   Nay, you need two—a
pinch of salt and a pinch of hunger.   This, remember, is
no laughing matter to a hungry bush preacher, for I find
the difference between English plenty and African paucity
is the old candid contrast between the relish of a man who
likes what he eats and the epicure Englishman who eats
what he likes.   Another African dainty these days is rats,
five little rats tied to each other by their twirling tails and
put on the famine market.   Snails, too, are a widely eaten
commodity long after every mongrel dog has been heard
to give his last howl on entering the gaping pot of gaping
negroes.   These snails are in much demand by Lubans, and
a brisk business is done per dozen—decimal dozen, I

BANE AND ANTIDOTE.
A great snake specialist.

mean, for in Africa $12 = 10$. Not a question this of the negro *blasé* palate but rather the pinch of hunger; sentimental repugnance loathes a shining and repulsive snail, but its nutritive qualities are exceptionally high. So, too, caterpillars. Not merely when famine stalks the land but tribally, the Luban gloats over these furry little creatures with a polite name. An apologetic African, with that day-in-day-out ache in the pit of the stomach, defended these extremes of diet in the clever retort: "Even in the dark, who ever forgot the road to his mouth?" This famine, of course, is the metaphoric dark night to him.

Here is an equally hungry fellow defends his doleful diet of boiled snakes by saying, "A hungry man will even burn his mouth." (The snakes, that is to say, are figuratively scalding food.) But as a matter of fact the *Lusato*, or boa-constrictor, does taste like delicate veal and is a famous Luban titbit. My friend Chivangwa has a lively collection of snakes of many colours and sizes, and these, kept in gourds, feed on flour and mice pending the gluttonous "snake supper." Every new moon he takes them out for dentistry, and instead of hanging them on a peg he prefers to coil them round his neck. Even antelopes they think inferior eating to snakes. This I found on sending a native back ten miles at sundown to bring on some venison I had killed, but on reaching the spot he drew blank, the antelope *non est*. Hours after, however, he lurched into camp dumping down some very toothsome-looking steaks in the moonlight, not mine but

some of his own prowess as substitute.   His story ran that
as he came shambling along on the return journey, lo! a
long boa-constrictor blocking the way.   Sprang at it, slew
the snake, seriously skinned it, and finally cut up these
steaks ; witness, my apologetic messenger in the moonlight offering me snake veal for the lost venison !

May I here right an old wrong about boas ?   For,
albeit the boa-constrictor is a world-word, it is quite
certain the glamorous associations of this awful name
are wildly astray.   By very common consent the boa-
constrictor, though " mother of all snakes," is the most
timid of African reptiles, the natives declaring that the
mere sight of man so unnerves him that you can go back
hours later and still find him dazed and stock still.   A
mere boy who spies this snake in the bush, before darting
off to bring up a man with a spear, resorts to the simple
expedient of plucking a spray of leaves and leaving it
dangling before the boa's fascinated eyes.

Not troubling with remoter contingencies, there lies
the fascinated snake lost in wonder at that swaying
bunch of leaves.   Gazing, ever gazing at it with a look
that looks whole dictionaries, " the agony of shyness "
this is called.   Meanwhile, scramble and scrape, the man
with the spear is speeding on to a sure victory—sure,
that is to say, provided ever and always the reptile's real
name is avoided in speech.   " Call him not Lusato," say
the natives, " call him *a coil of rope*, lest you break the
spell."   True, therefore, to this rule, the native who first
sighted it in the forest burst in on the villagers to report

the presence of—"a coil of rope," the ladies all remaining to smack their lips and discuss the juicy steaks of—"a coil of rope." Does not name equate nature? Change the former and you transform the latter.

Locusts, of course, are considered a Central African boon in feast or famine, and for all the world like shrimps. One can surely be a good Pauline Missionary and enjoy these, for were not locusts an Athenian luxury of old, and preferred by the Greeks, even to such dainties as succulent quails or best figs? You can see any day in Africa an exact counterpart of the Nineveh sculpture in the British Museum, for the sight of boys carrying long sticks to which are tied locusts is as common here as it was in Nineveh.

But, you say, surely the African woods are a well-stocked larder. We certainly find it otherwise, for curiously the vast and dense African forest is a poor refuge in the pinch of famine. Crammed full of poisonous tubers as it is, very many natives nosing all over the forest have died sad and sudden deaths by experimenting on a new diet. "Touch not the aristocrats" is the dread forest charge to children concerning all poisons in Africa, poisons being called "aristocrats" because you dare not touch them. A good old rule I find workable is the eating of any fruit nibbled at by the monkeys.

Unlike the organ-grinder's captive on a chain, these forest monkeys are fastidious eaters, and with endless supplies before them, they nibble at fruit, rejecting petulantly more than half. Besides, as a monkey's mouth is supremely clean without a tooth-brush, one can eat with serenity his leavings.

Very much of this, of course, was not by any means the normal Central African dietary, and the dining music was not always to the tune of *de profundis*. Nevertheless, my practical experience of purely native food for more than twenty years all points to its peculiar acclimatising properties, and it seems in some unarguable sense true that if you wish to be much in Africa, then the said Africa must be much in you. Certainly it is along the lines of an ideal African dietary that the " blackwater " problem will be solved. They challenge all puzzling diseases with the pungent query : " What has the invalid eaten ? " Hence their national saying (an unconscious Irishism) : " Eat one thing, and then you'll know what you have died of ! " Thus when he sees a European dip into so many different tins, the sage negro says triumphantly : " That is why you ' whites ' die off so easily : we Africans eat only one thing, so we know what kills us." For this is the meaning of that most curious name the white man receives from his negro—*Kaminamabweta*. Supposed to be a compliment of the first water, it means " Mr. Tin-Swallower." Thus you see this tin-swallowing by the European is the African's glory, for does it not mean an assured income as a carrier of the terrible tins ?

CHAPTER XVII

Our Eastern Exodus

"Behold I will do a new thing. . . . I will even make a way in the wilderness."　　Isaiah.

*　　　　　*　　　　　*

"Go through, go through the gates: prepare ye the way of the people: cast up, cast up the highway: gather out the stones: lift up a standard for the people."　　Isaiah.

*　　　　　*　　　　　*

"The voice of him that crieth in the wilderness, . . . Make straight in the desert a highway for our God."　　Isaiah.

CHAPTER XVII

Our Eastern Exodus

WHEREIN the reader, following the manner and method of Moses, pitches his tent towards the sunrising.

THE scene now changes to the East of the Lufira, for Babylon is fallen, Mushidi dead and done with. And as the hart panteth after the water-brooks so we abhor the old muddy wells of Bunkeya and break away East to the far-flowing Lufira. The slaves long ago took the bit in their teeth and ran off on their own; now, all alone we must make a fresh start on fresh soil, and round our cluster of huts the future great population will gather. Lofoi Valley is our first choice of a site, the Belgian fort being two miles down stream from our Mission camp.[1] At first blush, this proximity of Christ and Cæsar does not seem prudential enough, yet this of all things is the country's greatest need. Foreigners though they are, Government under any flag is the crying desideratum of

[1] The subsequent history of this venture is interesting. Mr. Campbell came down from Mweru with Mr. George and began at Mwena. Then Mr. Clarke came from the West, and he and Mr. Higgins branched off to start the splendid Koni station. Then Mr. Anton ; the final phase being Mr. Last, beginning at Bunkeya, and Mr. Zentler near Kavamba Lake.

the moment. Far from treating these Belgian new-comers to a cold, hostile stare, we rallied round their ensign and wheedled all sorts of negroes into a loyalty that has stood the stress of years. When there was no king in Israel every one did that which was right in his own eyes, and a like anarchy menaces us. Granted years of grinding autocracy and, be sure of it, the day the political pendulum begins to move it will go full swing to anarchy : *après moi le déluge.*

So off we trek East for the new start with many a haunting memory of the Bunkeya charnel-house. Our backward look at the dark den is full of sad regret that there we had been hammering away at the iron gates of Mansoul and never a surrender. Fishing, however, is Christ's own simile of this business of saving souls, and our farewell was as cheerless as that of the man who from dawn to dusk of a wintry day has fished a cold Scotch loch with never a nibble. Yet watch again the "dramatic neatness of God's methods," and how at eventide it can be light. Just then, in a brown study that was almost black, God gave me my first soul, a wild man of blood who had been an executioner in the old days. Smish was his name, the same in after years who became an honest elder and won two other elders. The sun is westering, and Mr. Lane and I have said good-bye to the doomed Babylon, of which place it was legally true that a Garenganze man could not die outside it. Stupidly, I had lingered too long at my good-byeing, and was in fact lost in one of the too many roads leading out from the capital,

On the Lualaba

when a voice reached me in warning. Was in no humour
to bandy explanations with any one, but here comes a man
out of the grass—our dear Smish of the future, who shows
me the way. So off we go together, never to separate;
this whole initial adventure being the parable of our
friendship in the future. Right away on that road I paid
him back in kind and showed him, the lost executioner, a
way he did not know. Now he knows it better than any
of us. Son of Belial though he was, I soon found that for
a native he had a delicate and scrupulous sense of honour.
Listened to the Gospel gingerly and with tight-shut lips;
no effusive reply but rather a constrained look of reflection.
And then came salvation for even such as he—from mean-
ness to nobleness, from limitation to enlargement. Smish
was his name, but "Gad" it should have been, for after
him "a troop cometh." Conceive how the old men of the
land looked aghast at the temerity of the young generation daring to link their lot with "strangers," this very
word (*Veni*) meaning "the folks you don't know where
they come from." "No," said Smish, "but I know where
these strangers are going to, and I am going with them."
So here comes the cleavage between the old generation
and the young, between the "hitherto's" and the "henceforward's." The former all eyes to the rear, adoring the
past, sighing for the might-have-been's; the latter looking
forward, alert and surmising, "'Tis better on before."
"Last words are lasting ones," and his dying prayer as he
lifted up his eyes to Heaven, death dews on forehead, was,
"Father, my journey is done—I come."

20

Nestling at the foot of the Great Range, here it is on the Lofoi River we cradle the Lufira Valley Mission. But it seems a cardinal defect of this place is a tendency to be drowned like a rat. Only the other day we groaned (or growled?) in the capital as we bought a few drops of water; now here is this feast-or-famine Africa giving us too much. The other night we were all in our first sleep when the great boom of on-coming torrent broke on the out-lying hamlets, and then comes a stampede from all directions to us in the centre. For we are known to be on the highest spot in the vicinity. There is, however, such impetuosity in the rush of the dark devastating waters that it becomes quickly evident we were all far too low, so the next thing is to rush for the nearest trees and ant-hills. In this stampede mothers lose sight of husbands and little ones, and those separated keep up a wild-beast howling to one another in the pitch dark from their different perches. No time for looking after mere material belongings, as in a case of water slowly rising upon us—nothing heard but that booming coming down the valley, above which were the shrieks, "Water! Water! Fly! Death has come!" The shrieking soon subsided into a brave acceptance of this that means to them so much of desolation, destitution, and death, for as the waters have already risen waist-deep in ten minutes, there is no knowing where it will stop. Shivering round a smoking and flickerless fire of green wood, there they stand on ant-hills—ant-hills we had always thought only a blight on the beautiful valley

scenery, but now precious life-belts for the whole
community.

Mr. Thompson and I climbed up on the roof of our
grass house after rushing about in the water, making
more or less futile attempts at salvage work—human
life, of course, ranking first—and you are hereby permitted
to think of this midnight perch of ours in wet garments
as indicating the most miserable night we ever passed.
We stick on to the high-pitched roof with pious pertinacity,
constantly pinching ourselves into wakefulness, for the
tendency to doze is very tempting, but in that event so
also is the other tendency to go clear over the edge of the
thatch into the flood.   A crescent moon rose about one
o'clock, lighting up a scene as bleak-looking as it was
cold and miserable : our little Mission settlement wholly
under water, only the tops of banana trees appearing to
mark the paths.   And not only our special spot, so flood-
proof as we thought it, but the whole country, as far as
the eye can reach, one vast pale stretch of water reflecting
the moonlight and looking all the more ghastly on that
account when we thought of the hamlets submerged and
tragedies enacted in the darkness.   The longest night I
ever spent in my life was on that roof-top watching for
the day, and never was sound so welcome as the first
shrill clarion of a surviving cock on a tree branch.   Then
when the Eastern sky grew red, and finally the sun rose
to answer all our questionings begotten in the darkness,
we were speechless, for here was a great lake—Mweru, some
called it who were born there.   Look ! glistening red in

the rising sun, whole herds of antelopes crowding each
other off the ant-hills, each paltry peak their true Mount
Ararat in the deluge. See, too, the swimming snakes
darting about, heads erect and fangs menacing. Add to
this a thousand rats drowned and drowning. The crocodiles,
too, have leaped the banks and are wallowing in new
fishing-ground. Fancy an oily crocodile with unconquerable
levity sailing in triumph into your submerged kitchen !
He does not need to cook to eat, albeit he has come to eat
the cook. It took three days for the waters to assuage,
and for more than a week everywhere we moved was
through sinking quagmire. On venturing into our houses
again to get a notion of the damage sustained, the awful
smell of decomposing food, etc., drove us back. To in-
ventory the losses is impossible, and after searching in
vain a reasonable time for anything once possessed you
give it up and reckon it among antediluvian possessions
and memories.

But again, let us ask the question : Is this proximity
of Fort and Mission prudential ? Now, here it may not
be amiss to suggest that the particular peril of most
Missions in Africa is the tendency of Government and
Mission to go their own ways, seeking as wide a berth
as possible. But this amounts ultimately to a peril, for
only with the civil power keeping a Mission in its proper
place can the latter be stripped of its false prestige.
Many a little Protestant Pope in the lonely bush is forced
by his self-imposed isolation to be prophet, priest, and
king rolled into one—really a very big duck he, in his

own private pond. Cæsar was not the only man who said he would rather be first in a village than second in Rome. Quite seriously he is forced to be a bit of a policeman, muddled up in matters not even remotely in his sphere. Now only this pinch of isolation forces such an one to act oddly, for many a godly man has blushed an *ex post facto* regret at actions more judicial than judicious. To call this provocative policy of isolation "potential popery" seems too strong an epithet, but a glance at Cardinal Manning's *Origin of the Temporal Power of the Pope* is decisive. If my memory does not trick me, I think you will find Manning traces this pestilential pretension to just such a simple source, for when, oh, when was the Bishop of Rome trapped into all the toils and terrors of the Temporal Power? Why, surely after the fall of Romulus Augustulus, in the absence of imperial rulers in Rome, the primitive Shepherd of Souls was forced (?) into ruling with the rod, the significant end thereof being a triple crown. Quoth Luther, "I am more afraid of my own heart than of the Pope and all the Cardinals. I have within me the great Pope Self"; to which we say "Bravo!" for well-beloved Martin.

*   *   *

Here come curious complications, and I a Missionary am compelled to become a Commandant. It is a fine saying and true that a shoemaker should stick to his last; how much more the Missionary and his non-meddling in politics? Yet all this, in Africa, though trite enough to be a platitude and logical enough to be an axiom, is easier to talk than live. Did not poor Pilkington up North die with a rifle in his hand repressing revolt? Did not Livingstone wear a Consul's hat? Remember, here in the bush you have no parading policeman who runs to your call; no clean-cut institutions of civilisation where each official is seriously saddled with responsibility. Unlikely things can happen, and at this point the most unlikely of all falls to my lot. Hard by our Mission camp on the Lofoi, the Belgians have built their Fort, the whole garrison consisting of a picked band of English Haussas and Dahomey men. But on the East the Arabs are hemming us in, so unless the Government makes an aggressive sortie as far out as Lake Mweru, these Arabs will certainly construe silence as supineness and be on us like a bolt. What's to be done? These are the days when the solidarity of the white race swamps petty national distinctions. Did not Julius Cæsar say that on crossing over to *England* he found the inhabitants of that island called *Belgæ*? Why should not these Belgians now have their revenge?

Unlike Cæsar, who encountered people called Belgæ in territory called Britain, these Belgians have found people called British in territory called Belgian. Witness, then, the curious sequel. In the dead of night Captains Brasseur and Verdickt sit down and write their last will and testament (poor Brasseur was killed in the second Arab sortie), and off they start towards the East, leaving me a poor half-and-half creature indeed: acting Commandant of the Fort with my soldiers to drill and at

the same time God's Missionary to the heathen. The
Central African equivalent this to one's next-door
neighbour in England shutting up house and leaving
you his key with a request to keep your eye on the
place. Only in this important instance your neighbour
happens to be the local Lord Kitchener, and the Fort
and garrison are all thrown on your shoulders—you,
a semi-saint, semi-soldier. Such is sad, bad, and mad
old Africa, the *ex officio* Commandant in you tugging
one way and the Missionary in the same " you " tugging the
other. The shrill call of the bugle and the soft voice
of the evening hymn—what a muddle of memories!
A pile of regulations, all law, law, law; the pages of
the Gospel, all grace, grace, grace. Imprisoning a soldier
for insubordination at morning parade, and in the evening,
under the diamond stars, preaching deliverance to the
captives. The weary suspense, too, of it all. The night
alarms besides; all the superficial feelings on the alert
on a moonless night. Then, the uncertainty—would
they ever come back, or would the Arabs eat up the
column? Must I defend the Fort to my last cartridge?
All these thoughts come to me with the impact of a
blow, the man within the man fighting the man outside
the man, Missionary *versus* Commandant. Although
I did two years' soldiering in Scotland, be sure of it,
there is uttered much ungrammatical and unmilitary
nonsense in the shape of orders. My corporal, however,
is a Haussa gem and saves me much trouble. So
eminently and unaffectedly a gentleman, I can trust

him on lonely night duty, our common bond of English-
manship being his choicest consolation. Always scrupulously dressed in navy knickers, red turkey twill, and
fez, he often tells me that he has resolved to die as
artistically as a regard for a clean uniform will allow.
The Arabs, moreover, are his co-religionists, and if taken
he prefers death at their hands—at any rate, they kill
you neatly and thoroughly with a knife. The maddening
rumours, too, are as dangerous as dubious, for my native
scouts vie with each other in running silly screeds off
the reel. Even granting a germinal grain of truth in
these rumours, the said grain grows luxuriantly in the
fertile soil of a black brain, and putting two and two
together they always make six.

Making allowance, however, for the wear and tear
of language, I guessed successfully some of the happenings
over the mountains. The twenty men reported as
court-martialed and shot turned out to be only a chief
executed in error. The annihilation of the column—
a terrible contingency for me—merely meant a sharp
repulse, demi-defeat call it. So the weary days wear
on, until my nerves are almost worn to a thread. The
great black wall of the range stretches North with the
vast savannah rolling miles below. How natural for
the mind to leap those mountains, then on, on to the
Lualaba; on yet farther to Tanganyika; up now to
the Nile and down to Khartoum where Gordon, great
lonely soul, fell so nobly. Certainly, he it was who
wrote the words that have become my pillow of peace,

his valediction to all weary outposts.   Almost the last
line he ever wrote : "The hosts are with me, Mahanaim."
For if it be good Hebrew to translate this word as the " two
hosts," then surely it is better to translate the mere words
into the worshipping belief that my little garrison in the
Lofoi Fort is encircled by the same shining legions of light.

But what's that ?   Ay, what is it ?   A yell growing
louder and louder, and craning my neck on the bastion
I can spy the sleeping Haussa quarters vomiting out long
strings of yelling women, the absent soldiers' wives these
who can bear the suspense no longer.   All night they have
debated the fortunes of war ; for ten hours they have
wrangled over an ugly rumour down from the hills, and
sit still any longer they cannot.   A huge Amazon leads
them in a wild war-dance, and lining out four abreast,
club in hand, they start at the double round the Fort,
roaring out a taunt-song against the Arabs.   Round they
go, once, twice, thrice, roaring out their wrath in song ;
every yell supposed to energise their absent husbands
and win the victory—cataracts of vituperation, torrents
of curses !   They cannot pray, and they have gulped
down their anger too long ; now for the solemn institution
of this early morning " curse "-meeting when they dance
the Devil's wild fandango.   Nearly naked and wholly
wild, the flap, flap of their pendant dugs is made to
rhyme with the thud of their feet and the flourish of
the clubs.   Then having encompassed the walls of their
imaginary Jericho three times, off the Amazons rush to
the river for morning bath, splashing among the crocodiles

with never a twinge of fear. The Devil's matins these
became, my morning hymn drowned by their morning
curses. Glad was I when, one day, far up the hills I
heard the bugle of the retreating column, and in an hour
they filed past to relieve me of corroding care.

But here, as elsewhere, the loyal law of compensation
avails. Distasteful business this soldiering was for a
Missionary, yet even here I get my royal revenge. For
years afterwards I was permitted to chaplain these
troops, many of whom were my old soldiers. A wild
lot they were: cannibals, hundreds of them, who
subsequently revolted and murdered their white officers.
When Baron Dhanis, the Belgian Commandant (an old
Greenock boy, like myself) broke the back of the Arab
domination, he little dreamed what a defeat he organised
out of his victory, by permitting the crass crime of
"converting" these cannibals into the soldiers of a
civilised state. In delusion and confusion he caused
these old Arab cut-throats to be enrolled *en masse*,
the veneer of the barracks, smart uniform and deadly
Albinis only helping to hide the horrible man-eater
wrapped up in this official envelope. Conversion, forsooth, this was called, as though the wolf in sheep's
clothing has lost the old appetite for mutton. No
wonder the march of events soon swept dozens of
young Belgians into the cannibal pots: Leroy, Inver
Mellen, Andriane, Louis Dhanis, and many others.[1]

---

[1] The subsequent régime by Governor Wangermée and his successor
was a true triumph of sane, solid methods. Bravo! Belgium.

The same grotesque contradiction could be seen when Baron Dhanis surprised and beat the Arab auxiliaries at the town of a cannibal cut-throat, by name Bantubenge. "He of the crowds" this cognomen means, and seldom have name and nature reflected each other so well. For crowds there were. Now, the Arabs were bad, but here is a brute who dines daily on "black beef," yet this is the very man to whose tender mercies the Baron handed over "hundreds" of young children ranging in tender years from two to seven, and even ten. Nearly all belonging to Kitalo, Dhanis committed the unprecedented error of trusting such a demon with the custody of these lost lambs. Bantubenge—ugh !—whose name denotes death. In a few days they were all dead, sold for a piece of handkerchief to his hungry cannibals. Not dozens of children but hundreds, for the Baron's own words are : "*Des centaines* de jeunes enfants de 2 à 7 et même 10 ans." This was the famous victory of the 5th May, but all these poor innocents delivered (?) from the *joug Arabe* would have been far safer with their old masters. In other words, and without euphemism, the terrible truth is that when these Belgians took such cannibals under their wing as auxiliaries, cannibalism became a thriving semi-official concern. They even condoned their eating of their own black fathers and mothers. One instance of this happened during the attack on Gongo-Lutete by a man from Pania. Stationed as guard, he shot a man in the dark and came in to report. In the interval the body was brought in, and what was the guard's surprise to find that he had killed his own father, "the author of his days." Now, although the Commandant gave orders for decent burial, what did the son do but pass along the remains to his comrades for consumption! Tribal taboo forbade him the meal, but he could connive at his own father's disappearance in the pots. The volunteer drummer of this expedition fared no better. He disappeared, and some conjectured that he had been killed by a lurking foe. Not at all. A day or two later he—all digestive apparatus and no conscience—was discovered dead in a hut by the side of a half-consumed corpse. Had eaten neither wisely nor well—dined himself to death, in fact.

Only a week later, a young Batetela, not more than fourteen years of age, came up to the Baron's tent when he was dining and borrowed his knife. No sooner the possessor of his weapon, he slipped round the tent, cut the throat of a little girl, three or four years old, who belonged to him, and proceeded to cook her. Put on the chain as he was, this punishment was neither adequate nor exemplary, for soon a number of children began to disappear in the district. Caught again, this time they found him with a bag hanging round his neck and the leg and arm of a young innocent. He was shot. No wonder many of these liberated prisoners felt they had really fallen out of the Arab frying-pan into the roasting-fire of, so-called, liberation. "Prisoners of war" they were called, most of them poor naked nobodies, the sport of each new political move in the country. The "nether millstone" class is their title, because they get all the crushing. Your big Chief escapes in Africa, and so do the negro gentry, only the scum of heathendom left to bear the pangs of imprisonment. Let them make a try for liberty and see what befalls them. A band of these miserables rushed off one day, hoping to break through to their old homes. "Deserters," they were called, and followed up ; but on asking the local Chief which way they had passed, he pointed eloquently to his mouth and smacked his lips in a way that told the whole story. They had all been eaten save one, and he an old boy of Hinde's.

More *révoltés* man-eating. Rapidly incriminating evidence is very soon forthcoming on this marrow-freezing theme. Here, at my feet, is a young lad, Lumba, his story at sunset appropriately set off against a blood-red sky. Parting carefully his clotted hair, he discloses an ugly hole in his skull, the dig this from a cannibal axe. As serious as mathematics he makes a careful count of the living and the dead, and quite eighty of his friends were cooked and eaten before his eyes—licked clean up, bones and gravy. Very young as he was, these blatant cannibals offered him his life on condition that he would eat his own brother, and twice the laddie shut his little jaws like a rat-trap and snapped refusal. This vile persecution ran on into two days, and if Monday saw him treated to whips, Tuesday was certainly reserved for their scorpions. Finally, making a wild dash for freedom, clean over the pot of his boiling brother, he sprang into the bush, the cannibal guard sending an axe whizzing into his skull—the axe, forsooth, that was red with his own brother's blood now drinking his. Yet still he ran on for dear life, a large ant-bear hole ultimately affording a very inviting shelter from the hue-and-cry in the forest. And next day he awoke from a long swoon the proud possessor of the axe that split his skull—but could also split firewood for a needful forest fire!

Enough of horrors, do you say? Well, yes; but you cannot give an idea of Lubaland without alluding to them—and I can only hint and indicate. To make hideousness more hideous, witness a man, Lukatula by name—history will spue out his name with disgust! —one of the Belgian *révoltés*. Supreme he among the children of Cain. All around Kavamba Lake he had it noised that the white men were a low lot because they ate fowls, for what was the domestic fowl but the village scavenger? Only human flesh was worth eating, for was it not true that only man was careful of what he ate? As, therefore, man alone is careful of what he eats, the argument ran that man should be careful to eat man. Pharisee to the last drop of blood in him, here was a serious sickener—human flesh the only pure food of the race! For long weary months this diabolic epicure had his scouts out, catching strings of little boys and girls, all doomed to the pot, all reckoned titbits! Figures are, I know too well, very tricky things in Africa, but it seems sure that the climax of all these uncanny realities was reached here in this sad Lubaland when Lukatula shut two hundred souls in a house and roasted them alive. An eerie, weird, and awful business to reflect on, here you have cannibalism in full flower and blooming in torture — two hundred men, women, and children penned up in a mud house, the terrible thatched roof sent roaring up in flames. But surely, you suggest, a feeling of shame shot hotly through the murderer as he beheld these two hundred Lubans *in articulo mortis*? The obvious answer is that what, to us, is a nightmare and tragedy is to him something far different—a whiff of roasting viands from the Devil's kitchen, nothing more. Quite civilised in his way, this man's favourite plate is appropriately an enamel soup-dish from the West Coast, centred with the King of Portugal's crown, and encircled by the Portuguese colours. A reeking mackintosh his fashionable garment under vertical rays, over which he slings a very horsy pair of field-glasses. Granted (and gladly) this was a very special blaze of barbarity, specially wanton I mean, what was the cause? Merely the shaving of the cannibal's head after a long spell of letting his hair grow long. Month after month had passed and Luka-tula's fast - grizzling wool was ominously allowed to grow unchecked, dark hints thrown out that the day of his head-shaving would be "the day of many tears." And come it did, that close shave of his head being equivalent to a closer shave to many whose lives that day were in jeopardy.

Here in September you have white African winter, but it is the whiteness of electric light and as hot as an engine-room. Compared with Africa our English shiver-

ing summer is not summer at all, it is only Richter's
" winter painted green." A woman, Mrs. Horns, tells me
that farther North she went with her sister to take the
village tribute to the Chief Chofwe, and they slept two
nights in the district capital. Chofwe sent along to their
quarters and regretted his not having a fat goat to send
them for the cooking-pot : was therefore compelled to
send them, with apologies, a shivering naked boy—as
substitute for soup ! Here it is this lady Masengo presses
a point to the honour of negro womankind ; insists that
no woman ever did eat human flesh, that the men only
do so, that a woman defies any man to bring " man-meat "
into her house, and that all her household pots are inviolate. This witness is true. The rule is that the
cannibal club resort to the dark " groves " (*Mushitu*), and
there they keep a special supply of large pots for their
revels. The town ladies are jealous of it all, and insist
that these men are unclean until the village priest cere-
moniously cleanses them after " the red mania." This
means that blocking the path of their return to the town
is the purging process by which alone the man " unclean
by a dead body " can enter his own house. Indeed, priest
or no priest, many a wife sues at law many a husband for
his man-eating orgies, any stroke of bad luck in her house
being traceable to the dead man eaten by her husband.
" The dead do not really die," say they. But no sigh of
sorrow, mark you. It is all No. 1, and a fear that the
dead man will haunt the living to his undoing.

Another aspect of cannibalism. All Lubans are not

as brave in initiative as the lion and the leopard, and hence the institution of the cannibal vampire, the human hyenas who feed upon the dead. These are the cowards of the cult who prowl among the tombs. Up here in the Butembo forest you have a weird old man living in the woods, a solitary and cynic, the human steaks hanging in the smoke of his faggot-fire. This old vampire once upon a time played the lion, and killed brother-man as fair prey, but now he has descended in the scale : prowess all gone, a vampire hyena, nothing more. Other cannibals eat the produce of their own vine and fig-tree caught in fair fight, but this old vampire can only haunt the dead. These tomb-haunters are curious in one respect. They, too, sing a dirge of exhumation, a curiously perverse song like the perversity of their "owl-deed" (*sic*). The idea in this dirge is a conciliating of the supposed dead man's resentment at being so disturbed in his sleep of death. This dirge is uttered in the moonlight with a sepulchral whine, and runs—

> " Va Jika mu Kanwa
> Panshi va tina Mwashi."

" We rescue thee, O corpse, from the cold wet ground, and honour thee with mouth-interment."

An old friend of mine, the Chief Swiva, had a creeping experience of this song, and was once very nearly cut up in error by these very vampires, all because he feigned to be dead. You doubtless demur and ask why any reputable man could, should, or would pretend to be dead ; but

that is where this too true story comes in.   The facts are
demonstrable data, "chiels that winna ding," and thus
they run.   The village of this Chief Swiva had the mis-
fortune to lie on the trunk road, and was thus much
harassed by passing Government caravans plundering his
people.   Of course, in those days, before the splendid
Wangermée régime, very many of the State soldiers were
frank cannibals who would travel with a smoked human arm
or the like tied to their load—Katondo, for instance, did so
at Muntemune and to my knowledge.   Thus the endless
rebuffs and indignities from such a horde of brutes made
Swiva long to *lala dimo*, as he put it, *i.e.* to die and be
done with it.   But suicide is an unworthy death for a
chief, and the negro is a creature of monkey expedients,
so he slowly matures a plan.   Why not a mock funeral?
Why not sham sickness and death and burial?   Do not all
the local spiders, dor beetles and genus *Elater*, feign death
like a fox when touched?   Thus the weary months pass, and
finally poor old Swiva sees no hope of peace ahead save in
simulating death.   This he resolves to do, and one daring
day the false death-wail goes up at midnight; a wail
this ostentatiously prolonged throughout the next day.
Visitors pass in and out of the village bemoaning a
faithful friend departed, and there, in the dark mud hut,
swathed in his sham shroud, lies the malingering old
Swiva, heaving gently to the systole and diastole of a
hard but sad old heart.   (The King is dead, O ye negroes
not in The Know, yet long live the King!)   But the
fiasco of it all is now about to be made manifest, for far

along the road comes the well-known yell of advancing
soldiers : a yell this that stabs Swiva to the bone and
makes the shamming corpse lie as still as the real thing.
And now they pour into the bereaved (?) village, the
cannibal song drowning the mock death-wail — what
next? The dance begins outside the Chief's house, a
dance jigged to a vampire song telling of the singer's
deadly intent.   Be assured, O my reader, that whenever
the *double entente* of that dark song reached poor
Swiva's ears, as he lay, tied up like a mummy in six mats,
he wished he were really dead, and not shamming it.
But Swiva is a man of sixty summers, and there lies the
wily old Chief motionless, still hoping against hope that the
wild protestations of his own people outside will restrain
the cannibals from making a sorry supper off his body.
Ah, now it is the song he so often laughed over begins
to be crooned over his own creeping flesh.

"We rescue thee," crooned the dirge, "O corpse,
from the cold wet ground, and honour thee with mouth-
interment."

What happens? Poor old hypothetically dead Swiva
through a chink in his mummy-wrappings sees the gleam
of a knife, and——nay, not one word more dare I add.
Sufficient if I hereby officially inform you that all the
smothered wrongs and amenities of a down-trodden Chief
were uttered in that one rending shriek of Swiva.   In
scorn, he tore the trappings of the grave from him, and
in deadly fear the cannibals tore out of the Chief's hut.
Needless to say, as from the dead, he did there and then

arise a model Chief, with a new-born dignity that would brook no nonsense. Ever since his day of simulated death Chief Swiva, in fact, has been very much alive.

Where are we, then? What are your cannibal's latent ideas of things? Or is this man-eating merely a vulgar expedient to satisfy the qualms of hunger? Here is a cannibal at my elbow who will tell us all. When I ask him about *Budiañane* (the technical term this), he temporises, of course, in the usual cannibal way. However, as he has exactly the look of the cat that has been at the milk, he soon breaks the sorry seal of confession. Now, all that man's story is simply the old bundle of contradictions, for the subject of cannibalism halves in two like an orange: on the one hand the greedy *omnivora* who must have broth; on the other hand a whole priesthood ritual with human flesh as the buttress idea. All this, of course, is typically African; for as we saw, see, and shall see, the concrete and abstract are inseparable: "shadowing" each other is the literal idea we see in the Bantu abstract prefix. The coarse concrete side of man-eating, then, is simply the African carrying out the " beast-precedents " to a legitimate conclusion. Granted there are beasts major and beasts minor, but the negro at once schedules himself down among the carnivora. Is not (he argues) human war merely man the carnivorous shedding blood like the lion and leopard? The big animal grabs at the little one even as the big negro swallows the small one: the deduction is therefore inexorable that you must *eat what you kill*. Again, and yet again, have I heard

cannibals taunt non-cannibals with the mere wanton
killing in war and yet not eating what they kill. This
taunt is technically embalmed in the phrase, *Shikani
Yanyoka* = the (wanton) hatred of the snake, the point,
of course, being that a snake merely spits its virus with
deadly intent to kill, and not at all with an honest desire
to dine off the carcass. Hence the great *Kansanshi*
cannibal club sings a song in this same strain at their
revels : but to catch the idea of this cannibal *apologia* I
must put the words into the melting-pot and recast the
song in our own English rhyme :—

> " Other men only kill like the snake,
>   They kill, *nota bene*, for killing's sake ;
>   The *Kansanshi*, however, make no mistake,
>   They kill to partake of a human steak."

Plainly, then, the taunt is obvious, and really amounts
to the plea that if people must indulge in the madness of
man-slaying, then they should have method in their
madness and follow up the man-slaying with man-eating.
" To botanise on one's mother's grave " is a poor sarcasm
to a cannibal : in Lubaland they make a supper out of it.
The idea, then, that *genus homo* is merely one of the
carnivora is deeply actuating them in their gruesome
deeds. Yet how wonderfully these folks listen ! Here is
a puzzle of an audience, for all seem to enjoy the Gospel
of Peace, yet sure am I not one of the crowd enjoys
the peace of the Gospel. They swallow the sermon but
reject the salvation—problem, to find the reason of this.

After plying them with questions, I find the answer is as old as the days when the common people heard Christ gladly. It is surely this : all other religions under the sun make man seek God ; this Gospel I preach whets their curiosity, because God is seen seeking man. Beyond all doubt there is such a thing as the scientific study of comparative religions, but Christianity is not one of them. There is only one Gospel : there are many religions.

*   *   *

I gladly drop the curtain on these sorry deeds, and would now proceed to business—the Master's surely—by pointing out that, with this new complication of revolt, our road North is as straitly shut as the road West. We have no alternative but to look East for succour. Yet, even there, the circle of Cain is closing in on us, for what is the East but the Arab headquarters ? We may seek to ignore them, but they never forget us. Indeed, precisely now, with cold, concentrated malice, they are shutting us in from three different points on the Eastern skyline : Muruturutu in the North-East, Shimba due East, and Chiwala moving up from the South-East. Chuckling with glee that their old slaves the rebel Belgian soldiers have voted for slavery, they are now advancing to join hands with the Biheans and wipe us out, the compact, of course, to be sealed in blood—our blood. Thus, North, South, East, and West, the Devil is making a bold bid to win back the vast Interior to its old allegiance to slavery, the Arab in particular being bent on having nothing less than a huge dividend-swelling concern. But if the sufferings abound, so too the consolations, and like a whiff of ozone from the Indian Ocean comes the whisper that the British are actually working up into the Interior. How my heart goes pit-a-pat at the news! One Arab, with a glassy stare, even tells me tremblingly that— news! news!—they have already laid siege to Mulozi's stronghold, and if we are in high glee he is in high dudgeon at the tidings. Like a toothless negress, who will never see anything to laugh at, this besieging of their Karonga headquarters is a hard knock at my Arab informant. Who will cash his ivory cheques now, seeing Mulozi his old pawnbroker is nearly bankrupt? The shrinking of the planet is proverbial, and here is another proof of the smallness of our globe. Our whole concern now is how to successfully wriggle out East by crossing the Arab lines and, *sub silentio*, join hands with our own British kin. The problem of route, however, is a *minor* one compared with the problem of secrecy, for in Africa a mere glance is like proclaiming everything at Charing Cross. With this triumphant reactionary majority hemming us in, the stern demand is to be as secret as the grave, for in Africa three can keep a secret only when two of them are dead. So, too, with any new venture such as this projected breaking through to the East, for every three conspirators you can always reckon on four spies.

Therefore, on the native principle of "not setting your snare while the partridges are looking on," I slip off towards the East like a thief in the night, the outline of a plan dawning hazily on my mind. All my movements are necessarily of the non-committal kind. Yonder, across the Lufira Flats are the red ramparts of Kunde-lungu. There the Lord maketh you to ride on the high places of the earth, a great unbroken wall of uniform height lying athwart the Eastern trail as far as the eye can reach. Beyond that tableland is Kavanga, "the Eternal Gates of the Morning," the Africa of the Great Lakes and our own English kinsmen. Why should not the West join hands with the East? And this is how we do it.

CHAPTER XVIII

Boring out East

"As far as the East is from the West."

*   *   *

"They pitched their tents towards the sun-rising."

*   *   *

"O, the little birds sang East, and the little birds
    sang West;
And I smiled to think God's goodness flows around
    our incompleteness—
Round our restlessness, His rest."

*   *   *

"All these things | "All things work
are against me." | together for good."
       Gen. xlii. 36. | Rom. viii. 28.

CHAPTER XVIII

Boring out East

WHEREIN, Mushidi being dead and done with, the perilous process begins called "boring out."

NEARING this plateau wall, the blue blur sharpens into bold black lines, and you soon find it swerving from a straight N. and S. course to form many a large "dream" valley down which roars an angry torrent from the watershed. "Box cañons" all of them, and shaped like a U, with occasionally a sharp-shaped V. The river long ago dug out these ravines and is now wriggling down the middle like an S. Hamlets crouching in the reeds on either side of the river-bed dot these valleys sparsely, the people all high-strung and excited. Mugavi, a nervous little quicksilver man, is very kind as we pass through his place, and there is a curious loadstone of affinity when black and white thus defeat Babel by chatting in a common lingo. You seem to walk straight into each other's hearts. To be tongue-tied as to the negro's language means that an unnavigable ocean washes between your two souls, cutting you off from converse:

was it not when Paul spoke to the mob in their own Hebrew tongue, "they kept the more silence"? The women are nearly naked, and seemingly not at all troubled with the European quibble of frocks and frills. One dowager, who queened the town, beat them all, but she only attained to short ballet-dancer's skirts of skin.

Here is a Nimrod chief, a man of muscle who boasts a good kennel of hunting dogs, the objects of his extreme solicitude. Their trophies are exhibited, from wild boar to roan antelope, and he starves them, paradoxically, to feed their ferocity, not, as he explains apologetically, out of neglect. One of the curious category of upstart "hunter-chiefs" this, the tendency being for even a stripling who has killed his half-dozen elephants to entrench himself inside a stockade of bamboos. Good shots, all of them, they vulgarise kingship and claim to preside over the destinies of their own hamlet—and the next man's. Meantime the real Lord Paramount sits stony and stern inside his own stockade, plotting young Nimrod's downfall.

This chief sends his two sleek young sons with me, "to see the Great Lake and River": it is their first journey in life, and they are all a-quiver with vanity at the prospect of actually seeing the great unknown East. So there, with the moon hanging overhead like a great Chinese lantern, we have a farewell meeting: all agape, they listen as I sermonise them on the sacred subject of a God who so loves their soul and so hates their sin. On the morrow, in the Kasanga Valley, a large house was struck with

lightning and several people fell insensible to the ground.
The owner of the hut turned up at my meeting and wildly
controverted some of the things I was saying on God's
love ; describing the lightning incident as " God coming
down with red eyes." The old African heresy this, that
equates "God" with "wrath" (*bukadi*). Instead of
catching up this negro on a mere technicality, however, I
at once conciliated my man by admitting that Nature
could be cold and cruel, but that "herein is Love : not
that we loved God (one fraction of a bit), but that He loved
us." Across mountain and flood, marsh and meadow, one
moaning voice is heard in Africa, "No man hath seen God
at any time" : that is all the so-called gospel of Nature
can do for the negro. *N.B.*—Short all these sermons of
ours must be, for in Africa if you exhaust your subject
you easily exhaust your hearers. " For a running deer, a
running shot" is their preacher's proverb on brevity, and
in fifteen minutes the sermon should be done—no, not
that ; I mean the preacher should be done, for often it
takes fifteen years for the fifteen minutes' sermon to
be done.

Curious that these "sons of the mountains" have
lightning conductors in the form of a tall bamboo, and
their idea is that lightning is not a fluid, but a dragon
(*Kalumba*) ranging the skies, and specially attracted by a
bamboo rod.

The "goatway" as it approaches the Kana rivulet is
laid out with such masterly cunning and trickery that you
dare not escalade the mountain except in the wake of a

negro who is "in the know." The Valomotwa can crawl
flat on their bellies year in and year out, under the trunks
of trees purposely felled to hoodwink strangers. Breaking
through grass, they walk backwards and restore each blade
to its natural position, defying wit of man to know where
they have gone. To-day I chanced on a mountaineer
doing this crafty thing, and peeping at him with oblique
glances of the eye saw his triumph of trickery. That tell-
tale grass he put as softly aside as a surgeon parts the hair
to examine a scalp wound, the result being a clever fraud
in trail-hiding. Even thus do your troubles multiply, for
the local negro is endlessly laying all his plans with consummate care in order to trap the pioneer.

But African troubles are like African babies, they grow
bigger if you nurse them, and the morning brings counsel.
Tumbling out early, you negotiate the Kundelungu wall
with the wind whistling through the trees. Most clutch
at a faggot from the roaring camp-fire, and up this
mountain staircase we wind, the said faggot held off to
windward so that the play of the wind sends a tongue of
flame licking the bare black body. Anon, and far up the
mountain, you hear a triumph "coo!" from the summit,
half taunt, half brag, from a dwarf negro who is first up.
The lean, lanky six feet of humanity in front of me laughs
at the idea of the dwarf being for once "the tallest man
in the caravan"; and probably our Tom Thumb was right,
after all, when he answered their taunts by saying, like
Lincoln, "A man's legs ought to be long enough to reach
the ground." Breathing as loud as a forge bellows, here

we are at last on the top, just in time to greet the sun
coming up over it at the same time as ourselves, a crisp
and cross east wind blowing in our teeth.   Rocks, grasses,
and trees have all caught the flame of the morning.
Yonder, far below, Kasanga Valley lies at our feet, villages
looking mere dots on a map, the river a thin thread
wandering through an expanse of green and gold.   Out
through the valley mouth the Lufira Flats stretch away,
far, far away to the West, the vast panorama dramatically
opening out to its very widest by way of tragic farewell.
For this, mark you, means a long "good-bye" to that
Western slave-track and the wide waste of lonely land
stretching out to the Atlantic.

Early the next day we reach the Eastern edge, and in
order to keep a resolve really to meet the Valomotwa in
their own holes, we left the trail in tow of one of the
sagest guides I have ever known.   I have the honour to
appraise you of the fact that we followed this falcon-eyed
" path-borer" as meekly as sheep follow their bell-wethers.
And the result ?   A long day's game at explorer's bo-peep,
rolling about among the rocks on the steep brow of the
range.   Thin saplings cut obliquely, and left half severed,
were the unerring guide all along the route, the sort of
" scent " this in a very heathen paper-chase.   Without
this key to the labyrinth our quest would have been
hopeless beyond all conjecture, but with it the eye gets
accustomed to the arrangement, and we are conducted
along expectantly from one cut sapling to another, until
noiselessly and suddenly we are really on them, escape

impossible. The men spring for their quivers of *bulembe*
(poison) arrows, opining we are Shimba's Rugarugas,
but I approach empty-handed and ask, scoldingly and
indignantly enough, what they mean by fleeing incon-
tinently from us, their *bona fide* visitors. As if by magic,
their demeanour is now cowed and respectful, as though
they realise the game is up ; for here, on the lonely frontiers
of the world, could they flee farther or higher ? Later,
and they are ashamed of themselves, treating us with real
Highland hospitality : we have outwitted their black
Vigilance Committee, and the whole visit turns out rather
resembling the proverbial month of March—in like a lion,
and out like a lamb. Moral : In Africa a storm can clear
the air and does not always prophesy bad weather. We
were not the predatory creatures of their dreams, and how
could I blame them for thus taking refuge in their " muni-
tions of rocks," then springing up to eat us, not to greet
us ? Did not our own early Britons flee back before the
advancing Saxons and hide themselves in the mountain
fastnesses of wild Wales ?

Another thing. It very soon leaks out that this hamlet
we have struck is only one of many—that, in fact, the
rocks, like rabbit-warrens, swarm with people, who file in
looking daggers and grudging us their secret.

How is this for a proof that the whole world is kin ?
Here, where never white saw black nor black saw white,
what did I see to-day ? Two little mountaineers, speaking
the pure Gaelic, are in hot and high dispute over some
childish matter. " All right, what will you wager ? " asks a

three-feet-high youngster whose brow is creased in a worried little frown. "I bet three beads," retorts his opponent, and forthwith they link their two little fingers of the right hand solemnly to conclude the *Chipikwa*, or wager. And all this with the customary placidity of the Epsom racecourse—yes, here at the world's end. To the tramp Missionary it is difficult to say whether one is more harassed or exhilarated in being so startlingly reminded of the solidarity of the race. Is it not the tempter's endless taunt that this negro of ours is too unlike the European even faintly to understand our point? Yet little do these toy gamblers guess that they are tying themselves up in the same bundle with all the absconding clerks, bank-tellers, cashiers, treasurers, trustees, and speculators who ever put their money on the wrong horse. Reflection : So the old round world is kin after all.

Gunpowder has never reached these simple folks, and the hunting is all done on tiptoe with silent poisoned arrows. They plead that one bang from a gun would be too tell-tale, booming along the valley. These cañons of theirs are whispering galleries, that, with a great awakening clang, echo and re-echo the secret of even the hunter's footfall. As free as a bird, there never was such a thing as game laws, the forest being called *Butala wa Leza*, or God's larder. The innovation of English game laws would be high treason, for do they not say, "The antelopes were made for man, not man for the antelopes"? Sure am I a black local parliament would, with the whole force of its judgment and rhetoric, annul all laws against hunting. Err

these negro politicians no doubt would in many pertinent
particulars; bring in a Bill they might, to call winter
summer and Friday Tuesday, but as for game laws! And
no wonder, for to the black man of the woods life's
limitations are too manifold to admit of such a serious
restriction as venison. The negro cup is small, so let him
fill it to the brim. And here, once again, around the
flaming faggots I send out the old shout of Salvation among
these Kundelungu glens. Although weary to the marrow
of my bones, the very thought of the rocks thrilling for
the first time with God's praise is enough to rouse an echo
thrill in one's cold old heart. As you muse the fire burns,
and then it is you pour out on them the flood of longing
entreaty, the whole ministry reacting on your sickly soul
like a bracing tonic. Thus do we drink of the brook by
the way. Why doubt that after many days the blessing
will come? Grey and gloomy and grand the forest arches
over us, each tree preaching to us the old sermon of the
oak. Which runs : The creation of a thousand forests is
in one acorn. After all, you may count the apples on a
tree, but can you count the trees in even one apple ?

(*Later.*)

Yes! and come it did, for fourteen long years afterwards wonderful news reaches the Lufira Flats from
these very hills. Down comes a man with a long
string knotted into more than thirty knots. Each of
these knots, be it known, represents a man or woman
who has professed conversion to Christ, and Mr. and

OLD "MRS. HITHERTO" AND LITTLE "MISS HENCEFORWARD."

Mrs. Anton went up to verify the strange news contained in this strange mountaineer's string "note-book." There they were, women in the majority, on the same range at Lofoi, praising God among the rocks ; by a sort of spiritual spontaneous combustion the heather was on fire. For the Word of God is not bound, and these lonely hearts were profoundly converted. In later years, on Lake Mweru, these women make the best Evangelists. Of a Sunday you can spy some old negro ladies toddling out to the suburbs, a six or eight mile walk, in order to pass along their good news. Look closely at one of these and you can see the dear old face wreathed in most contagious smiles, the very manner of her joy proof positive that she has got what the world cannot take away. With her there is no case of logic *versus* love, for lo ! love is her logic. Her manner, too, so nicely balanced between boldness and timidity.

> "Just knows, and knows no more, her Bible true,
> A truth the brilliant Frenchman never knew."

("Heart" is a word that the Bible is just full of. "Brain," I believe, is not once mentioned.) Theories are for the human brain, but the human heart must have a person, and woe to this old dear if her faith has not given her a Person to talk to all along life's weary road, for her own tribe now turns the cold shoulder on her. Say nearly sixty years of age (on the wrong side), she has wakened up to realise with a glad surprise that God the Multi-Millionaire has invested all His capital in

22

her soul. The night is fast approaching when for her
there can be no work, so off the frail old saint goes with
this great thought energizing her journey of Evangel into
a toddling trot. If life be indeed "a sheet of paper
white, on which each one of us can write a word or two,
and then comes—Night"—I say, if this be a just simile
of life, then, to pursue the parable, we may add that this
old lady has discovered her sheet of paper is getting so
small that she must economize space and write close the
remaining words.

Lady, indeed, one must call her, for if you overhear
what she says to her equals it is all besprinkled with
polite phrases : " But, Sir "—or " No, Madam," the whole
being normal tribal usage, not mere make-believe. You
might, in fact, be reading Boswell's *Johnson*, the respectful " Sirs " so marvellously many. To seek to
establish a ratio of success is, of course, invidious, but
personally I prefer the soft-voiced pleading of these
old ladies to the loud young man who winds up with
his seven last woes. For Grandmother is really a
weeping sower, and with tears in her eyes and Christ
in her heart, she warns of impending doom. Then a
sort of sob steals into her story, the sincerity of that
sob making the warning all the more solemn. In her
own sad experience, I know for a fact that one of these
old dears has discovered that tears are a true telescope
lens through which she can pierce far into the heavens
above, so no wonder she believes in being a weeping
sower, for tears cannot blind if they be telescopes.

Contrast many a young negro preacher who can cover such an amazing territory of Christian truth in his sermon, forgetful of the fact that to preach the ever-lasting Gospel does not mean to preach everlastingly.

* * *

The ant-bear (*Mpendwa*) very annoyingly burrows his holes right in the path, and the unwary traveller could with great ease break his leg in any one of them. So sly are these curious sloths, that many a native on the wrong side of forty has lived his life without seeing one. My man, a Lambaite, killed four of these scarce monsters in a most cold-blooded, efficient manner. With all their wit centred in their two-inch-long claws, they tunnel far underground, and the trick is to out-manœuvre him in his network of subterranean subtlety. Hibernating as they do for half the year, the solemn way they go to bed for their sloth-sleep has won for them the negro phrase, "drunk with sleep." Like five long red sausages, each six feet in length, there they were, packed in, snout first, thick tail pointing outwards. With a warrior light in his eye, my man wriggled into the tunnel with his huge spear and killed No. 1 in a long choking moan. Then followed the solemn "sealing of the tube," the process being repeated with the certainty of a professional until four out of the five all died by his long lance. An adequate English analogy would be to imagine the London Tube Railway throwing up quantities of fresh meat out of the earth! No. 5, how-ever, had sapped a new tunnel of escape, escape in this

case being not by exit, but a deeper burrow, defying man
to breathe therein.

Given good paint and a better painter, here you have
a mountain incident that would hang as best Academy
picture of the year.　Last night a native after sundown
was holding his breath as he picked his way down the
face of this precipice, eye and ear pledged to perpetual
vigilance in the really awful venture.　So engrossed was
the benighted traveller in testing every fearful foothold
that he was wholly unconscious of a hungry old lion
stealthily stalking him from behind.　Intrepidly venturesome, this man-eater had already gained on his prospective prey by taking two chasms at two noiseless
bounds.　Is there going to be no slip between that cup
of a ravine and this lip of a precipice ?　The astounding
answer is that here is a lion planning murder who
commits suicide.　Madly springing at his man over
the chasm, but not reckoning on the narrow ledge of
treacherous schist for a foothold, down he dashes over
the last jutting crag of time into the gulf of eternity,
a dark yawning abyss, hundreds of feet deep.　The next
day, far, far below, he was raked out by the people of
the plain, broken in every bone.

Eastward ho !　Left the toy-town in the rocks and
were soon buried in thick woods, which only once broke
on a " parkland " centred by a palm, the useful *Hyphæne*.
At 8.30, to the surprise of everybody, we stood on the
Eastern edge of Kundelungu Range and looked down on
the beautiful Luapula Valley stretching far to the East,

rolling away in rich slopes and watered by a thousand streams—" a delightsome land." First glimpses, though, are fictitious, and the boys who are ahead cheer us on. Swinging round a shoulder of the hill, we emerge from its terminal clump of trees, and, perched out on a last ledge of rock, away on the N.E. we spy our first and most wonderful view of Lake Mweru—a mighty sheet upon which the morning sun, painted as never Turner painted it, is shining like a mass of liquid gold. But who could dare to describe that colour?—" not colour, Mr. Ruskin, but conflagration." Even if it were possible, it would be profanation. With no East shore visible, and not having seen a sister-sheet of water like this Mweru since our last sight of the Atlantic, the sheer extravaganza of the sight makes one shout for joy. Born as I was by the seashore, now it is the curtain of memory rises, and this wide waste of waters welcoming us as we emerge from the long choking grass makes us feel as though we had escaped from a tropical trap. Away to the South, banks of morning mist are rolling up from the lagoons of the Luapula, and only very faintly can we guess Kasembe's capital, sleeping prosperously in the sun, on the British side. British, indeed, that soil, for the other day Rhodes painted all those trans-Luapula lands red on the map, a clannish colour the red sun repeats every morning it rolls up like a ball of fire. Here comes a dissolving scene which memory makes its own for ever, every moment a memento. For slowly, but surely, time that tempereth all things takes the flare out of this red flambeau, twenty minutes representing as many dissolving shades in the softening scheme of colour : step by step, shade by shade, working up from monochrome through tint after tint, through rose into pale lemon, through sea-green into the ultimate azure. Tell me, please, is plain Peter Bell my negro neighbour taking it all in as he looks moodily at vacancy ? Apparently, I am *observing* while he is only seeing, for a beam of light in the eye is not charged with thought, is it ? Or can it be that he, a landsman, is thinking of this Lake as the murderer of fishermen in their coggly dug-outs, the red sunrise symbolic of the red blood of its victims ? To him this painted poetry is the plainest of plain prose, for in cruelty this Lake is feline. It licks your feet and purrs very pleasantly, but it will crack your bones for all that—then wipe its foaming lips as if naught had happened. But the grandest bit of Geography in the whole landscape is the glorious West side, away up North towards Luanza, where the sharp headlands have given the West marshes the slip. Rising sheer from the Lake, these bluffs are seen buttressing the whole North-Western Coast, dozens of little streams vying with each other how to leap over the cliff gracefully with waterfalls like a white mare's tail. The last of these is a gaunt spike of headland called Chipuma, alongside which the river Luanza flows into Mweru—our home in the far future.

But in Africa you too, like plain Peter Bell, must get all your poetry out of the prose of life. So off we go jolting down the hillside, heading for the first town in the valley whose lights we watched last night winking out one by one. But we draw blank, for all have taken to the grass on our approach, fearing the advent of the Arabs, who are raiding the whole valley. Shimba is the Arab leader's name = Lion. The eerie stillness reigning in the abandoned town bodes no good for the morrow, so we dart on into the valley, heading for Chilolo Ntambo's. Quite a political portent in his way, this plucky man has strongly entrenched himself in the plains, resolved to break or be broken. Meanwhile, and in curious contrast, the scattered aboriginal chiefs are at their old game of hateful and baneful plotting ; hysterically crying out one moment, " Come and kill Shimba !" and the next rushing up among the rocks for refuge. Torn into tribal tatters as they are, the Arabs come on the scene and, of course, instead of killing the flames of negro faction, they kindle them. Then it is the old cry rings through the glens, the bitter wail of Rachel weeping for her children.

As fighting is again imminent, and Shimba is gathering for another attempt, I send on messengers to carry the olive branch, their business being to clinch the cardinal postulate that I am " a thing of naught " (*Wagere*). *Ergo*, being a mere pilgrim travelling through, they must not expect me to help them in this mundane matter of aiming a gun-barrel in their trumpery squabble. When I told this candid cut-throat that it was the honourable business of the Church militant to suffer blows rather than strike them, he seemed almost inclined to adroitly interpose a big black fist between his face and mine by way of testing the temper of my peace platitude. Pressing on, an armed escort emerges from the grass with a roar, but these brimstone blacks acclaim us as brother cutthroats and seem quite sure we will kill three negroes for their one. Once, twice, and yet thrice I break in on them with a disclaimer—no, they don't want my olive branch, for when I'm for peace, like King David, then they are for war. Tell them to mortify the flesh and they will indeed agree to do so, but it is their enemy's flesh they mean to mortify with a spear-thrust. Thus encircled by a ring of rascals, we trudge on, only to encounter escort No. 2 on the edge of their stockade den, the horrible huzzahs suggesting that this out-at-elbows Missionary is reckoned a staunch supporter of their war. Remember, all this is a mere ovation to my white skin, not white character, and it is not at all flattering to recall the fact that yonder red-haired hobbledehoy of an Englishman, smoking his short pipe at the corner of Seven Dials, would get as royal a welcome. Besides, ovation notwithstanding, you need not go away and fancy everybody in the town is thinking of you: nay, verily, he is like you, he is thinking of himself. Not even a very tiny idea had they in the back of their heads that Christ was *versus* Barabbas.

But in Africa I have long ago learned that you must put up with a great deal if you would put down a great deal, and here is no exception. Greeting the Chief, this kindly man has the kindly idea that he should decorously shake hands with me *à la Européen*, so for the first time in his life he experiments on a hand-shake. Then after laboriously moving my arm up and down for some minutes like a stiff pump-handle he lets it go, only to be seconded by his wife, a small and very daintily finished little lady. This dame, I suppose, thought she had made quite a toilet. Ordinarily dressed in a simple and strong homespun, to-day she thinks herself irreproachably gowned in an old ragged and coloured blanket, marred with as many patches as blotches. Why is it that, right down from the days of Mother Eve, as soon as a woman arrives at self-consciousness her first thought is of a new dress? In the local homespun she would have been handsome, but now she is horrid. A sprinkling of loud yellow patches on a red ground is her ideal. They despise even fine lace, think it a rag, and call it "a lot of holes tied together." Alas! evil communications do indeed corrupt good manners, for in half a tick this new stiff pump-handle salute with high and low is *de rigueur*. But Chilolo is a real and reliable sort of a man and would make a good impression if sketched when he is speaking in his firm and yet quite unostentatious way. If dissimulation is the mask of the soul, then sincerity is its face, and I like the transparency of this old hero. Smoking a meditative pipe, he told the tale of these Arabs' entry into the country on the old plea of honest trade. Told of their picking a quarrel after a thousand hateful impertinences. Told finally of attack and repulse in quick succession, with the promise of a real big battle on the morrow. Such, then, is "the man behind the gun," a desperate enemy but a fine friend. An African this

who in many things is far and near belauded as a Chief
with a delicate and scrupulous sense of honour, and
certainly Mushidi showed his usual shrewdness when he
gave this man long ago a kind of governorship (*Diyanga*)
of the Luapula Valley.

But these bellicose blacks have hearts of adamant
where God's Gospel is concerned, and only met my appeal
with mortified glances. Every man of them said in his
heart—and a horrible saying it is—that God was a fool
to leave His Son to die. In Luba the very phrase "a
fool's death" is rendered "a sheep's death" (Isa. liii. 7).
Chilolo's son, a young exquisite, was as solemn as a
sermon when he said that no black man would believe in
such a God. And here was I, all alone in that hot den,
with lacerated feelings and blistered feet—ah, how a
Missionary suddenly shrivels up into himself with one
whiff of such loneliness. But I cannot go back, so I must
go forward—and what a goal, the linking up with our own
English race from East! Any day something thrilling
may happen, for coincidently with our moving in from the
Western Atlantic are they not also boring up here into
the Interior from the Indian Ocean? The exact picture
of this exciting thing is to be found in thinking of us as
engaged in the excavation of a tunnel, and here we have
at least reached the delirious point where we almost
begin to hear the pickaxes of the excavators at work in the
other side of the tunnel! Of course the plan of route
ahead is not even optional now. It seems it has fallen to
my lot, and I hope to my delight, as well as my duty, to

strike Mweru at its South-Western corner, and negotiate
the first trans-Lake voyage in dug-outs.

But here it is a long line of lion incidents occur, the
curious persistency of the thing being like the African's
proverbial rain that never comes but it pours. At any
rate, they seem to be all the fashion, whether biped lions
or quadrupeds, for here is this putrid scoundrel of an
Arab calling himself Shimba = The Lion, and even Chilolo
claims the suffix-surname Ntambo, which also means
"Lion." Certainly the roaring in name soon became a
roaring in reality. Forewarned of trouble ahead, in the
phrase *Ntanda ya kava*, "the forest is on fire," we
began by camping early and building a strong skerm, as
war-parties do. That night, however, we drew a blank,
the only incident being a troop of elephants rushing past
at sundown, making a noise like thunder. Plunging into
the fens near by, they bathed for more than an hour, and
with glee seemingly. Nearing Mbovola's village, however,
we find the villagers outside, frantic with excitement, and
bravely roasting a large lioness which had daringly leaped
the fifteen-feet-high stockade and killed a woman ; move
on and into this village, but just as we enter at one side,
down goes the portcullis gate with a smash at the river
entrance, breaking the leap of the large male lion ac-
companied by two little ones, all seemingly bent on
avenging the lioness. Then, day and night, the drums
din their deafening noise, all hope lost of your sleeping up
arrears of the past wakeful nights.

Nor will the villagers let us off the next day, so here

we rest. This bereaved and famished lion having made up his masterful mind to avenge his consort, twice attempted to spring the stockade, but was driven off. Thus our first fears were justified of a long lion trail, and the links soon became many in the chain of prophecy. The appalling rinderpest has killed off all the antelopes, hence the famished lions are forced to raid the hamlets and play for higher stakes.

Farther along, Mbayo, in the same valley, very pluckily killed a large male lion with an elephant-spear. Well primed with liquor, this tall native met his man-eater at the village gate. Just as it sprang for him, he fixed his spear as an infantry soldier does his bayonet on the command "Prepare for cavalry," the lion running himself through the heart in his spring. The famished fraternity came round during the night, and those royal rogues actually ate up their dead comrade, making much noise in the mastication. It is madness to send our little boys to draw water or fetch firewood here without an escort. But the end is not yet. Farther along in that same valley—to be exact, at Kapara's—a great lion was killed measuring thirteen and a half feet from tip to tail. He, poor fellow, was a shaggy veteran with blunted teeth, starving seemingly, for his ribs were looking through. This lion must have welcomed death, as his poor right paw was a swollen festered mass, a large acacia thorn deeply embedded in the quick. Thus we bowl along into the savannah, the rank grass, ten feet high, shutting out view of everything save a little blur of blue overhead. After a few hours of this kind of work, needle-pointed grass seeds showering down, the long stalks rebounding sharply on the face, a kind of smothering sensation is the result, and you wish for just one whiff of ocean ozone. With hundreds of spear-pointed seeds sticking out of your shirt it is easy to become a very porcupine in temper as well as appearance! The science of walking through grass of this description which overhangs and hides the path is very simple, what a poet has described as " following some fine instinct in the feet." Like a blind man who cannot see the trail, you throw forward your feet in a pawing manner, pull your body after them, and feel along in this fashion. Boasting of carnivora as it does, this savannah is a lively, dangerous place, and one has to be always high-strung and vigilant in the long grass. Even down to the shore of the Mulungwishi River where we embarked, these lions dogged our steps, and actually farewelled us with a double episode. It was on this wise.

In the far distance grey Mweru Lake was hoarsely threatening a storm, and the scudding clouds revealed a furtive moon. There, jammed into the thick aquatic grass, lay our canoes for the morrow, the beach so tangled that we, for the night, were shut into a tight little skerm to save our skins. At one in the morning an ominous scrunching, and the famished lions are eating our canoes. Eating our canoes! Very vaguely and at random I aimed for the matted clump of marsh, but even this guess shot caused the noise to stop with alacrity far too sudden for it to have been a miss. Then came day-break and the discovery of our nocturnal damages ; as for the canoes, the breakages were merely in the singular and not in the plural, but how singular—only the fifth boat crunched to pieces! So, too, the lions; one only had been wounded, and she caused a lot of trouble before she died. Shimpauka, one of the right sort, followed her up but lost traces in the tangle, then stupidly let go his best charge at a buck, reloading with only a poor pinch of powder as he presumed he had lost the lion. Hardly, however, had his gun spoken when he discovered his stupid error. For there, sure enough, and only a dozen paces farther ahead, lay my lady, not nearly dead but merely nursing her broken leg. If she offers battle (and she must), then she will fight and fight to the death. Then the terrible trouble began, for the dense growth had spoiled matters and forced him to see this thing through —retreat impossible. So he drew a careful bead on the lioness, the thought maddening him the while that here he was firing a stupid squib, sure only to jag the exas-perated beast into mad recrimination. And what do you think? There you see the doleful duel begin in which, tit-for-tat, the wrath of a man is matched against the wrath of a lioness. Their blood is up. On rushes the beast and on rushes the black! The strong, strapping fellow, in a frenzy of determination, and longing to get it over, hugs the huge lioness in a strangling grasp, and over they go on the ground in a whirl of man and lion. The lioness has dug her claws into the mass of muscle on the man's back; and the man, smarting with pain, grips at the lion's carotids like a vice, only, however, to get his three fingers crunched off. But his right hand is free, and still he clings with all the tenacity of terror to that beast's throat—yes, clings to conquer. A gasp, a dying gurgle, and the lioness owns up to the lordship of man—choked stone dead. To this day, all you can get out of the maimed hunter is a hissing intake of the breath, and a sharp clenching of his teeth, with the staccato whine: "Oh! if I only had had one tiny point of steel to jag her with; yes, even a nail or a needle to claw her when she was clawing me."

But all this is exceptional, you say. Incredible as it may seem, this getting into grips with *Felis leo* is not at all uncommon. Here is my man, Kasansu, who has had almost the identical experience, only in his case no shot is fired, the lion frankly and fairly under-muscled. This same long grass did it all, for although doubly armed with gun and spear, the lion and the man were in grips before the latter (startled, indeterminate) even remembered that he was armed—disarmed rather, for in panic both spear and gun were thrown to the winds. The beast, of course, was too terribly fresh to succumb to mere throttling, so, when they rolled over, Kasansu, by a clever wriggle, got on to its back, and gripping the nape of the lion's neck, willy, nilly, pinned his hairy head on the ground. Believe it, there was much champing of the bit on the lion's part at this curious compulsion to eat humble pie, but the man's roaring for succour had brought on the

scene a young fellow whose only weapon was a hoe-handle
—wood, only wood, when steel was the clamant need.
Nevertheless, the youngster, after much entreaty, was
persuaded to come on with his stick, the lad's haunting
terror being that Kasansu out of sheer exhaustion would
let go his grip of this licking-the-dust lion. But it all
ended in victory. Crack! crack! crack! and the lion's
skull was soon broken by this simple hoe-handle. In
later days a relative of this lion in the same district—
"Charlie," they called him—died only after running up
a big butcher's bill of nearly sixty dead natives. To be
exact, fifty-seven.

(Later.)

Blood still dogs us, and here comes another death, a
weird one. Picture my boy killed by such an incredibly
unlikely animal as the ratel, a sort of skunk that feeds on
honey. I can well conceive how the whole thing may
strike the reader of this chronicle as absurd. It happened
at Mungedi's, and the curious tale runs that this three-feet-
long badger gets systematically drunk from an angry
alcohol he distils from the beehives. Living as he does so
wholly on honey, the ratel has learned to sample it in all
stages of fermentation, and finally has struck the idea of
making his own distillery! This he does by digging a
pot-like hole with his three middle claws on the wet bank
of a river. Now he rams home the honey with a careful
admixture of water, and off he goes to await the issue of
the loyal law of fermentation. In two days or so, back
he comes to find his alcohol foaming up out of the hole,

and in a few minutes Mr. Badger is rolling drunk. The
liquor swimming through his veins like a glorious fire
makes him mad for murder. In height not much more
than a foot, anterior claws say two inches, here is my boy
killed by a drunk skunk. The skin is so tantalizingly
loose that if you grip it, he can actually turn in it and
grip you. Another instance of Africa being a topsy-turvy
land, an animal being doubly a distiller and a drunkard.

*　　　　　*　　　　　*

Beneath all this opulence of colour there lurks the
sinister thought that *Palpalis* is ambushed in every green
clump, transforming it into a weeping willow. For this
vile fly means sleeping sickness, and sleeping sickness
means a wipe-out. Now meandering through mossy
glades, now thundering down the gorge, these Congo
tributaries really ring hollow at heart. Only the birds and
beasts have a good time down here. There, serene in it
all, the black darter sits sentinel on a snag jutting out of
the water, and sunning his dark shining-green wings out-
stretched. Oblivious of the masked murder all around,
clouds of snow-white egrets with bright yellow bills in
the still reaches of the river fly lazily up and down
to their favourite feeding haunts. On, on you glide
down the gorge to the steady dip of your paddles,
the river brawling over the rocks and preaching as we
pass. True for you, Father Congo! In Africa we do
find that a Christian is not a canal cut out by a foot-rule;
not a canal, but a river. And a river has its deeps and

23

shallows; has its floods and shrinkages; is, in fact, God's own parable of a missionary. It only passes on what it gets. It only babbles like a baby when it is shallow. And it ever darts strongly and surely for the sea when too full for sound and foam.

CHAPTER XIX

Kavanga : the Gates of the Morning

"There's a legion that never was listed,
    That carries no colours nor crest,
But split in a thousand detachments
    Is breaking the road for the rest."

*   *   *

"I propose one more society in the Church—an S.S.S.S.—or Society for the Suppression of Superfluous Societies."   E. P. MARVIN.

*   *   *

"Good it is we have no Society guaranteeing a stated salary. For cut off as we are from our nearest bank by one thousand miles, the said Society would be politely and cleverly baffled how to send our quarterly remittance.

FROM AUTHOR'S LETTER.

CHAPTER XIX

Kavanga : the Gates of the Morning

*I*N *which the lost-in-a-forest traveller
learns that the Lord of Eternity is
the Lord of One Hour.*

B UT the amalgamated worries of Africa seem all shut
into the three days we are lost in the savannah,
groping and guessing our way. Cutting back from
the Luapula, we adopt the very risky but necessary plan
of striking pathless across country. Through forest-land
heading all the while for a certain far-off faint blue point
on the tableland. "The Plantations of God" is the
admonishing native forest name for what to me was a
trap. Here it is you put your foot where never even
black man preceded you, and here too you learn the
lesson of all the twists in the African trail. It is the old
line-of-least-resistance idea, for day after day you must
accommodate yourself to the new and changing aspect of
country lying across your track. A shag leads off by
blocking the way, and the shorter the shag the more
dangerous it is, because hidden in the grass. Your boot
saves you, a white man, but even then you would rather

save the boot, for you only escape a cut at the expense of cutting your own precious foot-wear. Now it is that this leather covering appears to the barefoot native both a marvel and a portent, for instead of thinking that the boot merely covers the foot that wears it, his idea is that those few inches of shoe carpet the whole forest with leather. A good lesson this, that even in the smallest boons of life there is nothing like the widest point of view, mere inches multiplied to miles. Literally only so many inches, but actually they cause the whole earth you walk on to be covered with leather, so it all depends on how you look on a little thing. This tale of jags, however, is only one per cent of the story, for the remaining ninety-nine of your caravan boasts, not boots, but that delicate pneumatic tyre—a bare black foot. Hence all these doublings and twistings of the negro trail, for your naked companion must go gingerly along this never-trodden ground, every wobble being out of deep reverence to some hidden shag or jag in the dense growth. For in order to avoid a pneumatic puncture, he must feel his way along, as against the white man with his leather "clogs" (*sic*) who can cut across country crunching down all oppositions. Then after the shag comes the stupid young ant-hill demanding another wriggle from the traveller, but this is minor compared with the long detour round a fallen tree : is it not easier to dodge than dislodge it? This means a twist twenty feet round the end, and long years after this tree has been burned out of existence the pawky path still per-

THE TRAVELLER'S TERROR.

petuates that very tree's downfall in the same old bend. Often, too, as a happy accident of environment, wide, roomy elephant-ways open up before you seductively, so off at a tempting tangent you go, although conscious of the cowardice of the thing. For how could a roaming elephant know your path? Then the blue landmark on the plateau looms out warningly from an opposite point in the skyline, compelling you to play the man and plunge again into the nasty scrub. Finally, all this high-stepping is so fagging that we lie down under a tree and rest like the Seven of Ephesus : a night in which you dream of being lost, for ever lost in some mad maze—of wandering, for ever wandering in a wilderness of woe.

No wonder on the morning of the 20th of June, the awakening is almost a glad thing, lost though we are in pathless bush. At least the erstwhile dreamer can console himself with the faded adage about dreams going by contraries, and you spring from your couch on the ground, proud, at least, you have shaken off that feeling of utter lack of volition ever haunting a dreamer. But a tabloid for your soul is as necessary as an anti-fever tabloid for your body, because after a day of jagging thorns we had a night of jagging mosquitoes. (To get "keyed up" for the day is our bush phrase for the true tonic effect of a tabloid of quinine.) These blood-suckers make you rise, tingling with fever, but here comes the tabloid for your soul : the Book of Hosea opens at the sunrise words, "*His* goings forth are prepared as the morning." No doubt, " lost " is the true tale of our folly, nevertheless there you have the honest "Bible" of the route, a prepared path for a prepared morning. The curative property of that simple sweet line was wonderful. So away we start once more, and right off get soaking wet in the thick dew—not the modest dew of an English meadow sward, but dew distilled ten feet from the ground on spear grass and showering down on you like a spray-bath. One native taught me a lesson in this thick dew as to "counting my blessings" even in times of trial. "God is good," said he, "for the thickest dew in Africa falls in hardest drought," a reminder that God in all lands "tempers the wind to the shorn lamb." But, at least, in this drenching dew I have a coat on my back, whereas all my poor fellows are shivering nude, so they deserve the palm. Indeed, as you tramp along, here is a point steadily and surely gaining ground in your brain, to wit, that this man Friday of yours is a most companionable comrade and much more real as a man than his wordy preacher. On the march, for instance, his thirst is the real thing, and not the ill-tempered craving of an Englishman ; so, too, with hunger, his is the hard-gnawing sort, the deep hunger of faintness he gladly satiates with the sundown meal of coarse mush. Ah, "ye have heard of the patience of Job," but know also that here are men of grit and tenacity of purpose. Cold numbs, hunger gnaws, and they, down at the very bottom of life's hill, give never a twitch or twinge by way of grumble. In comparison we, as a grumbling, greedy race of Europeans, are all self, self, self, from the soles of our feet to the top of our crown.

Nearing noon the boys fire a broadside of their match-locks into a dense cavalcade of elephants, a mere pinprick in the armour-plating: £10,000 of ivory on the move—what a sight! Each tusker with five or more wives according to the length of ivory. The tusks, too, of varied sorts and colours, some not at all normal, and one great bull with only one tooth. Another has a freak tusk, and while the normal one gleams gracefully up in position, its twin tusk twists down in the opposite direction, the great beast looking a horror. But remember, animals though they are, this is not a mob but an army, and one great bull seems to lord it over the whole battalion. In response to a most aristocratic wave of his trunk, like a Field Marshal's baton, away they rush straight ahead, clearing for us, not a path but a royal avenue. The coincidence of our far-off landmark, the steel-blue wall of Kundelungu, coming for once into dead line with the track of this army corps of elephants, is surely eloquent of the goings forth of our God being prepared as the morning. Here at last is your prepared path—and made by elephants, too.

But there is more to follow. Not for nothing are these woods christened by the negroes "the Lord's Larder." "Plantations of God" is their second name for the same idea, and as the native would not dare to dream of driving God out of His own garden, why should I? "Every beast of the forest is Mine," said The Same, Who proves it by sending this densely packed herd galloping true for objective. (Why recognise God in

great things and exclude Him in small? Why forget
that the Lord of Eternity is likewise Lord of an Hour?
Was not the microscope discovered at the same time
as the telescope?) But—I repeat it—there is more to
follow. Let those who deny the efficiency and sufficiency
of Faith for desert diet just wait one moment and watch
how these very elephants feed us. A mere way in the
wilderness is as nothing to a table in the wilderness, and
spread out like lunch at a picnic, " God's elephants "—
the negro phrase this—doing it all. Picture this big
blundering Jumbo made of God unto us not merely our
advance-guard to cleave an onward path, but an elephant
it is that providentially becomes our kitchen gardener in
the wilds. Remember, or you have missed the point,
the last and nearest patch of cultivation we have left far
away East along the Luapula, yet here, hidden in the
desert—can I believe even one of my five senses?—
like a vision from heaven we emerge on a glorious surprise
of green pumpkins that eye of man never saw—an " elephant garden," they call this green Goshen. For one
measureless moment I could not believe my eyes—
elephants, the notorious robbers of green crops, now
paying back the human-kind in their own stolen vegetables. Yet how easy and elementary the explanation.
Hundreds of miles away, along the green banks of
Luapula, a band of these rogues had raided the squash
gardens in the moonlight; then, having cleared out the
field, off they rush for the forest, far, far from the
dwellings of man. But however excellent Jumbo's

digestion, these obstinate pumpkin seeds would—well, would not digest, hence these glorious gardens all from stolen fruit. Natural law in the spiritual world, verily.

At night in the woods we built a large fire, a mighty roarer five feet high, fed with logs eight feet long. The great blaze flares through the night, and at daybreak we slink out, in the raw morning air, to rub our fingers at this all-night (and all-right) blaze. But we soon find that these parts are alive with tsetse, so the only way to avoid their tormenting sting is to go off in the moonlight, travelling six hours—not per day, but per night. High in the west hangs the monster moon as white as a new half-crown. But our path, remember, is fringed with an endless grove of trees, and the moon weirdly throws their sharp black shadows on the ground. Peeping out from these ghostly traceries of trees, we guess here and there the tiny ribbon of trail hardly hinting its presence, and this elusive little path is our precious all. Only eighteen inches wide though it be, it is a sure guarantee of real standing ground, everywhere else a mass of shags and jags. Newcomers laugh at it, call it "the corkscrew," "crooky-crooky," and other naughty names; but in later years the man who ought to know is he who "bikes" it. What, a "bike" in such a tangle? Yes, why not? Hypercritical as he is forced to be, he is pledged to praise it with a reason! For, *nota bene*, the negro and the cyclist are bound in a common bond of horror lest they puncture their double Dunlop tyres, the negro's bare toes being as perfect a pneumatic tube as the cyclist's. So, when that bare-footed black tiptoes it through the bush, dodging every suspicion of a jag, how unerringly can a bike follow where his tender toes have trod! Thus the very serpentine shape of that path is its choicest character, for every twist and turn indicates that Mr. Negro has dodged a shag or thorn, and how could a white man afford time to turn back every blade of grass to discover hidden holes and obstacles? A parable all this of our African life—the black man leads, and we follow. The best place to prove all this is out West, a mere mile out from any European's "station," for he, good man, generally scratches a wide road out from his gate. And long before a break in the trees shows just the peep of his gable, this pioneer road tells of a white man ahead. But does your negro use even this new-fangled clearing with its almost painful Roman straightness of aim? Oh yes, but only in his own old wriggly way. There, right *in* the new road you spy the same old twisty trail, a path within a path, a circle within a square; the African still dictating to the white man, still utilising him up to a certain point and then throwing him over. Parable, indeed, for is not the negro's way of walking like his way of working? Plays with us and our methods, taking just what suits him, rejecting all the rest.

The 26th of June is our third day of this kind of thing, and the facts and the philosophy of the situation alike point to a new enemy attacking us in the honey-

bird. Our meal-bags depleted, the bewitching cry of
this bird quite disorganises the march, one man after
another dropping out of line to follow its lead. Finally,
the percentage of this defection ranges so alarmingly
from zero to a hundred that we call a halt for stragglers,
as it is extremely dangerous to lose sight of one another
in this wilderness. To your great surprise and greater
indignation, one, two, even three hours pass in waiting;
man after man dropping in with a lordly gift of whitest
honey and a pleading, propitiatory smile to atone for his
crime. ("Own up and pay up," remember, is the forest
rule.) Would gladly buy for instant, indignant use some
of that wax Ulysses stuffed into the ears of his sailors
to pass the Sirens safely. Now it is you resolve never,
never more to enter on such a ruinous game of travel
as this "heads—I win, tails—you lose" groping and
guessing in pathless bush. Oh, those shameful hours of
fret! fret! fret! Did not John Wesley say, "I have
no more right to fret than I have to curse and swear"?
Surely this is the kind of facetious forest described by
Gordon Cumming as a forest of fish-hooks relieved here
and there with a patch of penknives.

One sight I saw there, far from human ken, and
never shall I forget it—a sort of glimpse away back at
prehistoric man. As far as cold ink can do it, let me tell
you what I saw—a theme this for blinding tears. There,
leaping about from tree to tree, exactly like a monkey,
was a horrible human being stark naked. A poor woman
this who had lived nearly all her days as an animal

amongst animals, the bony fingers like talons of a hawk being all the weapons of her forest warfare. The body cunningly coloured like the grey bark of the trees in which she lived, you can scarcely for a moment locate her, until you catch sight of the black eyes gleaming like coals of fire. Then comes a shriek followed by a fierce cataract of what the natives call "monkey curses" (*Mafinge akorowe*), and off she springs from tree to tree, twisting her face into a grotesque sneer. She has forgotten how to speak with human modulation and can only screech, a literal proof this of the Spanish saying, "Live with wolves and you will learn to howl." Then a snatch of curious song reaches us from the top of one of the highest trees, a song-dirge containing a half-hint that she was rebel against her race, with a reason :—

> "The black stork croaked into the town
> A truth that made the folk all frown;
> 'Twas a message weighted with grief:
> 'The Earth is God's: man's a thief!'"

She had fled the dwellings of man, poor soul, driven mad by the injustice of her own tribe, not a human being now, but the "black stork" roosting on branches and shouting in rebellion against man the robber, "The Earth is God's: man's a thief." Here is a proof, surely, that insanity is often only the logic of an accurate and overtaxed mind. Even the tough blacks with me nearly wept at this sight of sorrow ; and one old philosopher, after a solemn and dignified pinch of snuff, said, "Truly the human race is only a huge beehive : we, the human bees, go in at the same door, but we don't sleep in the same rooms." Nor did this old orator doubt that God would visit her tormentors even in this life with condign punishment for their evil deeds. Only he was careful to explain how this judgment might *not* come. "They will not," said he, "become mad, but they may become too wise, for God sees to it that those who steal bananas must pay for them in honey." Rather like what Anne of Austria said: "God does not pay at the end of every day, my Lord Cardinal, but at the end God pays." Or to mix metaphors a bit. Here we have the old error, that because the lightning zigzags it does not know where to strike. These leafy bowers, though, were palatial compared with the cold ant-bear burrows this poor woman slept in when the forest was aflame with lightning heralding wild torrents of rain, her only diet raw wild ants and rawer snakes. There in that living tomb of clammy clay she passed the wild weather, a curious watch-dog contrivance being the capturing of a jackal (*Mumbulu*) which she tied as sort of sentry to the mouth of her lair.

> "Oh, dwarfed and wronged and stained with sin,
> Behold! thou art a woman still!
> And by that sacred name and dear,
> I bid thy better self appear."

Cringing forward conciliatingly in her direction, I tried to edge nearer, but no good! The least suspicion of my approach made her frantic, and off she sprang from branch to branch like a wild thing. Fail though I did, like a stinging whip-lash to the conscience came the thought that we might have saved her had we been only in the country in time.

The pathless forest breaks occasionally, and for a stretch of three hours or so you see it thinning out; not now the dense dark thing of the morning, but dotted over with large acacias, mimosas, and Euphorbias. A curious example of the grotesque in vegetation, these candelabra top each sugar-loaf ant-hill with the humorous hint that after sundown they will be lit up as forest lamps. The stiff spokes have the insidious suggestion that they were artificially hammered out of bronze, and, child of the desert as this tree is, surely the Tabernacle "pattern" (Ex. xxv. 9) lampstand was moulded therefrom? What suggests this most forcibly is the odd Borassus palm here and there towering in the background of these same Euphorbias. Here at least we know where we are. Did not this very ventricose palm pose as the mason's model for the swollen column of the ancient temples of Egypt? And is not Egypt the door of Africa? The Hall of Columns, for instance, of Seti I., what is it but only so many Borassus palms petrified in a row? The same thing this as the Greeks modelling their porticoes and peristyles from the date palm. If, however, these candelabras hint at the bizarre in Nature, farther on we encounter the tragic. Monster cobra-like Lianas hold giant trees of great girth in their death-grip, the victims in every case nearly strangled, and holding out pale, pathetic arms, preaching to us as we pass. Was ever parable so eloquent of sin strangling the soul ?

On and on you forge, the tiny track left behind scarcely making any impression on the stubborn grass. Dare to drop your penknife, compass, or anything, and never was needle in haystack so hopelessly lost. Yet even here your negro is an eye-opener, and once again the gulf is seen to yawn between white and black, between Mr. Know Nothing and Mr. Know All. Watch what happens. You make a dive into your pocket for—say, —your compass, and lo, the conviction stabs you that it is lost Very vaguely, somewhere away back in that maze of forest it fell to the ground—nay, not the ground, for that, too, is almost as lost as your compass below the thick tangle of undergrowth. Yet here is a lynx-eyed group of blacks actually daring to describe that hopeless maze of country for miles far to the rear. They know that forest as though they had planted it. As though they had planted it ! Shooting back in memory to the last point where the compass was in use, there they are chattering out an astoundingly intimate description of that mad tangle, tale of twists, loops, and detours. Precisely as a London policeman lecturing Hodge ticks off on his fingers the requisite number of streets he must pass in order to reach the British Museum, so too with these negro blood-hounds and their topsy-turvy forest. Now only a blurred and exasperating memory to Mr. Musungu, here you have them stringing it off like so many London streets. This sort of thing : " Yes, back to that last ant-hill, not the minaret-shaped one but the dome. Then beyond that, the calabash tree with the broken arm. Farther back now to the sycamore with the hollow in the trunk, the hollow one (N.B.) and not its brother at the side. Beyond that again the clump of bamboos in the dip—yes, the same clump in which the guinea-fowls rose." And so in thought away you go, back, far back through that tangle, the native having made a mental cinematograph of the intricate twists and turns as he passed: trees, grasses, hollows, and stones all assorted and ticketed in the archives of the black brain.

Who will say summarily and simply what all this "thinking black" means? Wherefore these superacute senses of the raw bush negro? Here is the African's own answer as scratched down in my note-book from his own lips, the third person singular being originally in the narrative nominative. True to the Roman saying that there is always something new coming out of Africa, the negroes here pretend to have made the great discovery of the ages—a sixth sense. This they call *Chumfo*, and sure am I it reveals a whole continent of undiscovered negro character. Why is it this negro can smell his way along? Why is it a black man miles away can get wind of your doings? What is it that silently tells him all the mixed motives of things, their why's and their wherefore's? Why is it that two can only keep a secret in Africa when one of them is dead? Answer: The mighty sixth sense. But what is this sense No. 6? As a matter of fearful fact, here we have something very serious. What is it? The negro answer is that the so-called sixth sense is only the lightning collapse of all the senses into a sudden instinctive unit: not $5 + 1 = 6$, but $5 = 1$. This away at the dawn of cognition is their definition of what we call instinct. Instinct, that is to say, is the whole five senses collapsed into that unit of sensation which may be represented by the formula: $5 = 1$. Now, it is this unity of savage soul that accounts for the marvels of the bush life. He can smell his way. He is all alacrity. His wisdom is not syllogistic but unconscious. Those five gateways of the soul we call "senses" are wide open to Nature, and the "marconigrams" stream in as divergent Five to collapse at once into convergent One. Ask him to argue the point and he would smile: arguing is the five-senses side of the subject; at the centralised one-sensorium he only *knows*. This, too, is the reason of the sanctity of all dear "grandmother" philosophy among the sons of men, for "Granny" does not argue the point *à la* J. S. Mill. She lets Mill patrol the five gateways outside, knowing that they all radiate in on her central point of instinct :—

> "I do not like thee, Dr. Fell,
> The reason why I cannot tell."

Mill would have voted for Dr. Fell and proved him lovable : "Granny kens muckle mair." And thus the last is first, mere logic beaten by instinct; for in God Most High have we not the apotheosis of instinct? The

24

Divine Omniscience being intuitive and independent of logic certainly partakes rather of the nature of instinct than of reason. True for you, Dr. Holmes : You can hire logic, in the shape of a lawyer, to prove anything you want to prove.

CHAPTER XX

"Great White Lake"

"Where the sand has drunk hot tears
From the brimming eyes of millions
Through the long ungracious years."

*   *   *

"The tired Lake crawls along the beach
Sobbing a wordless sorrow to the moon."

*   *   *

"Gone down the tide:
And the long moonbeam in the hard wet sand
Lay like a jasper column half-upreared."

CHAPTER XX

"Great White Lake"

*I*N *which there devolve on the reader the duty and delight of daring the first crossing of Lake Mweru in dug-outs.*

*L*AUS *DEO*, this longest lane in all our wanderings has its glad turning on the 27th of the month. With a great gush of gratitude, we fell in with a tiny tell-tale track gradually growing more defined as it led us out through a dense forest, thick with the lordly *Ficus Indica* and the larger acacia. White with blossom these latter were, as though holding high festival, the forest jubilant. Emerging at last, we look down on Mulangadi's far-stretching sorghum plantations lying in the rich valley of loam watered by the Lwizi. "Well done!" everybody shouts as we realise the real extent of these sorghum fields, the white tops waving visible as far as the eye can see. What a cheering *coup d'œil* for famished men! Mrs. Experience in Africa is, no doubt, the best because the only teacher, but I regret this excellent school dame always asks such terribly high fees. When will one learn even her A B C of expert travel?

We broke another old law of African exploration which
insists that when the last stream is reached you should
cross and camp on the off bank; and here is our penalty
this morning, for the Lufukwe has burst in the night, carrying away bridges and destroying the cornfields.   Moral:
In Africa, to-day's "won't" is to-morrow's "cannot," and
now what shall we do in the swelling of Jordan, how shall
we negotiate the crossing of this turbulent tributary?
Well, somehow or other, after two hours' swimming and
battling back and forward, nobody distinctly remembering
how, we get over at last.   Shall always remember the
little boys bobbing about in the turgid water, frantic all
of them with cold.   Two went swirling down-stream like
bits of cork and were nearly drowned.   Pushing on, we
reach a hamlet and get the meeting of the week at a most
unlikely place.

The Chief, a Sanga hunter of great prowess, I found in
the hands of his wives, who sat in affectionate proximity
to their lord, doing up his hair into a most fantastic
coiffure.   Purring away like a big black tom-cat on
having his fur smoothed the right way by a skilful hand,
his funny face looked out on me from a forest of hair.
And by way of a looking-glass he, feeling immeasurably at
peace with mankind, occasionally cast vain regards into a
large bowl of water that, he said, "shadowed" his black
beauty.   Well, this big, vain, soft-hearted fellow, if not
vulnerable himself, led us out again and again in the
Gospel; and there was the Chief Kapwasa from up-stream,
just over his shoulder, taking it all in.   But truth is not

ours to pare and bate down, so they had to get it—the Evangel of a heaven above and a hell below. This Chief dances round about me with boisterous cordiality, his sole word of greeting being "I! I!" A poor enough welcome if he knew it, for is it not excellent Latin for "Depart! make yourself scarce"? Away back to Adam, I am their first white skin, and the most complimentary description of our lobster-like integument is this: "The skin of a baby." It gets more serious, however, this pigment puzzle, but the final decision is benighted enough: "God," say they, "must have passed through Africa in the dark and did not see us properly, but when He reached you whites it was light, so He did not miss any of you. Ye are sons of the day." The same idea this as when the Chief, desiring to let me know I was very clever, said, pointing to the solar angle, "Yes, you were born at half-past seven in the morning!" a dense negro being told that he was born at twelve o'clock midnight. Contrariwise, the negro having been made in the darkness, some of the night got worked into the composition of his body, so, black is he born and black he behaves. This twist West, though, is a detour, and we must again head for the East.

Mweru, the "Great White Lake" as it is called, is still some distance off, yet here it is a surprise sheet of water flashes out from among the trees in the North —Lake Musengeshi this, and a discovery. Sailed round it in dug-outs; took soundings all over; mapped it by prismatic and watch, and baptized the thing "Mary

Lake "—Mary for my mother and Lake for itself. Almost as big as Lake Dilolo, a curious thing about this hidden lacustrine gem is that it is only thirty years old, a sort of glorified lagoon, and born in a night   The mother Lake is Mweru; but one mysterious year the Luapula swept a fearful flood into the Lake, the water rising so high that it leapt the low ridge of hills at the South end, drowning the inhabitants and roaring out its shame into the basin of this future Lake.   Thus Mweru paid for it all in creating a small rival, the assuaging waters, land-choked, being, so to put it, forced to open shop as a private firm, Mary Lake the new signboard. Signboard, I mean in the literal sense, for half-way on into the Lake we sighted a giant tree of dense foliage, and there in the bark we cut out the four letters of the new name, a memorial to all generations. Pushing on now, we breast its low girding hills, and here is the real thing at last, a wide world of water. Known to the mob as Mweru, this Lake really boasts of the " boa-constrictor " title " Mwerumukatamuvundanshe," for in Africa must not a big thing have a big name ?

We billeted at a fishing kraal, an aged, ill-smelling place, owned by an aged, ill-smelling man, the person probably Shakespeare described as having " a very ancient, fish-like smell."   Shook his head a hundred times before I was done with him : could not make me out at all at all, and seemed very sure I was as bad as mad. Nevertheless, his heart was better than his head, for in order that his hospitality might incur no reproach he presented me with two fowls—two formidably fat fowls, and may I be as fit to die as they were. The dear old Gospel had a poor reception—rousing rejection rather. Told him I had come to allure to brighter worlds and lead the way, and he hinted that I might take my way and clear, then his, oh! his would be a brighter world. The question is a fair one whether I did not antagonise my old friend with a too abrupt mode of preaching and failure to polish down the asperities of speech. We live and we learn, I trust, and the greatest of all lessons in Africa is wisdom to adapt the "how" to the "when." Alas, as you will see, subsequent complications proved too sadly that he had every right not merely to snarl at but to shoot me. And thereby hangs my tale.

As though divining my thoughts, this old man turned the tables by starting the oldest wrangle in Africa—given canoes hidden in the reeds, and an impatient traveller, to find the "how" and the "when" of your voyage.

All my men, poor landlubbers from the Western plains, refuse resolutely even to think this trans-Lake venture. Looking out disconsolate at Mweru, they recall their own Lufira ditch and see here the skies coming down to open and swallow the black specks of canoes. *Po pa pera dikumbi* they call it, "Where the firmament ends," and they argue that if the sky ends there, man must end earlier. "Why, I ask you, by a threefold why (*Patatu*), should we dare this voyage?" said one of these solemn-faced sacrifices about to be offered up. With no book but nature, every little picture is to the negro Christian a parable; and here again, looking out on this vast expanse of skyline, you get some more of his "thinking black" philosophy. He has been shut in all his life to the plains, never saw such a pitiless waste of waters. He looks, and looks, then a dreamy thought comes into his eye and he sighs, "Ah yes! what a tragedy that we humans can *see* far farther than we can walk!" In other words—how little our life agrees with our lip! How little our word squares with our deed! To top all my trouble, yonder is Kilwa Island lying off in mid-Lake, the robber's den from which this Arab Shimba launches his bolts. Darting about like black ducks, you can see his scout-canoes patrolling the Lake, and the problem now stands how to slip past these lynx-eyed blacks and cross Mweru. The very dirt on my calico coat (a thing my boy tailored for me) is now a boon, for one startling speck of white in a canoe would tell tales. Remember, we have Arabs behind us as well as Arabs in front, and, as Lord Macaulay puts it, "Those behind cry 'Forward,' and those in front cry 'Back.'" Therefore, on we agree to go, and God be with us on the waters!

Dawn of the 4th of July saw us shooting out into the hot and oily waters of an uncharted sea, Mweru at this end describing many strange curvatures quite unknown to the R.G.S. Capes, bays, and deltas all foreign to the map, yet old-fashioned enough to the negroes. My cook can turn a phrase as neatly as he turns a pancake, and on taking in this vastitude of skyline he said, "Who ever fought successfully with God? He killeth even aristocrats." Yesterday we were in the grips of revolt—no, never, never more to agree. Here we are to-day kinsmen dear, bound in the common bond of fear that the Arabs may nab us. I felt then more than I had ever felt before the essential kinship of men. Clouds of water-fowl rose on our approach, so dense that blindly banging with a No. 12 we bring them down freely. A spur-wing goose so falling nearly killed one of my men, the point of spur being a terrible dagger, and quite serious enough to brain a black at one blow. The estuaries, however, are the certain postal address of Mweru birds of every hue, and from far and near the congeries flock to a glorious dress parade. To commit that bit of bright-coloured scenery to paper would be impossible, the thing is all too grand and elusive. Pelicans, grey, white, and salmon-pink with yellow pouches—as serious as a sermon; whistling tree-ducks, black and white, zebra-barred and chestnut; dainty lily-trotters, black and white, golden yellow, chocolate brown; bronze-green cormorants and black darters; kingfishers, crowned cranes, curlews, sandpipers, *Ibis religiosa*, spur-winged plovers with yellow wattles, black water-rails with lemon beaks and white pencillings; herons galore, large grey herons, purple slate ditto, Goliath ditto. Last, not least—yea, king of all, the rosy flamingo, rare as royal, and peeping selectly out above the papyrus. One of these birds I cannot place, Nseva they call it, and they flock so thickly that they are a proverb for a united phalanx of patriots. Runic rhyme this proverb, and Englished thus :—

> "A thousand Nseva rise at once,
> Each one refusing precedence."

Any one of an arithmetical turn of mind, I invite to consider carefully the following figures indicative of the thickness of this flock—at one bang 114 (one hundred and fourteen) fell to the right barrel of a Greener.

Most wonderful of all, some far-travelled storks are there, daring birds that have shot far down from the North :—

> "Wild birds that change
> Their season in the night, and wail their way
> From cloud to cloud down the long wind."

Feeding on snakes, frogs, and fish as staple diet, the long Southward journey gives them an *en route* chance of a crab here, a shrimp there. In hard times, where sterile stretches of desert must be crossed, their crop and stomach are crammed full of shells. It would seem a wild exaggeration to suggest that these storks ever saw Egypt, but not far East from here the whole truth of migration came out. True, a bird cannot talk, but what if one day it brings a letter, to wit, a light metal ring bearing a number and date fastened to one leg? And what if the said ring proclaims the said stork to have been liberated away up in North Germany? The ounce of avoirdupois fact

contained in this metallic message dangling from the dead
stork's leg is surely worth the ton of scientific fiction
written on this subject of migratory birds—yes, Prussia
is the name on the ring, and 5th July the date thereof.
There is another link, too, in this story, and that immensely important as indicating the actual stork-route
into Africa. For, be it known, this stork had a brother-
bird released from Northern Germany in the same July
with the same metallic data. But he, poor bird, is not
made of steel and was shot in Tunis, just as he was
entering on the Great African panorama—a needless
death seemingly, yet how necessary as a link in our chart
of bird-migration! For here we see what really happened.
Sailing South out of Prussia, full speed ahead, over Bavaria
they go, over the Lake of Constance, South, ever South,
until the Alps are cleared. Leaving the Adriatic far on
the left, down into Lombardy they dart, right over
Florence and out into the Mediterranean with stately
beating pinions. Africa is now ahead, the land of sun,
sand, and surprises beckoning them on, but Tunis sees the
death of Stork No. 1. (Alas, man and stork alike, how
often, O Africa, hast thou killed a new arrival with one
such brutal knock-down blow!) But Stork No. 2 knows a
thing or two, and he plans a route far from gunshot
range; nothing less than the taking of Africa in its
longitudinal length, and sailing serenely down the middle.
Not many shot-guns there, quoth Mr. Stork. So there
he starts on his long African journey, fifty solid degrees
of latitude ahead. Out of Europe into Tripoli, out of

Tripoli into the Libyan desert: sand, only sand, rolling like a sea; sun, only sun, parching and pitiless. Think, now, this weary Libyan, the only water in wells, and the only wells far and farther between. Think, more desert and vaster, for now he enters the Sahara, where enemies of the air begin as well as enemies of sun and thirst. But still he sails on, sleeping in a salt marsh one night, roosting up a yellow acacia tree the next; but oh, what joy when he reaches a lake! So fond of a bath is the good fellow, he sometimes goes to sleep up to his knees in water; in high icy lands they are often taken out in the morning, frozen in all night. Still South to the sun he comes, crossing over a branch of the Nile and sailing over the pigmy forest; but we are all pigmies to Master Stork, so high in the air is he, so low down are we. And now he is nearing us, for away to the East he can spy the blue Tanganyika, while to the West the great Congo twists and turns like a great water-snake. Through these two he comes, and away far below he can see a curl of blue smoke from a passing village; sometimes spies a group of hunters out in the wilds cutting up game; sometimes, too, he sees a lion kill a zebra. And now here is another expanse of blue stretching out to receive him, for what is this but old Mweru with our chimney smoking away on the Luanza cliff? But the end is not yet. Veering S.E., he heads for his doom, and one crack from a shot-gun ends it all, life's panorama done for ever —story ended, stork ended in a flutter of flying feathers thus ! ! ! ! ! ! ! ! ! ! !

But let us continue our voyage. Gliding past these birds, a huge aviary that beggars all description, on and on we fare; then somebody spies certain suspicious specks of black far out to sea—Shimba's scouts, probably. At this point there is much ambiguous whispering, then a mild mutiny breaks out as to whether we dare push on. Ten, twenty, and thirty minutes pass, and now the black hulls of the canoes are seen bearing down on us for all the world like tiny torpedo-boats : the leading log makes straight for my boat, a miniature replica of the old sailor's print of the *Arethusa* bearing up to engage the *Belle Poule*. But it is a mere scare : these are Arab scouts who sail up quite close, offering the Fontenoy privilege of first shot, then, having verified who and where we are, away they dart back to report at headquarters in the island. The result of that encounter was as sad and sorry a thing for me as could well happen. For when Shimba saw that we had given him the slip he swore a sudden vengeance, put to sea with a flotilla of dug-outs, cut across Lake to my old fisher-friend who grudgingly gave me the canoes yesterday, burned his village to the ground and dragged him off in chains. Not much cause for congratulation here : my visit has been a visitation—see, away in the distance the village in flames ! Can you wonder at that old man for years and years shooting an envenomed glance at the very mention of my name ? What a monstrous enigma it must have seemed to him, my preaching of peace and claiming to be an ambassador thereof, whereas the net

amount of peace we brought to that poor town was—fire
and sword, and the old patriarch dragged off in chains.
True, we had outwitted Shimba, but what a fly in the
ointment!

Happily, this cut-throat soon finds out he has gone
a little too far, for an escaped fisherman runs away
West with the tidings, and after nearly a week's journey
bursts in on the Belgian Fort with a haggard and agonised
look to tell the tale. Now it is Commandant Verdickt
dares a deed that proves him to be the bravest of the
brave. Following in our wake, he strikes the Lake at
the same South end, crosses over to Kilwa Island in
crazy canoes with a handful of men, and dares to try
to carry the Arabs' stone fort by storm. Forlorn hope!
Himself in loud white jacket, a target for the elephant-
hunters, one of his traitor soldiers dares to wipe off an
old score with his own corporal, killing him from the
rear. This means, of course, a pitiful stampede, and
poor Verdickt, after living a charmed life, is nearly
drowned on the return journey. But the veil that
hides the future in Africa is indeed woven by the hand
of mercy, for had we known, dared we move? The
way of man is not in himself, and here is our harmless
little journey spelling out blood, blood, and yet more
blood.

On and on we sail, blissfully ignorant of it all, our
second day on the Lake giving promise of surprises.
The old canoe-man is a marvel, talking all the way
pettingly to his log; calling it by its baptismal name,

and forbidding any man aboard to whistle, lest he bring the wind. The poise of this paddler is a marvel, his stroke so rhythmic and sure that he can carry on for hours without making a false move. Late in the afternoon we see symptoms of approach to land; not mainland, however, but rather a large unknown island answering to the terse euphonious name of "Tangled Isle" (*Disokwe*). Beyond this we sight the real East shore, finally grounding among the reeds at Lukanga. Stiff as buckram, we spring out of our cramped-up canoes, and fall into Livingstone's old trail when he came up to see Mwonga: the Doctor's compass and watch survey is delightfully accurate; has a look of plod about it. Heading North towards Kalungwizi, we foot it many a weary mile. Then one glad day I hear the tootling of an old cracked bugle, and, at last, through the trees, across the flashing water, behold, a bunch of ribbons, once the dear Jack of Old England! All that follows in quick delirious succession is marked on my mind with vivid distinctness, a memory for life. Run down the slope with the innocent joy-bells of my heart ringing, and drop into a canoe: far too excitedly, though, for we get nearly drowned in the turbulent crossing. Then, as in a dream, a white man, eyes dancing with delight, grips my hand, and we can scarcely utter a word—he from the Indian Ocean and I from the Atlantic. Thus West and East join hands. This, be it known, is one Bainbridge *vice* Kidd, who died before my arrival—the same poor Bainbridge who was to die a

few days after I left him. With all our many months'
hoardings of enforced reticence, did we sleep that night?
No! we talked the sun up. Sitting inside the snug
bastions of the Fort, the soldiers bring a pile of faggots,
and there we splice the two ends of our East and West
cables, comparing notes. Only representative of his
Queen, there he is, day by day, looking off into our
wild unknown Interior, two big business-looking revolvers
ever lying on his table, and full of forebodings. Gazing
moodily over at our *terra incognita*, little does he guess
I am "boring out" to join him.

A few weeks ago his chief had been buried in the
grave hard by our fire, and—he is to follow suit in a
week. The poor fellow pours out his soul into the night;
for, burdened with responsibility, he is now a miniature
edition of Great Britain in breeches, the death sentence
in his power, and he too, alas! in the power of the death
sentence. Kinder to me than a kinsman dear, he—the
same man who in England would have treated me to
a stony British stare—he, even he, had mercy on my
limping along in old slippers in the rain. Gave me a
shirt, gave me hose, gave me medicines. Miniature
edition of Great Britain indeed, he not only represented
England's Army and Navy, but, quite unconscious of
the inroads I was making on his slender stock of supplies,
I fear I treated him as though he were an agent of the
other Army and Navy—Victoria Street!

But it is only past midnight under the solemn stars
you get past the outer fringe of things, right home to

the soul of a man. Loneliness is at his heart like a knife, and now is the time to push the right royal claims of the Lord Jesus Christ. Far too long have good folks in England sheered off delicately when these subjects are approached, but only by facing them can we conceive what a trap Africa is to a newcomer. Arriving as many young men do in this land wholly unawakened to the graver issues of life, the first glance they get amounts to a moral slap in the face. Perchance even the scarce Missionary he meets is of a sour, mournful type, who has missed a glorious deed of helping this newcomer. Too often it is a fact that this Africa robs a Christian man of his victor's song and leaves him a broken-spirited jumble of distraction. But the fact is, a mere Missionary in Africa is lost in its vast mileage, a poor pin-point in the immensity, and the lonely Europeans are long miles apart. Then he wakens up to find what an elegant fiction is that loose talk in England about the joys and manliness of a "man being alone on his own feet." Fleeing from cities and the "fight for bread" of congested towns, he soon discovers the value of dear old English ways. Even the starchy fads of fashion are seen in a new and almost favourable light. At sundown his thoughts, like homing pigeons, travel fast and far across the seas to his native land. He dreams of the old dainties and decencies of life and longs to be there. He drops that nonsense about a clerk in an English office being "chained to his oar-pen like a galley-slave." Finally and comprehensively he

25

sums up a hundred African needs in the dear old phrase,
" the thin crust of conventionality." Then it is England's
boy shrinks suddenly into himself, the awakening being
rude and poignant. Nor dare a Missionary, who serves
the God Whose name is Jealous, be silent, for He hath
cursed the man who "winketh with the eye." Gentlemen, to ignore is to wink, and thus to palliate, so
"suffer the word of exhortation."

CHAPTER XXI

A Page of History

"Father Nile presents his compliments . . . and begs leave to inform the world that the Father, at the suggestion of the Reverend David Livingstone, has removed his head-quarters to a delightful region [Lake Mweru] about eleven degrees South of the Equator, or Equinoxious line, where for the present he is to be found by his friends. Carriages to set down at Cazembe, a couple of hundred miles or so South of Burton's Lake Tanganyika. N.B. You are heartily welcome to any refreshments which you may bring with you. Niggers about here don't need to be shot."   Mr. Punch, 1869.

*   *   *

"Cartographers in Afric's maps
  With savage pictures fill the gaps,
  And o'er the inhospitable downs
  Place elephants instead of towns."

CHAPTER XXI

A Page of History

W HEREIN the reader, now in glimmer now in gloom, watches these negroes work out their destiny in the darkness.

AND now, having " bored " out East, let us take our bearings : where are we ?

In this all-encompassing gloom it is vital that you fasten on one fact : by so reaching the shores of Lake Mweru, we now see a faint streak of light shooting up from Lake Nyassa and along the Tanganyika plateau. Like a beacon light visible at sea from far, we strain our gaze towards Nyassa, gladdened to know that yonder is God's lighthouse of Livingstonia, shining true. And lighthouse, remember, is the true metaphor to symbolise Dr. Laws' work out there ; lighthouses do not ring bells and fire cannon to call attention to their shining, they just shine on. Likewise Livingstonia. Nor are our Eastern hopes futile. For many a day that transport link with Chinde succours us, albeit the real route of the far future is due South to the Cape.

Will my good-natured reader again let me write in the first person singular? for the next link in our story is the day when we came round the North shore, a white man and a handful of blacks. The date is November, 1893. We have crossed the Lake in canoes and are now heading back Westward, seeking for a Mission site on the Eastern edge of our Garenganze country. My crew and I go to sleep curled up on the sand of the North shore of Lake Mweru: that is to say, when sleep comes our way. In the white horses roll foaming, almost getting at us, and the African lets a long-tongued flame from the faggots lick his skin. As the wind increases its whistle, each of the fisher-lads quietly scoops a grave of dry sand into which he descends, sweeping back a few inches depth of sand by way of blanketing. Huddled thus all in a heap, oh the confidential chats we have! Natives, I find, like you to poke into their little histories, and generally the most ordinary-looking little boy has a career of crosses. One lad of sixteen said that when a boy he used to hear of God far East among the Romanists, but his family crossed into English land, and, said the boy, " Who ever heard of God among the English?" But against this put the remark of a young Roman Catholic pupil as he pointed to his brass crucifix: "Yes, I wear God round my neck." Our appeal to a man to break with the dark tribal past only evoked a song about potatoes, which I construed as indifference. On reducing the song to writing, however, it was not noisy, empty doggerel, but a preaching parable

LUANZA
The Mission Town Built on the Cliff
overhanging Lake Mweru

of my appeal. Said the song : "Lombe, you remember, introduced potatoes, and what was reckoned poison is now staple diet." This is *their* way of expressing my desire. Yes, they treat the Gospel as though it would poison them ! But who would have guessed that a man singing about potatoes was really pleading for an acceptance of the Gospel? By the by, this mention of diet reminds me of the curious tendency in Africa to enter a long spell of monotony in one kind of food. In the mountains you are dosed with honey, and in the plains the everlasting fowl is your fare right round the clock—just a little too much of *toujours perdrix*. So, too, on the Lake here, it is fish, and fish, and more fish :—

> "A paddle, a row or sail,
> With always a fish for a midday meal,
> And plenty of Adam's ale."

Finally, on the North-West shore, near Luanza, we made a find of a charming slice of English-looking territory, the Chief coming up with a red fez stuck impudently on his head, and claiming proprietary rights to the soil. He might have been a Duke of twenty descents, so tall his talk, so short his stature. Well, after long hours of the old parrot cry of "property in danger," we finally settled the *meum* and *tuum* of the thing, and next day was appointed for the delivery of the titles. This curious ceremony opened with the angry roar of the Chief's drums that lent themselves to anything but dulcet harmonies; then we all crossed the boundary brook and climbed the bluff, a great ring of roaring blacks being now formed round a noble tree—"the tree of witness" this was called.   Here the Chief, nodding affably to me, stepped out into the centre of the ring and asked me to join him in the " signing of the title-deeds."   For all I could guess from this ring it might have been a prize fight that was planned : can it really be, thought I, that instead of settling the matter in black and white, it has to be finished in black and blue ?   As matters turned out, however, our conveyancing ink was Napoleon's kind —gunpowder.   For, cutting out a large square on the tree, the Chief called on me to fire a bullet into the mark ; then, with an air of amused paternity, he, with a bang, planted his copper bullet alongside my lead one.   So there it was, "signed, sealed, and delivered," the living tree carrying in its bosom the two " witness-bullets," the human ring round it a warning to all men that this tree was inviolate from the woodman's axe.   Postal address : Luanza, Lake Mweru *via* Chinde.   The cliff rising sheer from the blue Lake, a narrow ledge of flat land for our township, the Bukongolo Range walling the town high at the back and sheltering it from the wild west winds, that is Luanza.   The other day, when the present King Albert of Belgium came along, we sat on the cliff verandah looking across to the far British shore, and I asked him what he thought of our outlook.   " Oh," said he, " here I sit imagining myself at Folkestone looking over at Calais."

*   *   *

Here it is, then, on this bluff overhanging Mweru, we settle down in the dark to hold on to the country—motto :

Work, wait, and win.[1] To " pioneer," I know, is a word as
much abused as used, but note what it means to us here.
The Arabs have wiped off all the hamlets from the map
and driven the Shila folks to the caves in the Bukongolo
Range—problem : pioneer a population first of all. Kuva,
the Lord Paramount, owing to the stress of war, is hiding
away somewhere in the rocks of Bukongolo, and we must
fish him out of his cave—problem : pioneer a kingship in
our need. Here, too, on the cliff there is no trace of
a village, everything swept before the Arab bands of
raiders—problem : pioneer a township. Nor hut nor
tent have I—problem : pioneer a house. Nor food nor
vegetables nor fruit—problem : pioneer a garden and
orchard. Nor book nor written speech have they—
problem : pioneer a literature. Etcetera, etcetera. This
" etc. etc. " representing the needle-to-the-anchor kind of
business in which you are a jack-of-all-trades and very
particularly master of none. Too many irons in the fire,
no doubt, but in they go—shovel, tongs, poker and all.
We did not come out here to eat bananas, and these are
the words I wrote in chalk on the first mud walls of my
pioneer cabin—

> " The compass was not invented by an astronomer,
>   Nor the microscope by a natural philosopher,
>   Nor the printing press by a man of letters,
>   Nor gunpowder by a soldier."

[1] The first to rally to our help at Luanza was Mr. Campbell from the
West, then Messrs. Arnot and Cobbe from the East. Next came the first
lady who ever penetrated these wilds, Mrs. Crawford, her party including
Messrs. Gammon, George, and Pomeroy. After this came the " John Wilson "

Quite a cheery reflection this for Mr. Robinson Crusoe Africanus.

*   *   *

But who said it was four thousand miles to Old England? Mocking at mere mileage, there goes the homely tapping of a woodpecker, each warm-hearted tap! tap! tap! hinting that round the next bend of the Lake the United Kingdom of Great Britain and Ireland may come into full view. Nor is this all. Flir-r-r! goes a covey of red-legged partridges trying on the same happy hoax, the very birds apologising for the long lapse in letters, and sending us these home-felt sights and sounds of theirs as substitute. The poor little Mission garden is also a policy of make-believe, and resembles Stevens' Indian one, the most pathetic thing in a whole land of exile. The native trees and shrubs and plants with huge leaves flourish rankly. But the poor little home flowers, the stocks and mignonette and wallflowers! They struggle so gallantly (like the Mission lady and Mission baby) to persuade you that this is not so very far from England, and they fail so piteously. They will flower in abundant but straggling blossoms, but the fierce sun withers the first before the next have more than budded. It is a loving fraud, but a hollow one. The very wallflowers cannot be more than exiles. Yet here in this affectation of a garden you have the pulse of the

party, the only remaining member of which is Mr. Higgins. Then don't forget Miss Jordon! Both winning and wise, Mr. and Mrs. Higgins have held on all these years without release, the last stop-press news being that their far-off Luanza house has gone up in smoke.

whole African puzzle. For granted you battle with and win a feeble flower from the silly soil, where is the perfume? And precisely as you sniff in vain for the old whiff of the mignonette, even so with the emigrant English-man. He too loses his bloom and fragrance, and Africa soon robs him of his genial smile. But he that hath ears to hear can get a thousand such sermons all over Africa, and every day. For instance, learn a parable of the fig tree. Glance at those Mission doors, a pioneer effort in carpentry. The good fellow made a dive into the adjoining jungle, and after felling a fig tree he laboriously ripped the planks for his first doors and tables. The which is a perfect parable. For that wood was as green as the Missionary who cut it, and after a few months those tightly fitting boards, so full of sap, shrank into yawning cracks, a sorrow and an eyesore. How like the fresh young Missionary, the first year how neat and trig; the second, how warped and shrunken! For as long as sap is sap and sun is sun, the latter will soon suck up the former, and the Mission door will be like the Missionary who made it. Learn, therefore, a parable of that fig tree. When its branch is yet young and tender, and shooteth forth its leaves, then ye know— that it is not the time to make doors and tables! Their very word for "leaves" has a Biblical ring in it. It means "the tellers," the idea being that they mark the change of seasons, and all appeal to the leaves, i.e. "the tellers," as proof positive that the season has changed. Thus the phrase, "When ye see the leaves then ye *know* that summer is nigh," is as African as it is Biblical.

Nowadays we are all better off and dine on a better diet—better off, yes, but are we better? Sharp is the contrast between a London " slummer" and the modern African Missionary on his highly respectable station. Pause half a moment and consider. Note this curious new word "Station" we begin to use in Africa, a new word for a distinctly new idea. You will search the dictionary in vain for its meaning, and the Acts of the Apostles too. Yet this term can with special fitness stand for the idea, because this is the thing that anchors the Missionary. Not a sheep-run nor a railway station, but a *Mission* Station—in a word, an isolated estate some hundreds of yards or acres square on which the Missionary lives as magnate of the district. Station in name and station in nature is such a place, for it forces the preacher to be as stationary as his station : the native must come to the Missionary, and not the Apostolic contrary. And what if this lightly-come lightly-go negro runs off seeking pastures new ? *How can the stationary Missionary follow him?* The danger is that in this Africa ever on the move, this Africa peopled by roaming tribes, the natives spasmodically scratch the soil in one valley for three or four years and then flit to new districts for new fields. Remember rural Africa cannot boast one plough, only hoes ; and this is fatal to fixed population. He only scratches the soil and then moves on ; not one of them will play the man and dig deep. Nor has he any coal, only forest faggots, and these he soon runs through, owing to his deforestation for corn-growing. Here, then, in lack of firewood we see another factor driving him on. Face this moving-on problem.

Up go the stately buildings of the white man and down go the mud huts of his black neighbour, No. 1 just getting in as No. 2 is moving out. Alone the Missionary finds himself, the clannish coalescence of his parishioners outwitting his plans. Leading up to this point, all has been hypocritical silence, and the foreigner with innocent serenity thinks his black neighbours are a fixture, so he settles down to build, which also, alas! means building to settle down. "Strangers and pilgrims," yes; but the Devil has all the pilgrims and Christ all the strangers, for we saints are anchored with impedimenta when the sinners—the natives—are up and away. There on the off-bank of a brawling stream you have the *pro tem.* native village only a few thousand yards distant in measure but many thousand miles in mind and manners. Behold the grotesque contradiction of the thing!—a middle-class Missionary acclaimed as the local Carnegie, staggering rich, no poverty of the Cross, no stigma of shame, but contrariwise a grovelling negro lauding him as lord and master—a poor enough start for the dear old Gospel. So very much is the African a servant of servants that he outwits the Missionary, who should be a servant of all; and here in this initial wrong Christ is wounded in the house of His friends, Christianity equating wealth, not poverty. Bring the African to book

on this subject, call it all a blinding delusion, tell him
you are really as poor as he thinks you are rich ; I say,
tell him this, and into that negro eye of his comes a
magpie gleam accusing you of mendacity.   To split a
hair on the difference between real and relative riches is,
to the naked negro, an unworthy juggling with words—
are we not "the people of God," and does not the very
name of the Creator mean greatness and prestige in local
lingo ?

*   *   *

But let us look at our Lake now.   For six months
in the year there is a South-Wester thundering in
on our shore, a wind adversely in the teeth of our
schooner [1] when travelling up-Lake.   Beginning in April
and blowing through the dry season, the monsoon is
so distinctly rainless that the season commonly takes its
name from it.   A good guess at Meteorology this, for,
blowing over the highlands of the Transvaal as it
does, where could it get rain from ?   The commence-
ment of rains coincides with the change of monsoon.
A deterrent on the water, this same wind is a saving
boon on land, blowing in on us on the bluff when the
heat is at its height.   Not the wild salt winds of the sea
with famous curative virtues—oh no !—for when a man
has incipient fever they strike a chill to his marrow,
generally bringing the attack to a head.   Towards
October we approach the change of seasons, when we

---

[1] Well done, Greenock !   Across sea and land loyal hearts sent that
splendid iron boat, and for years it was indispensable.

have our greatest meteorological disturbances on the
Lake, and on the cliff at Luanza we need all the hold
we have of the rock, the wind heralding torrential rains
sweeping down the gorges in wild rugging gusts. Looking out to the Lake, you can descry a hardy fisherman
nursing his "dug-out" in a grey, cruel sea: exactly the
opposite of the old Francis Drake style, these canoes
have high viking prows, and sterns almost flush with
the water. He has christened his log by a lucky name,
and when far out, talks pettingly to the boat as his own
familiar friend. Transacting, as he thus does, in honest
ways, the honest business of a fisherman, it is a pity
he spoils it all by a curious mid-Lake ceremony called
"the cursing." What this amounts to is bluntly a fierce
cataract of oaths in which he apostrophises all the dead
men in the Lake. Singling them out by name, he curses
them with all the gall and bitterness of a presumably
doomed man—the presumption being that, all alone as
he is in far mid-Lake, the dead men will drag him down
to the deep. Then there is a pause, but the stubborn
silence of the Lake only stiffens him in his resolve to
keep cursing. Making a clean circle of the Lake hamlets,
he challenges all the dead chiefs by name, the volley
of oaths (*Mafinge*) being to the accompaniment of a
curious rat-a-tat noise he makes with a drumstick on
the side of the boat. The livelier the fish rug at his
two long lines tied to his two great toes, the louder do
these curses rend the air. Sure, if ever food needed to
be "sanctified by prayer," these fish, the fruit of cursing,

deserve a purifying "grace before meat"! Yet what
shall we see the great Kazembe do with these very fish?
Will he, too, not dine to a cataract of curses?—the very
fish cursed in their catching being again cursed in their
cooking.

But here, incredulous as it may seem, the wheel goes
full circle once again, and the erstwhile curser can now be
heard singing a solemn *Te Deum*. Yet this fisherman,
remember, claims he is only cursing *demons*, for forthwith
with the same mouth blesses he God. Certain it is that
for centuries this quaint old song of deliverance has been
sung as a cast-iron formula by all Shila men who were
capsized but came safe to land. Greeting him with song at
the *Njiko*, or landing-place, all the women-folk burst out
into a "God-song," as it is called, the escaped fisherman
joining them in the chorus. Simple enough in its diction,
the whole value of this praise-song is to be found in its
archaic terminology, the very grammar of the thing being
steeped in most ancient twang :—

> "O God, the minnows
>   Had nigh feasted on me;
> But Thou, O God,
>   Didst rescue me!"

Then, when the "praise procession" reaches the hamlet,
first among all his treasures to be produced is the great
"horn of salvation," as it is called, a horn this crammed
full of charms, and in symbolic idea a real cornucopia.
All life's successes are ascribed to its mediation, and the
"horn is exalted" accordingly. This song of deliverance

idea, remember, is not peculiar to one tribe only, for the very vilest type of cut-throat negro does the same thing. The infamous Rugaruga, for instance, whose very name on the Lake became, as we have seen, the verb to murder and loot, these too have a cast-iron formula of "God's thanks" when they escape in war. Say a bullet whizzes past his ear, and at once, conscious of having been saved from death, he interjects the ancient prayer: "O God, my Deliverer, never again will I revile Thee!" Not a chance idea this, please note, but a technical prayer, proving once more that God hath not left Himself without a witness, even in the darkest hour of a dark land. Right in from the far Ocean, piercing the darkest hole of Africa with a shaft of light, is this all-pervading knowledge of God-Creator.

Without labouring the point, I have already urged that the most obdurately deaf negro (deaf to your entreaties, I mean) would resent with extreme asperity any notion that he denied the immortality of the soul: *that* is not arguable. Let me prove this by describing one memorable meeting I held in that same Kalamata's town among the cannibals, a meeting held on the day subsequent to my seeing a man eating human flesh. You wonder *how* these hell-hounds can understand the Gospel ; especially if the fugitive preacher has to push on past their place a few miles before his camp for the night is reached. Well, here is a typical meeting on virgin soil, and you, my reader, shall judge whether Paul spake not the truth when he wrote that "God hath not left Himself without witness."

The deep-voiced sycamore-drum calls them in, an ugly, verminating throng almost *in puris naturalibus*—there behold! the uttermost man in the uttermost parts of the earth. (Yonder, too, on the throne of God, do not forget the Christ Who can save to the uttermost.) Supporting me on my near right is the Chief, as Chairman, with whom I propose a loud Socratic dialogue, not as preacher, but merely inquirer, with note-book respectfully open. No skimming, skirting, and shirking of difficulties here; I simply ask and he simply answers; why not? " A big horse takes a big fence," and this big black is on for big business. Note, please, also, that I have given— on the strength of Paul's above-quoted words—the bold initial guarantee that I will neither intrude nor innovate one new-fangled idea in the meeting. The theme for the day is " GOD !" and having got a thousand voices to hush the ineffable Name three times, we settle down to Bible-business. Well, to anticipate, it turns out that the subject of our choice is a gold-mine; not only about God is it but from God too. Asked their name for *Him*, the answer comes sharp and short from the Chairman-Chief, " *Vidie Mukulu*," *i.e.* the great King. And here comes the opening in question No. 2 : " You, the King of these parts, tell me, please, what *your* kingship involves." Answer—a long string of kingship paraphernalia : Primo, a King has laws; secundo, a King has a *Chipona cha Chidie* = a judgment-seat; tertio, a King has subjects, loyal or rebellious; quarto, rewards and punishments, and all rebellions quelled within his borders. And now comes the Missionary's opening, for had not **a** thousand voices, *nem. con.*, declared that God was the great King (*Vidie Mukulu*[1])? Sharp and sudden, you flash in upon them the question, "And so *God* has all these kingship rights too?" Now is the momentous moment for the appearance of the Holy Bible. "A King has laws, has he? Well, here they are, the great King's." "A King crushes rebellion, does he?" And so on you go, rigorously innovating n-o-t-h-i-n-g, but merely building on their own adjective "great" governing their own noun "King"— God demonstrated a great King preaching great peace by the great Lord Jesus Christ to His subjects in revolt. Thus out of his own mealy mouth you judge Him a great King; even to this man-eater postulating a great Judgment-Seat, great Laws. All this, too, far, far in **a** Central Africa beyond the reach of any Mission by whatsoever name named. How vivid many a Pauline statement becomes! Run down the Acts, and note those Apostolic speeches; to a congregation with its vellum copies of "Prophets and Psalms" these were profusely quoted. But when Paul took his plucky plunge into Gentiledom he ever preached and practised God nigh at hand, God touching their Gentile lives at every point: yea, in God they lived and moved and had their being. Quite a different thing this, remember, from the folly of pretending to preach to the God *in* a man—how can God be in the soul when Paul says, "At that time ye were *without* God"?

---

[1] This great God-title is most interestingly found even in the far North, beyond the Luban language limit.

26

The only God in a negro is the god of this world, the Devil. But look at our blue Lake again.

To speak of Lake Mweru's "trough" as geographers do of Tanganyika is wrong, for although the Bukongolo Range rises sheer on the West, trenched to a singular degree with brooks and streams, all leaping into the Lake, yet Mweru is not the big evaporation-vat that Tanganyika and every other locked-in lake must be. The Lukuga drainage notwithstanding, Lake Tanganyika water is notoriously nasty. In spite of all that salt, sulphate and carbonate of lime, and sulphate of magnesium dissolved and washed down every year by erosion of water, the whole is soon in motion and joins the Lualaba exit-flow, every cubic foot of water entering at the Southern doorway having to pay toll at the Northern exit. As though guarding this exit doorway, there is a patrol of pugnacious hippos, known familiarly to all natives. The old patriarch of this clan is a disagreeable veteran who often lies sunning himself at full length on the flat rock just midway across the Lualaba mouth. He definitely hunts men, and has shivered many a canoe with gusto. The *Vasayila*, or harpoonmen, have for years exerted all their blandishments on his tough, tight skin, but he has lived to a green old age, rich in honours. Of course, there is sorrow on the Lake, as all the little fishing hamlets know well, and often a dug-out puts out to sea never to come back again, the forementioned ring of hippos having all to do in the matter. For this reason, no native has

been known to cross Mweru direct, all insisting on making
the detour round the North end. Along the shores, the
canoes dart about like wild-fowl, while far out you can
descry an odd, daring Shila man, his dug-out appearing
as a dark speck, rising and falling on the crest of the
wave. "Nursing" his canoe he calls it, and even in a
grey, cruel sea that game of pitch-and-toss he plays with
the Lake is a safe thing, even in the angriest storm.
Down dips the dug-out into the water-trough, only to
reappear riding the wave with the safety of a duck. A
mere log, it must mount every wave, nor dare it cleave
even one : no wonder, therefore, it curtsies so deeply to
the blast out of sheer respect. He is making a try for
something good for supper and has, all the while, enshrined in his vision, the picture of the log-fire with wife
and children squatting round. Long before Europe got
wind of the idea, these canoes were fitted with invisible
marconigram apparatus, for the most tenacious legend
of these fishermen is that they are perfectly *au courant*
with their wives' doings at home. This mysterious union
is so real that any act of infidelity on her part is doomed
to react prejudicially on her fisherman out at sea. Thus
all cases of drowning are brought home to the "guidwife," just as, on the contrary, she accepts with smug
complacency the tribute of being the efficient cause of
a good haul of fish. For during all the time of her
husband's absence in mid-Lake has she not kept the
dozen "taboo" rules sacredly? She dared not, for
instance, raise her hand to the shelf in her hut, nor

dared she shake hands with any one. To cook food was also severely taboo during her fisherman's absence, nor could any stranger cross the threshold in his absence. This last custom, indeed, is so rigid that the tribal name is derived therefrom, the fisherman always drawing a circle barrier round his hut to debar entrance in his absence. Hence Shila = to draw a line, from which the *in extenso* tribal name comes, *Vashilanandanediango*. Thus the Lake-dwellers boast of a name as long as the Lake's own title.

Such long names are quite a cartographic curio, and are explained by the Central African idea that as name equates nature, therefore anything big must have a correspondingly big name. Hence it is these great Lakes of the Interior all boast long "boa-constrictor" names unknown to map-makers. For instance, as we have seen, the plain Mweru of the R.G.S. maps is only Mweru in the same short sense as Tom = Thomas, or Will = William. Only, however, in the serious debate of the forensic negro elders can you hear Lake Mweru called by its full-dress name of *Mwerumukatamuvundanshe*.

Obviously too big for plain workaday speech, this long comet of a name loses its streaming tail, and brief, blunt Mweru is the normal usage. Nor is this a fancy freak peculiar to one corner only. Take the good Livingstone's own Bangweulu as another example. In his anxiety that people should not call it "Bungy-hollow," he himself was "out" in the spelling of his two final vowels. But the important point to note is that even this longish name is only a mere apocope, like its twin-sister Mweru. For the Tom = Thomas analogy is as nothing to the fact that Bangweulu is only the curtate form of the real name, *Bangweuluwavikilwanshimango-mwana*. If you laugh at the fisher-folk for such a long-winded title, they will quote the proverb, " Big thing, big name." And if you still refuse to bow to the sanity of the idea, they clinch their postulate with the sister-proverb, " Little beef, little juice." Now, although this seems mere black verbosity, these long names are really a philological boon, deciding at a glance the real inner meaning of the Lake's name. A geographer in London without the clue of this full name could toy with his pencil for weeks, trying to solve the meaning of brief " Mweru," and would fail, because the solution is all locked up in this hidden longer name. For instance, the Mweru mouthful, parsed literally, is unerringly rendered " Great-White-Lake-Locust-Drowner " (*i.e.* too wide an expanse for locusts to dare to try to cross with impunity). So, too, with the geographic mouthful repre-senting the true name of Bangweulu. This only means " The-Lake-so-stormy-that-it-must-be-propitiated-by-the-voyager-and-so-wide-that-you-must-take-provisions-aboard-for-a-trans-Lake-voyage." So, for orthographical pains you get philological gains, and the names are as easy to parse as they are hard to pronounce.

CHAPTER XXII

Black Man = Black Manners

"The thing that hath been, it is that which shall be : and there is no new thing under the sun."

Solomon.

* * *

"When I was a boy in Gaul I beheld the Scots, a people living in Britain, eating human flesh ; and although there were plenty of cattle and sheep at their disposal, yet they would prefer a ham of the herdsman or a slice of female breast."   Jerome.

* * *

" For are ye not as the children of the Ethiopians unto Me, O children of Israel ? saith the Lord. "

Amos.

CHAPTER XXII

Black Man = Black Manners

WHEREIN the reader finds that the African so debases his surroundings that the surroundings take revenge and debase the African.

IVORY is pouring into the villages, and with it come the fine old fellows who tackle Jumbo, following him up even into the marshes, where they run a risk of being snapped at by a crocodile. An odd elephant has been known to avenge man and teach Mr. Crocodile a lesson, one instance having occurred when I was at Kashobwe's. The elephants came down in the tropical effulgence of moonlight to bathe in the fen-marshes, their gleeful splashing quite lively. Timid little baby calves shrinking on the edge and refusing to plunge, the mother coming up and squirting a shower-bath as their share in the fun. Comical little rogues these, standing about four feet high, skin falling in folds and far too big for them. There they are, looking exactly like a dozen youngsters wearing the coats and trousers of their elder brothers. This submerged marsh, however, be it noted, is alive with "crocs," and these

reptiles quite coolly commence to nip poor Jumbo's toes,
forgetful of the fact that Jumbo's trunk is Jumbo's glory.
At any rate, Nemesis falls like a bolt from the blue, for,
smacking like a long whip, down comes that elephant's
trunk, twisting round the crocodile's tail, and—tableau!
With one half-shriek, half-squeak, the long greenish-
yellow croc is sent flying over the marsh—flop!
splash! thirty yards off.   That deft tight grip the tusker
took of the huge reptile's tail, and the way in the moonlight he waved it theatrically aloft like the figure-of-eight
smack of a whip, doubtless made that crocodile unto the
third and fourth generation resolve never again to nibble
at an elephant's toes.

The mannish type of woman here even tackles a
crocodile, and Madam Luban is not too finicking in the
choice of a weapon.   These ladies are quite deft with
the short national knife, and two of them attacked a
crocodile in best Amazon manner.   They had gone down
to the fishing-weir to empty the wicker baskets when
a lurking croc shot out at them with a snap.   Taking
advantage of the fact that when this beast misses a first
grab he must pause to unlock his teeth, these plucky
women attacked him with their two short knives and
finished him in a few minutes.   But what a weird
business, the long yellow crocodile writhing with his
wounds, and snap, snapping his white teeth in chagrin!
The two women flowing with blood yet never a wince;
two paltry penknives doing it all.   And all the while
yonder is a heron fishing on a sand-spit, chuckling with

glee. Quite the largest of these Saurians ever seen hereabouts was found farther up, dead by its own act of folly. Nor knife nor spear killed this monster, only its own vile voracity : the crocodile killed the negro, and the killed man killed the crocodile. Washed up on the bank, the dead monster lay four feet high—not long— with a tell-tale human armbone sticking out of its chest. The old fisherman who acted as sort of "Crocodile Coroner" on the occasion, clearly and convincingly proved that the reptile, instead of making one sure bite of his victim, had snapped off this arm then grabbed a second time before swallowing the first. Thus in murdering the man it committed suicide, the ragged end of the humerus boring through to tell the tale that it had stuck athwart the gullet and worked right out. "King over all the children of pride" as it is, little did the old fisherman guess what a grisly pun he made of the crocodile's name by dubbing them "the Undertakers" (*Vakoka Panshi*).

But to return to our mighty Jumbo.

Mere beefy bulk, though, is nothing in forest prowess, and this same ponderous elephant positively trembles at the thought of a tiny leech. And no wonder, for many an elephant dies an awful death from a leech sucking the inner membrane of his trunk until the monstrous tusker is maddened to death. Goaded to its doom by a tiny leech, like a locomotive thundering down the line, off this six tons of madness rushes at fifteen miles per hour—"Any- where, anywhere, out of the world!" You can come across a huge clearing in the grass, where the writhing giant has nearly beaten his own brains out, the agony all centred in that finest and most delicate of all his organs, the "marconigram" trunk.   Yes, one tiny leech can puncture that huge balloon of beef, the vulnerable point this vaunted trunk.   On Lake Mweru this is called "the leech doom," and is the cause of that curious ceremony all elephants perform when they come across drinking-water. This function is called "the benediction" (*Kupara*), and the elephant passes a scared, wistful gaze over the sheet of water, at the same time waving his trunk like a mesmerist again and again over the solemn, treacherous pond.   But the trunk, as a matter of fact, is no magician's wand, but the supreme headquarters of Jumbo's cunning, and supplying him with, not so much a sixth sense as a *sensorium commune.*   Instead of "praying" a sort of grace-before-meat kind of petition, as the native suggests, he is really wringing from the water the "leech secret." Certainly the merest soupçon of leech-treachery is enough, and with one trumpet-roar the idea of disgust is so strong that it gives him momentum for a fifteen-mile run.   Is this the reason why an elephant has been endowed with a trunk?   I mean, if clear water is so needful to Jumbo, then does not this very length of trunk permit him to drink from the bank without entering the water and thereby stirring up the muddy sediment?

(*Later.*)

Again I say, Bravo ! for the men who risk life and limb following them up.   The average African hunter is a stalwart who works hard, walks far, and is named "friend

of the forest." What splendid evangelists these wandering
Nimrods make! Take an instance. An elephant-hunter
gets soundly and profoundly saved, so at once God claims
his witness far afield. His elephants, of course, claim his
presence out there too. Away beyond the edge of
cultivation he goes, following up the spoor of his elephants;
dipping down into gorges, skirting precipices, sinking into
bulrush bogs—

> "To preach as never sure to preach again,
> And as a dying man to dying men."

Then he comes back to tell us all about it at our
Saturday night prayer-meeting, a weird tale of the lonely
bush and the stately goings of our God. It would test
the most skilled in mental acrobatics to explain away
such personal intervention of Almighty God to and for
that hunter of His. "What will prayer do for you?"
laugh his old hunter chums. "All that God can do for
me," is the royal reply. The misses as well as the
hits are all reported as occasions for praise. And his
favourite Bible proof is that "the Lord preserveth man
and *beast.*" Listen to his quaint exegesis—*preserveth the*
man when He grants a hit, *preserveth the beast* when He
grants a miss! That is to say, locked up in the custody
of this one verse you have all the fates and fortunes of the
hunter and his prey: God for the man, yet God for the
beast—yea, God all and in all.

But one flash reveals the diamond. And this exhorter
in the prayer-meeting soon gets to close quarters with his

younger brethren, the local preachers. "You think," says he, "that this preaching in your own suburbs is evangelising Africa (a mere radius of a few miles); but in my wanderings I come upon an Africa you know not— lost villages in the far bush, groups of towns that never saw the map. Oh, my elephants lead me to strange corners and among stranger folk. They lead the way and I must follow; and sometimes, lying across our track ahead, we see shafts of ruddy light shooting up, and here we are on a long-lost village. Once in olden times it was fabled that they had a visit from a Northern tribe, but since then they have lived and died lost in the bush. So what do I do? I let my herd of elephants escape, and stay with these scared-of-eye Africans—did not God lead me to them? And if God's way is our way, will not His joy be our joy?"

He has lost his elephants owing to this intercepting town—

> "But all through the mountains, thunder-riven,
>   And up from the rocky steep,
>   There arose a cry to the gates of Heaven:
>   'Rejoice! I have found My sheep!
>   And the angels echoed, around the throne,
>   'Rejoice! For the Lord brings back His own!'"

Thus he tells his tale. His profession is elephants, but his confession is Christ. And who would compare profession with confession—what are literal elephants to spiritual sheep? Not once but several times has he broken in on such old-world folks—a true Mission to the lost, far truer than many a high-sounding enterprise born

in a committee-room or baptized on a platform. Watch
him, this apostle of the Nimrod cult. A veteran of life's
battles with a war-worn face, there he stands in his plain
loin-cloth, the very plainness of the old hunter being a
plainer rebuke to the young generation of over-dressed
Christians. He adorns the doctrine, and they are too
apt to adorn themselves. A mighty hunter *before the
Lord.*

As we have already seen, of course one swallow does
not make a summer in Africa. But (if one dare execute
such a straddle on cross metaphors) here is a straw that
indicates the current among the cannibals. I refer to a
curiously foreign feature of life in here, a great tribal
meeting on sanitation summoned by the deep-voiced
Nkumfi, or sycamore-drum, the Chief taking his seat by
my side and seconding everything. Being thirsty, I
proposed to indulge my baser nature with a cup of water,
but found it filthy with contamination. If "Afric's
sunny fountains" would only roll down water instead of
sand at times, it would be a decided improvement.
"Golden sands" sounds poetic, but in Africa we must
get all our poetry out of the plain prose of life, and this
trek I have drunk red water and black water, yellow
water and white water, but worst of all was this green
stuff to-day. Ah yes! I believe in "holy water"
provided it is of the right kind. Pushing investigations,
we soon find out that here is a vast tribe living on a
dunghill of disease, the whole insanitary condition of
the place a clear case of ten thousand dirty men shaking

their dirty fists in Nature's face. "Dirt-cheap," as a phrase, may be excellent English, but here in Lubaland dirt is not cheap, oh no, but costly, disease-gendering and deadly, in fact. Hence this curious innovation—a lecture on sanitation. Here they gather, massed in their thousands, my business being to pulverise prejudices. It turns out a famous gathering they will never forget, that seething black cloud melted from the distrust of an attack on old heathen ways of life to excited acquiescence when the thing was taken right out of our hands and made law. Shot after shot rang into the hill behind the town by way of ratification, and towards the end I darted in with—Christ crucified. They are utterly delighted to know that *we*, in the night of the Druids and later, were as bad as they. It was very good of them to let me down so softly, for my sanitary address was more poignant than polite. In order to convey the truth with entire fidelity, I had, in fact, dredged the dictionary for adjectives with some sting in them. Besides, we must remember that these dirty doings of theirs all enshrine great traditions, and I was really combating prejudices of a most bristly kind. However, at glad last, a ray of intelligence actually pierced the mists of the cannibal brain, and the whole mob caught at the extremely elementary idea that there is a weak futility in poisoning yourself with filth. Yet once again I admit that Aristotle was right, and that this one swallow does not make a summer in Africa.

Of course, crooked Nature has likewise trapped the

BLACK MAN = BLACK MANNERS 441

Mweru negro into very crooked sanitation—the old
story of the negro debasing his surroundings and the
surroundings taking revenge by debasing the negro. A
hundred huts packed together means that a smothered
incipient cough beginning away at the corner of the
hamlet is, in a few days, heard infectiously cough, coughing its way round the beehive town. But if so with an
elementary cough, how about the infectional terrors of
sleeping sickness? In Lubaland, as I now write, whole
towns are being wiped off the map—the *Nodder* they
call that disease. So, too, smallpox licks up a whole
population, the disease sweeping through the land like
the annual grass-fires. Here, then, we see them crowding
and verminating in their filth. Living in crowds they
must die in crowds, like the flock of five duck you can
shoot with one cartridge from that same stockade. For
the Luban duck are like the adjacent smallpox Africans,
they stupidly flock thickly, a half-dozen easily falling to
one shot. In Lubaland one burning arrow silently fired
into that grass village did literally burn the whole of
the mushroom edifices out of existence—a perfect type
this of what inflammable diseases do all over our weary,
Christless land.

Such, then, is the precious price they pay for the
plan of higgledy-piggledy. For the crooked ways of the
crooked negro have not yet been exhausted, and long ago
it must have been obvious to the most superficial reader
that this crooked sanitation must also breed a crooked
set of morals. Laugh at the Missionary as the modern

traveller must, we dare not hide the fact that the soul
of all improvement is the improvement of the soul.   The
infectious cough going round the town is only the type
of the infectious immoral gossip—there is no secret
hidden in that whole grass town.   The hundred huts are
only a whispering gallery, and what is told in the Bantu
ear is made known on the Bantu housetops.   Mere bairns
are corrupt and tainted at the cradle, life has no more
secrets for them.   Preach against it, and they only poke
the proverb at you, " What baby lion ever trembled at
his father's roaring ? "   Pour out on them your most
withering scorn, and they nag you thus : " If the tree has
grown up crooked it is because no one straightened it
when young."   Thus the negro river of morals is fouled at
its own fount ; the said fount being, so to speak, not a cool
mountain spring high up in the clouds, but rather one
of their own hot springs hiccuping down in the sweltering
plain.   Even the Missionary who makes a clutch at
these waifs being swept past in the current of sin can
only give them two hours or so of corrective school
training ; but, alas, against these few and fugitive hours
in the day you have the retrograde lapse of twenty-two
hours into heathen hovel-life.   Think of a whole heathen
family packed like pigs in one tiny little beehive hut !
Still clinging to forest figures of speech, they call these
tots of theirs *Tunsaala*, or twigs, elders by parity of
reasoning being big branches on the tribal tree—a happy
Missionary metaphor this to encourage any one working
in Africa among the young.   " For," say they, " how do

you set the camp logs blazing in the forest if not by first of all coaxing a few tiny twigs to catch fire, the six-feet-long logs soon flaming furiously from this humble initial ignition?" *N.B.:* The young teach the old, the twigs lead up to the branches, and the chips of the old blocks will send the said old blocks blazing. It's coming, oh, it's coming!

This packing of the domicile into one den, remember, is only an enlarged photo of the domicile packing itself with mush at supper-time. The same family who crowd each other out in one tiny hut is likewise seen crowding round one tiny pot, the big paws and the little paws all digging into the thick porridge in the same ratio as a soup-ladle and a salt-spoon. The negro argues that God, in perfect design, has dieted mankind according to the divine gradation in the size of human hands. Baby cannot eat too big spoonfuls if he uses his own little fists : "Little meat gives little sauce" is the native apology on this score. There is probably a moral in all this peculiarly pertinent to our poor prayers, to wit, what God gives us is better than what we can take. A Luban child asks her aunt for some pea-nuts. "Take a handful," says the elder. "You give me a handful, auntie; your hand is bigger"—to which we say, Bravo! for little Miss Salt-spoon, who scores an easy first against Mrs. Soup-ladle. Here, then, once again, you have a fruitful source of disease—a common pot with a dozen fists of varying degrees of cleanliness all putting the public health in jeopardy. Like the little bechive roof of his hut, with

27

all the matchwood rafters shooting up and converging into one apex, so, and much worse so, with these human hand-ladles and spoons, all shooting into the centre of gravity, all digging out from the mass of mush their voracious supper. Speaking is taboo at this sacred season. "Table-talk" is only the happy lot of other lands who boast of tables, but Mr. African dines on the earth that boasts of seed-time and harvest, and in the first instance gave them that bountiful meal. But the high crime and misdemeanour of the town is to dine alone—their very word "criminal" has this meaning, "Mr. Eat-alone." Such a one is a thief and has gone over to the wild beasts. For the notion of people assembling in order to absorb food is certainly not a natural idea: the lower animals never invite each other to dinner—on the contrary.

Here, then, is Africa's challenge to its Missionaries. Will they allow a whole continent to live like beasts in such hovels, millions of negroes cribbed, cabined, and confined in dens of disease? No doubt it is our diurnal duty to preach that the soul of all improvement is the improvement of the soul. But God's equilateral triangle of body, soul, and spirit must never be ignored. Is not the body wholly *ensouled*, and is not the soul wholly *embodied*? Too often in Missionary literature the writer talks about these "humble abodes" of his black parishioners, whereas the real phrasing of the matter is that they are more *humbling* than humble. The more grandiose our Mission stations, the more striking and impossible the native huts. The louder, too, the call to gut out these clotted masses of tropical slums. Ignore this as Africa's burning question, and you commit the sad old folly of the Middle Ages—I mean when the Church built big cathedrals and men lived in hovels. Ever since those days back in Bihe when I lived with Mr. Negro *chez lui*, I have a plan simmering in my mind, a plan that involves long one-street villages lined out for miles. The thing can be done, and we Missionaries should do it. Oh yes, we are here for souls, but—I repeat it—the negro soul is as wholly embodied as the negro body is wholly ensouled. In other words, in Africa the only true fulfilling of your heavenly calling is the doing of earthly things in a heavenly manner.

(Later.)

Penning, as I do, these lines long years after, here on my table is a measuring-tape that witnesses the success of this idea. That tape has helped to line out *six miles* of street frontage along our tangled Mweru. A whole tribe pluming itself on its dirty dens actually, *en masse*, took the idea up, burned its old huts and built long one-street hamlets along the edge of the cliff. Even the preposterous Lubans caught the idea of the thing, and the last developments in 1909 are a wonder. Writing on the spot, let me tell what happened. I am off these three weeks at a Luban town, living with a negro in his own mud hut; we go halves with the domicile and are in close touch. Just one year ago I had a rousing time here, then passed on, and seemingly after long years things have come to a head at last. Found them, as a township, a dark mass of dilapidated huts, and the problem was how to get them out of that hole and give them a fresh start. That was a year ago. Now all is so changed that " marvellous " is the true adjective qualifying the truest of nouns—*change*. After many years' tentative work in Africa, there seems (from a letter before me) a serious concession that it has been largely along wrong lines. The error lay in training exotic carpenters and joiners, who at once deserted their own tribe and went far ahead, to return never, never more. The clamant need is confronting the tribe as a whole, and " housing " it along sane, simple lines—two- or three-roomed cottages, that is to say.

To get a whole town so to arise after the sleep of centuries is a very thrilling thing; there is a quiver in the air, and you feel in a very true manner you are getting nearer the root of things. They do it all, their own houses built by and for themselves. Then away at the end of this new town of theirs, you can see the roof of the Bible-school, the point this where we link up the spiritual with the temporal. Man can see to the *housing* of a town, but God alone can see to the *homing* of it. And, remember, in the old dens of darkness the fount of life was poisoned : no home, no holy felicities of life—a human pigsty. The children of these holes we daily clutched at as they were daily swept past us, but the Mission school only has them for two hours, as against the long reactionary remainder of the day (and night !) in

LUANZA.
A Specimen of Town-planning.

heathendom. Hence this happy solution in the housing of the people, with the hope that God will "home" the people we have "housed."

Of course in fighting filth of this sort you must be ruthlessly efficient, and one old man even took the field and defended my action when I could scarcely do so myself. Kinder to me than I could be to myself, he, referring to the breaking with many a past custom, said, "How can you enter through an old abandoned doorway without first breaking the many cobwebs blocking entrance?" A concession this—and from a very old high-and-dry Tory—that their ancient ideas were cobwebs, nothing more. And here is my reward this trip, for I am now living with a raw Luban in his own three-roomed house: mark you, in his *house*, when a year ago you could not have slept in his town, the pestiferous hole being nigh mortal.

These lines are penned to the flicker of a tiny lamp burning linseed oil: not true linseed, really sesame, and not a bad light. This oil is grown for us by the Lubans: a new crop is just being planted, and these oil-growers speak about "growing" our light for us. Thus literally "light is sown for the righteous." Who ever heard of the Israelites having mineral oil? Obviously it must have been sown; and Christ the Light was sown in sorrow too.

But what about tools? you ask. Talk about economising your hardware—here is a snapshot I saw to-day, eloquent of the penury of centuries. The negro

—one of the illustrious family named "Smith"—was squatted under a tall clump of millet thirteen feet high, two old worn-out garden-hoes in his hand.   Mere "scrap-heap" iron now, they had done the season's farming for him : witness the waving millet in the background. "Now," quoth the negro endearingly to his broken scraps of hoes, " you have made unto me a harvest, and, go to ! let us make an axe to build a house wherein to dwell." So, sure enough, the transformation is soon going on apace.   First of all he manipulates two antelope-skins into a bellows, and then (dressed in skins himself) he starts to blow as loud as his bellows.   Then comes the funny business of a funnel for his blast furnace ; this moulded out of mother earth like the blacksmith himself.   Then we reach the item of coals—a heap of red iron-wood reduced to charcoal, which he soon puff-puffs into a blaze. And lo, the fire being now as red as it is ready, this son of Tubal Cain throws his two bits of hoes into the furnace and grips his hammer.   But what is this hammer ?   A nice round stone.   And what the anvil ?   The hammer's own cousin—another block of stone.   There are tongs, too—five, six, or seven strips of thick green bark all at hand, bark that bends at will into any shape of tongs he desires.   The very greenness of these bark tongs is their major value, for when, in welding, they bite the glowing iron, instead of burning like a match these tongs simply spit out their native juice, so that each pair of tongs can bite the red iron three times before ignition.   "Fighting flame" is what this Smith-by-name and Smith-by-trade

negro thinks he is doing, and the paradox of his poverty
is that he can always boast a wealth of these stone-age
anvils, hammers, and tongs, the very iron having been
dug out of the earth as a stone.

Thus he whirls round in his circle of existence, exactly
like the earth he dwells on. For the earth opened to
yield the iron—that made the ore—that made the field of
grain—that made strong the man—that made and unmade
the hoe—that made the axe—that made the cool cottage
in which he dwells : verily, *this* is the-house-that-Jack-
built. Why wonder that this model black strokes himself
down with complacency in the borrowed words : "Take
us all, professions and trades together, and you will find
by actual measurement round the head and round the
chest, and round our manners and characters, if you like,
that we blacksmiths are the only genuine aristocracy at
present in existence"?

More about polygamy. Things certainly get "curiouser and curiouser," as Alice had occasion to remark
in her travels in Wonderland. Among the Lubans man is
reckoned such a frigid monster that a woman is graciously
permitted to cook his meal, but may not eat of same.
She is caught in a cobweb of *Mbala* laws and by-laws, a
stringent point being that she cannot even speak during
the whole period of cooking and consumption of food.
Only after her giant is refreshed is this "covenant of
silence" formally annulled by the breaking of a stick
or straw into three fragments, each fragment kissed by
the lady as she throws it away, and then the remaining

third bit is broken between them. Sequel: three
pretences of shaking hands, the fingers not meeting,
however. And all this mummery at food for ever and
a day, and after every meal, the man receiving his
homage with a smug complacency. This kissing of the
fragments of stick by the lady-love is, of course, the
only kissing known in the tribe, for one of their bits
of banter against the white race is that they "lick each
other" as a greeting. The same woman this who has
built her own house, including even the final touches
of furnishing; the firewood and pots all her own finding
too. Let a Missionary pitch his tent in this town
and soon swarms of these ladies seek his serious
opinion anent their crooked conjugal relations. These
ladies suffer manifest distress and keep buzzing round
like a swarm of bees; snip-snap for hours, the African
women beating the men at putting posers. Now it is
one understands why, in the *only* negro lady's conversation contained in Scripture, it should be noted that
she asked (even!) Solomon "hard questions." From the
days of Sheba's queen they are all alike pouring out
puzzle-speech the livelong day. Wave them off, beseech
them to stop, implore them to change the subject: oh
no, all their gabble is concerning the holy estate. My
rule is to tell all such unblushingly that the woman
who wants her husband to be different generally wants
a different husband. Very often, though, the men are
brutes and to blame.

The usual story is that the plaintiff is Mrs. No. 1,

that she married him long ago when the world was younger and he and she at the mating age. Then came Mrs. No. 2 ; a pause, then Mrs. No. 3 intrudes on the friendship of Mesdames Nos. 1 and 2. According to this lady, it seems a mistake to say it takes two to make a quarrel, for here you have a woman arguing that two wives for one husband would be passable. What she does declare to be deadly is this terrible triangle, for just as it takes three straight lines to enclose a space, so seemingly it takes three wrangling wives to make a quarrel. At any rate, soon enough, the husband's snappish retorts tell No. 1 the tale that she has been superseded—yes—she who for so long took hungrily the crumbs of affection that fell from his table. The upshot of all this matrimonial muddle seems to be that ideal wedlock is considered only a solid bread-and-butter arrangement, and the best cook wins the worst of husbands. No royal glance of love ever (?) flashed from mate to mate, and the woman who ousts another woman only does so in order to enslave herself. Yet for centuries this has gone on, a concubine cook exerting all her blandishments to win a man's stomach, not his heart. Is this the reason why the word for stomach (*Munda*) is the same as for "heart"? No simple fireside virtues in demand here. Cook, only cook, and soon enough they find that the love that has ends, quickly has an end.

But there are more horrors here, and all suggestive of this land of uncounted tears. Between me and my

night's rest, lo, a heart-broken little girl weeping her
eyes out in the long grass. The spot is tangled, and
there is a rough overgrown heap—her mother's grave.
This orphan is seven years of age, and in the adjacent
village she was belaboured with blows to force her to
marry an old negro rake. So, with tear-soaked face,
away she darts from the dwellings of men, out, away
out to her mother's grave in the bush, one moan and
one only: "Oh, mother, why did you leave me out
here in the land of perplexities?" (*Pano pa kanshia*).
This led to a stormy encounter with the old *roué*, and
if anger be "a punishing of oneself for the fault of
another," then was I sorely punished. Without any
beat-about-the-bush circumlocution, here you have the
darkest smudge in a dark history—the baby-brides of
Africa. Here is a curse that must be faced and fought,
all the angels of God fighting for you. Yet they can
argue even this. Trying to talk me out of my
abhorrence, they insist that "baby-betrothal" is only their
tribal system of "Life Insurance," the idea being that
if the child comes to an untimely end then the husband
must pay the insurance money. But they forget to
say that "Mutual Insurance" is the real idea, and this
cuts both ways, the child having to pay for her old
husband's demise. Here, then, is a so-called Insurance
really *ensuring* one thing—the misery of the tiny
widow.

Our Sera neighbours over the hill are a bad lot.
There I found more people buried alive. But is this kind

of thing really authentic? The answer is that the best
sort of African proof is always that genuine thing you
yourself stumble over in the grass, accidentally. Here is
an instance. Down in the Sera plain I put up for the
night in a random hamlet on the edge of the bulrush-bog.
At sundown here come a crowd of merry bairns round
me, as happy with their white visitor as a cat in the
fender. But now for a change of metaphor. Then they
begin to prattle like starlings, putting many a poser to
poor me, big questions from little folks — why not?
Should not a big horse take a big fence? Next we
exchange names as per Luban courtesy. The first little
girl of my gossip is much more strikingly well dressed
than all the crowd, so much that one opines she is a
personality, the local magnate's daughter perhaps. But
when I probe inquisitively about her nice beads, nicer
calico, and fantastic hair-coiffure, it soon begins to dawn
on me that this really harmless interlocutor is painfully
embarrassing. Had village elders been around, of course,
I would never have got wind of that tragedy at all, but
here are a dozen precocious little chatterers telling me
the tale. Describing, if you please, most graphically how
they killed this little *mode de Paris* girl's mother at the
last funeral. That she is no Chief's daughter at all at
all; and that, in fact, she has only been paid so much
"hush-money" for her mother's death, witness these
blue beads and fancy calico. Mother had gone on the
long, lonely journey with the Chief, who had always an
escort in life, and must not be deprived of one in death,

the orphan child receiving "solatium and damages" for her mother's sacrificial death. She herself, though, would grow up, only to be one day fuel for the same fire. So much for the tell-tale vouchers you stumble over among the villages, and the next best criterion is the thing you *overhear* in Africa. Remember, the "Socratic method" of fishing for facts, by questions, is Africa's greatest peril : is not an African only an echo of his querist ? (Besides —oh, pitfall for the unwary—unless you conjugate your verb of interrogation in the subjunctive mood, you don't ask a question, *but dictate an answer*.) On the 7th January, down the Lualaba, I overheard and jotted down a "sacrifice" talk going on : the white man is supposed to be sleeping, and this is what comes over his shoulders. Chimunwa's brother stretched out his lame leg to his listeners, then tenderly and approvingly patted its only four toes. Quoth he : "Ah, you may laugh at 'Game-leg' (*Chilemakulu*), but proud am I to have only four toes." "Why ?" chorused the company expectantly. "The lack of my fifth toe on my left foot," answered he, "is my life. They were going to make me one of the sacrifices at ——'s funeral, but a sacrifice with a blemish won't do, so I got off scot free." The point again made in that talk was that as in life the dead Chief owned the country and its inhabitants, it was obviously absurd to think he should be allowed to go all alone on the "long journey" of death without company. Then came a snatch of pure Bantu which unconsciously was a literal quotation from Isaiah : "The bed is shorter than a man can lie on in the world of the dead." This, to prove the loneliness of the tomb and the need for company.

To press again for the reason of all that murder is to receive this time a utilitarian explanation. Piercing below the stratum of the sacrificial idea, you reach that deepest deep in human nature, the law of self-preservation. It is only the African Tsar's plan for securing himself immunity from the anarchist's bomb—merely the King's threat that if they kill him, then in revenge he will die, dragging many down with him to the grave. Hence the negro song of warning—

> "As the forest trees rock
>   When the wild winds blow,
> The King's death is a shock,
>   For how bloody the woe!"

But is there no glint of sunshine in it all? Yes—and very much yes. Life is full of contrasts in Africa, and one such bloody sacrifice was really the means of breaking a bad heart of adamant. This was our pioneer elder of the Garenganze church, the late Smish, who was an executioner in the old days. Behold him hurrying to her premature death a young mother with her babe, when the poor doomed woman at the grave's mouth took the baby and, forgetful of her own impending death-pangs, sobbed out, "Oh, deal kindly with my bairn!" (*Ikala viya ne Kana Kami*). Smish never forgot that stab— I mean the royal glance of maternal love this mother flashed to her bairn was never forgotten. Poor baby, on being torn from her, did not know how he stabbed his dear dying mother in the expostulating cry, "Mama! Mama!" Years after, in contrition of heart, the memory of that dying sob stabbed his soul, and when he heard of Christ praying for His enemies he thought likewise of that dying woman's prayer.

Watch how we conciliate these cut-throats. Picture a tall hunter of powerful build, with a smile that would frighten a bull-dog. But when his tale is told, it is a wonder he has a smile at all. Have not two years dragged past since his right arm was torn to pieces by the bursting of his old "five feet of gas-pipe" gun? The story runs that, being a big brave black, he had enough of the child left in him to want his weapon to go off with a bang; so, one day in hunting, he loaded up inordinately, the charge of powder nearly a foot deep in the barrel. Of course, the bang that should have flattened the elephant on the ground burst back on the hunter, and the biter was bit. Thus began the twenty-four dragging months of agony, when the quacks from far and near exploited the gaping wound until the one became many. At last, we come on the scene, and the problem now stands how to break this ring of rascals and cure our man. Well, plucky Mrs. Crawford, after much judicious wheedling, finally conciliated the whole gang of kinsmen, the stoutest objector being the man's own wife, who resentfully sniffed a very gem of a sniff in protest. To the last, this good lady—one of the well-meaning, fussy type—turned up her nose at the idea of a "death-sleep" operation; but this turning up of her nose was not to be wondered at,

for the said snub-nose is naturally adapted for that purpose. Yet was she a kindly little body, and no doubt it
was out of genuine affection for the sufferer she resented
the terribly business-like look of the table and gleaming
instruments. Just as a peaceful cat dozing in the sunlight becomes a thing of bristling wickedness and fury
when an enemy comes on the scene, even so Mrs. Hunter
and her dislike of this "death-sleep." But, at last, we
won her round. Result : a splendidly successful ampu-
tation of the arm by my pioneer wife, the poor hunter
getting the first moment of peaceful calm in two years
when he entered that soft fleecy cloud of chloroform.
Then after three days, all the premature wrinkles of pain
smoothed out of his brow, and once again the old *joie
de vivre* flamed up in his face—a triumph of antiseptic
surgery. In the coming years, no doubt, when Africa is
a gridiron of railways, smart brick hospitals will grace
these latitudes, but no surgeon will ever boast of such
fame as this "death-sleep" lady and her pioneer
operation.

The scene changes, and here is a whole town in the
terrors of toothache, my dental patients numbering not
ten, twenty, or thirty, but actually more than fifty. "The
lion of the mouth is roaring" is the tribal phrase for toothache, and the only remedy known is to attack the tooth
with an axe. That is to say, they bring the tortured
negro up to the axe, then fitting in a plug of hard wood
against the stubborn tooth, the axe crashes against the
plug, sending the tooth, in some cases, down the man's

throat. No wonder when the theory of my forceps spread
abroad the whole town tumbled to the thing with joy, one
woman with perfectly good teeth running up like a mad
thing and distorting her mouth for me to operate. " Oh
no," explained she, with a soft sigh, " I have not toothache, but the lion of the mouth will roar after you are
gone." The raw bulk of my dental patients, however, had
one sing-song plaint translated thus into honest, thick-
skulled Hodge dialect : " You needn't mind which, they
all aches at times." Yet this is the tribe that boasts the
ancient proverb, " The teeth have no substitutes," and the
very notion of an Englishman wearing false teeth sets
them frantic with excitement. So ho, the ancients were
out, for the teeth *have* excellent substitutes. The Luban
fad in the fashion of teeth is that the four lower front
teeth must be knocked out, and any of the household not
so maimed is compelled to shut the door every night as a
punishment.

On the Garenganze shore of Lake Mweru, and nestling
at the foot of the Bukongolo Cliff, you find the average
fishing settlement hidden in a cloud of millions of
mosquitoes. The typical hamlet lies at the north of a dark
glen down which runs a mountain stream, and on the
Lake side it is shut off from view by dense pith-tree
forests, a weird picture these, approximating to a mangrove
swamp. Year by year, the rich foreshore along the foot
of the cliff is growing in size, the mountains sending down
boulders and also a rich diluvial soil which mixes with the
beach sand. This amalgam is a garden land passing rich

and, owing to the inroads of Mweru, just the desideratum
for rice-growing. For such a huge expanse of water, the
crocodiles are surprisingly scarce, an African river always
boasting more than a lake. This penchant for rivers by
" crocs " is seen even on the Lake, where the confluence of
any stream is a sure, almost the only sign of the enemy.
And no wonder the fisher-folk coined the phrase " stealing
water " from Luapula. In order to strike fear of these
oily lurking crocodiles into the hearts of their young
people, the ordinary message a mother delivers to her
child is : " Go and steal some water from the crocodiles ! "
This persistent dread of being snapped has given the Shila
child phenomenally quick eyes, and their mode of mani-
pulating the water-jar has almost an element of jugglery
in it. I remember one dark day when a fisherman lost
his child by a crocodile, and on going out for his nets
found that there too they had forestalled him, a huge one
having torn his nets to tatters. Nor does the fatalistic
negro even attempt to better things for the tribe. The
elephant's penchant for " warranted pure water," however,
is often a means of its death, the harpoon-trap being
usually set in his tracks leading to water. Here is an
example just at my elbow. There is a great roaring outside, and it turns out that a young lad, Walepa, has killed
a monster elephant. Ever since Mrs. Crawford put this
lad under chloroform and cut off his arm, Walepa had
been thought useless, but he certainly killed his elephant
in a most ruthlessly efficient manner. The negroes who
plume themselves on having two arms are now showering

28

compliments upon him, punctuated with hand-clapping.
The boy had heard that elephants were coming to drink
at an adjacent river, so setting out with his brother he
struck their trail leading to water.   Taking advantage of
an overhanging high tree, he climbed and set a trap-spear
overhead, the missile of death pointing " dead-on " the
elephant's trail leading to water.   But how was he to
make sure that the spear as it crashed down would pierce
a vital spot ?   This he planned most slyly.   Climbing the
tree with a small gourd of water, he asked his brother to
stand with back bent full in the trail below.   And now
for the stroke of genius.   He forthwith proceeds to sight
the spear by aiming at his brother's backbone with the
dripping water : drip ! drip ! until a drop finally struck
the backbone.   What next ?   The heavy spear is now
aimed " dead," and the youth descends, as he naïvely puts
it, " to see what God will do with a boy's spear."   Sure
enough, a brief hour sees the whole boyish plot crowned
with fruition.   Shivering with fear, the crash of approaching elephants is heard, and the monster bull, as it trumpets
near the water, receives its death-blow from the descending
barbed spear.   The negroes glory in that filthy, frothy
meat, but it is not edible to Europeans.   It would need
not a cook, but a magician, to prepare it.   The ivory is
valued at sixty guineas.   But King Leopold's long arm
reaches out for all the ivory, the resultant revenue to
be nobly devoted to charity—the charity that begins at
home.

Ranging the Lake with your eye in April, you can

descry a curious procession of Sindbad-the-Sailor floating
islets, "Bob-abouts" (*Visera*) their name. Really clotted
masses of papyrus, duck-weed, and Phragmites, these have
been swept down by the Luapula current, the rug and tug
of the eddies tearing them from the parent bank of the
river. So launched in the first instance on their long
voyage by the swirling Luapula, this same current pilots
them far down-Lake, their destination being any of the
capes jutting out to debar farther advance. Funny fact
though it looks, it is really these floating islands that have
crowded Kilwa in mid-Lake with leopards, and the islanders
tell the tale quite circumstantially. There came a dark
day when, like a pirate flying the black flag, one such
floating island grounded on the South shore of Kilwa with
a young male leopard aboard, a poor quadruped Adam
this, without an Eve. One year passed and yet another,
and lo, a charming lady-leopard came across, cabin
passenger, if you please, in the cosy depths of another
floating island. At this point in the fisher narrative the
naked old "Admiral" of canoes sticks his hands into
imaginary pockets and drops his jaw. Need he add the
sequel? Both at the mating age, that quadruped Eve
really robbed them of their Eden, for are there not now as
many leopards as negroes on the island? The theory that
these leopards swam across such an expanse of Lake is
absurd, albeit a leopard is the best swimmer of all African
Carnivora. The snug depths of these floating islands are
shady and seductive enough to account for such curious
cabin passengers. But better far than all this is the

splendid shelter all such afford to a poor fisherman in a dug-out when struck by a white squall. To avoid sudden swamping he darts his canoe, nozzle first, into the soft pulpy island, and away they sail together, island and canoe, the fisherman as dry as a kiln in his cool shelter of rank floating grass. "Life-belt Island" we named one such, for it saved a sailor's life. Here is a native who believes that God could not love His Son, since He gave Him up to die. His reason is that his grandfather was the famous Mwalumuna, who taught what true paternal love was. When far out on Mweru his canoe foundered. Letting his wife sink, he battled on and on for hours in the rough water, with his five-year-old son now on his back and now on his breast. Sunset saw them safe on Kilwa Island among the Arabs, who laugh at the idea of such risk of life. Their proverb runs, "If the water come like a deluge, place thy son under thy feet"—a reference this to the Arab tradition that when Noah's rebel sons felt the flood gaining on their mouths to choke them they put their sons under their feet.

The hippo is a great factor in fisher-life, and poor young Duvivier was killed off Mulonde River by a wild one not far from our door. The majority of Mweru hippos have been galled off and on by the harpoons of the fishermen, and the only safe shot is from the land. Duvivier had given his animal a first shot and was hoping to draw upon it decisively when the maddened brute charged from beneath, so that probably the brave young fellow was engulfed in its mouth, for I could not find his body after dredging for four days. The curious fact in connection with these Mweru hippos is that they are grouped in austere "schools," called *Matanga*, the various schools all known intimately and boasting of personal names like *genus homo*. Thus the old grandpa hippo is "Mulonde senior," while grandma is popularly known as "Mrs. Kafulo," the sons and grandsons all boasting of a serious "postal address" appellation. Great excitement prevails among the children of the fishing hamlet when a bumpy-faced little baby-hippo pops its head above water to proclaim its advent into hippodom. A queer little caricature of a hippopotamus, heated wrangles take place among the youngsters over its christening name, and I found one small boy at Mulonde offering to fight the whole crowd (in the order of seniority), rather than yield his nomination for the brand-new pink hippo-baby's name. Feeding as they do at the rate of five bushels per night, the poor fishers' fields are raided recklessly; but a Shila man only shrugs his shoulders and, pointing out to the waves of the Lake, says, "Yonder is my well-furrowed field!" The same idea this as when, paddling his canoe, he claims to be "a miller of water" instead of a miller of flour. This serious fact as to a hippo's fixed domicile is only proved by the occasional seeming exception when a young bull-hippo "marries out" of the school. For although he hives off and marries into another school many miles distant, yet whenever he is badly wounded you can see him putting out to sea, and blowing like a porpoise as he steers straight for the old "postal address." In the grip of an imperative intuition, that homing hippo makes a bee-line for the old place where, as a pink baby, it was christened by the fishers' children. It is a Medo-Persic law among hippos that they must die where they were born.

But to return to our Lake-dwellers. These Shila fishermen are plucky salts who hunt the hippo with harpoons on their "coggly" dug-outs. The Lake is full of a very pugnacious sort, which crush their canoes on occasion. On the 3rd July, at the South end, a boat of hunters shouted to me to come and help, and sure enough on coming up with them I found, like whalers playing a whale, they had a hard hippo in hand. He had received two harpoons and was making away with them both—tugging at the rope like a dog pulling at his chain. The local hippo clan had turned out to the rescue, surrounded their less fortunate fellow, put him most loyally in the centre and kept him there, defying the hunters to break through their clannish circle. It was a real sight to see that belt of big heads keeping hippo guard. Once and again the men broke through, evoking only reverberating roars from the enraged guardians, and narrowly escaping a capsize. On came the sturdy "dug-outers" with loud, ostentatious splashing. On came the heroic hippos with a rush to the tournament. And what a kill ! Floating usually four hours after death, this one died in the sulks and his brethren of the hippo school tucked him away under the tangled papyrus.

Farther along a bull-hippo charged me in a dug-out in his best swashbuckler style. Waited for him quietly, as in two or three plunging springs he came on, bowling and bellowing in rage ; then got a bullet in through his open mouth. A momentary and momentous hush, then up he comes with a suffocating, explosive noise, spouting blood. Anon, taking the whole Thames-at-Westminster-Bridge width of the Lualaba, he floundered and writhed in his death-struggle, lashing the placid water into foam. The final act was to throw himself theatrically up in the air, then, with a sucking swirl, he sank like a stone. The curious touch about it all is that these hardy blacks are naked to the blast, the idea being that, as they *must* get wet, a cold clammy calico clinging to their body is worse than a natural and normal nudity. In fact, these droll Shila folk take this matter of dress so seriously that they have worked out at a solution exactly the opposite to ours. For the same man who fishes *in puris naturalibus* can be seen, under broiling vertical rays, sporting two blankets, our nude fishing friend being now rolled up like a huge sausage in his coils of calico.

A smile got the better of me when old Nyemba began to speak seriously of "his goats," meaning the local school of hippos. This note of proprietorship in his possessive pronoun was smile-provoking when one reflected that the said hippos claimed old Nyemba's fields so very much as *theirs* : does not each hippo sup on his five bushels of vegetables per night without asking the

Chief's permit? On leaving, I reminded Nyemba of this by way of a parting quip; but a challenge of this kind rarely finds him reluctant, so the old man bade me condescend to wait a moment for obstinate, ocular proof that the precious hippos were really his. In relating what happened, I confine myself to facts, eschewing imputations. The Chief mysteriously whistled up all the local ladies, and made them group themselves on the end of the island, the water, be it noted, as clear as plate-glass, and for hours no hippo visible. Had not I been searching for hippos the whole morning, prepared to shoot upon the least hint of a ripple? Well, at the Chief's magician signal this band of women sent out a weird shriek to the water, and as by a miracle a school of five black hippo heads came up to the glassy surface with a gasping roar as obedient salute. One responsive glance they gave at the group of women, and in a second all was calm again, the hippos bobbing below water. Real living hippos, truth to tell, albeit I had spent weary hours trying in vain to sight even one for our larder, all declining obstinately to show up. Yet here was old "black art" Nyemba with a school of hippos, so to speak, hidden up his sleeve, the homelier diction of the sleeveless Luban for this phrase being "hidden up in his armpits." But the old Master of Ceremonies resolved to "rub in" this idea of his proprietorship of these hippos, so once again he made assurance doubly sure. "Try again, my girls," he shouted to the women waving his staff like a magician's wand; and once more,

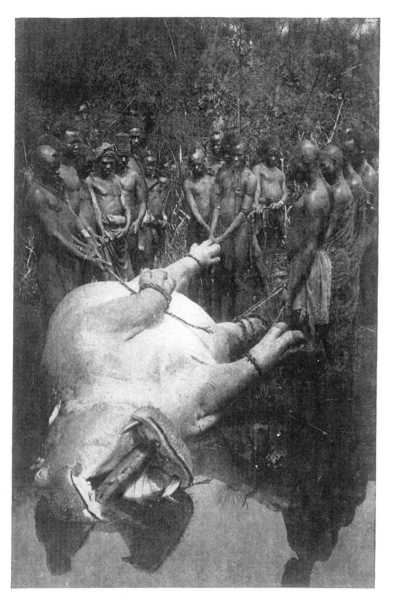

FOUR THOUSAND POUNDS OF BEEF.
At 6d. the lot.

like a gramophone record, the same magic shriek rent the same still air with the same magic appearance of the hippos. I spent the whole night wondering what this *homo*-hippo league meant at all at all, and—and I am wondering still. Call it "black art" if you like, I prefer to think of old Nyemba as an artful black : the phenomenally long time these huge hippos were submerged is not such a puzzle after all, for it seems as if the hippo's very ungainly bulk is in its favour. That is to say, with lungs full of air, his specific gravity thereby becomes almost equal to that of water, with the result that he can coolly walk or run along the bottom of the river-bed as though it were dry land.

With a land of this sort that can boast not one butcher's shop, sometimes the Missionary with his own right arm can open up a long-shut tribe by a happy kill of hippo—fancy thousands of pounds of beef for one bang of a gun. The killing of one such monster gave us our first footing on the Luapula. By a long detour of miles and months here we come out on the Luapula, striking the left bank a few miles below the Falls— object : to pick a Mission site at Johnston Falls.[1] Advancing from the West this time has made the muddle, for the off-bank is agog with excitement, my quondam friends "turned to be my enemies." Across the stream they throw many a dainty morsel of black logic : "You

---

[1] Mr. Pomeroy began here, then came Mr. and Mrs. Anderson, then Mr. Campbell and others. The second phase of this station was when Mr. and Mrs. Lamond and Mr. Sims retired back from the river to Kaleba, Mr. and Mrs. Campbell branching off to begin work on Lake Bangweulu.

came" (this is the sort of thing) "from the North only three months ago, and now you come from the West, therefore you are not you." My answer, of course, is the eager echo: "I certainly am I, but you are not you, because I guard the *entente cordiale* (*Chipwane*) while you set it at naught." There goes Chief after Chief filing past on the off-bank with the biggest muster of guns he ever made, every man of them munching this apple of discord, "Why advance from the West, when you came from the North?" A reminder this, that in Central Africa nearly all the polemics arise from our negro's prejudices as to a suspected point of the compass—instance, Sir Alfred Sharpe repelled for coming from the East, and Hannington murdered because he entered Buganda from Busoga. Nor avails it to reply like a wordy windbag. Deeds are the only eloquent words in such a fix, so I produced quite a knock-down argument by—inviting the whole tribe to dine with us. Depend upon it, the world's slums are all alike, slum street, slum town, or slum tribe, and the simplest solution is—to open a huge soup kitchen, free tickets for Chiefs and slaves. This is that line of least resistance so inelegantly rendered in the Luapula alliterative proverb, "Brow of brass, but belly of butter." Curious way of capturing a tribe, camping on its utmost border and asking your enemies out—to supper. Without money and without price those soup tickets—and no wonder! For the net local cost of my four tons of hippo-meat worked out at the round sum of—sixpence. Eight thousand nine hundred and eighty pounds of meat, not at 6d. per lb., but the whole 8980 lb. costing a single and solitary sixpence.

This is how it came about. Slipping over to the hostile bank by stealth at sundown, I killed a monster hippo in its very best days. Tried the temple shot, and the bullet zigzagged through the brain—magic bullet that, for did it not metaphorically slay also the enmity of my hundreds of enemies? Listen to yonder glad cry on the off-bank; the news catches on, drums beating and clouds of canoes darting across in the dusk to verify the kill. Canoes, *nota bene*, yet there were no such things in these latitudes yesterday—oh no, scarcely knew what a canoe was. Now, where the carcass is, there are the vultures gathered together—and in boats, too. Yesterday they shot angry glances at us—now, picture the same softened eyes with that dreamy look one sees in a kitten's when it smells frying fish. Yesterday they were lolling in the sun, a tribe of indolents. Here they are at a later phase rushing on this beef with the tense concentration of a crowd making for the refreshment-room at a station where the train stops three minutes. But do not quote too quickly against them Paul's "whose god is their belly"; do so, and you are at the bad old business of beating a cripple with his own crutches. He has got a reason, and here it comes. That is to say, such a serious chemist is this negro, that if you give him plain flour with no "relish," he will go to bed hungry rather than touch mere carbo-hydrates without the adequate albuminoids. In other words, that ravenous shriek of his you

hear at the hippo banquet has one meaning only—
Nitrogen ! Why is it that the African alone has special-
ised here and coined a word for " meat-hunger " (*Kashia*) ?
Why a special substantive if not that there is a specially
substantial craving behind it ? He ravens on that meat,
his very blood and bone crying out like chemists for the
needed nitrogen. Red raw flesh covered with blood is the
thing beloved of the negro—torn off the animal just after
it has been shot, muscles still quivering.

CHAPTER XXIII

"The Year of Love": an Epilogue

"For while the tired waves dimly breaking
    Seem here no painful inch to gain,
Far out, by creeks and inlets waking,
    Comes silent, flooding in, the main."

      *   *   *

"The noisy waves are a failure, but the silent tide
is a success."   PHILLIPS BROOKS.

      *   *   *

"Such a tide as moving seems asleep,
    Too full for sound and foam."   TENNYSON.

CHAPTER XXIII

Epilogue

(Luanza.)

KNOW ye, therefore, that unquenchable hope was crowned at last, for the glad year 1905 was termed *Mwaka wa Lusa*, or " the Year of Love." Somebody drew blank when he said that Hope makes a good breakfast but a bad supper, for there is no throb of joy akin to the darkest hour merging into dawn. For look what befell us. At Koni, Johnston Falls, and Luanza it was the same story and the same time.

All these sterile years the Gospel had been stored up in Garenganze folk mentally, like so much sound money that returned no interest. They listened, and they watched us with their ferret eyes, and, of course, they had their difficult questions to ask, yet answer some of them we could not. I admire your African, because you can never get out of a difficulty with him under the fog of a definition. He may have a funny figure-of-eight twist in his query, but it is always to the point. Alas ! the average white man's remarks to the negro, though lacking *point*, are always *pointed*. The story of these long sterile years of sowing was supremely simple from the African's standpoint. Intruding, as we had done, into his darkness

473

with our Gospel of God, the said Gospel made too preposterous and impossible a claim upon him. Hence his blunt
black challenge to the Missionary : " Well, you just sit
down here and live your Gospel for twenty years or so,
and *then* we will believe you." Thus, for nearly a generation, did the negro's face set in those obstinate lines of
Christ-rejection so well known to us, and it has taken all
that time for the truth to get home to his hard heart that
all our Gospelling was not the mere effusion of a passing
excitement. This " pegging away " is what the African
calls " the pertinacity of a fly," the compliment being
equivocal, as most African flies have a sting in them.
Some flies, like some Missionaries, even give " sleeping
sickness "—a curious sort of jag that must be if it makes
you sleep instead of wakening you up. And " sting " is
the very idea in bush-preaching, for the unblushing sin
forces Evangelist to be as plain as John Bunyan. Hence
that negro obstinacy, and, if you have only pertinacity
enough, the said obstinacy can easily work out at
malignity. Mr. Pecksniff has not yet been born in
Central Africa, and, as we have seen, the nude negro has
nude speech : one cheery old gentleman used to exhort
us in the *pros* and *cons* of this attack of ours on the
citadel of the negro soul. " Remember," said he, " if you
hit the body only on one spot you will soon raise a lump."
This is true enough, for although you can easily laugh and
chat yourselves into the good graces of a negro, yet
remember *that* is only the nominal surface black man you
have conciliated. Scratch this coloured Russian on the

subject of sin and you verily find a Tartar. The hint of obstinacy is seen in the very set of the jaw. No, mere sophistry will not break him, and only the power of God can make him throw the doors of his nature open to the Christ. But the "raising of a lump" is only one side of the "pegging-away" story, and the very cheery face of our old exhorter was enough to make you ask where his lump was after so much sermon-tasting. "But," says this old man, "there is another aspect to this Gospel-thumping of yours, and remember also, O white man, that if you beat the drum on one spot only you will crack it." Sure enough, the very next day one of the biggest drums the Devil owned in the country was cracked. B—— was a notorious thief who had been in the Belgian chain more than once, and many a time he had wept, not the tears of penitence, but of revolt. For years, with a customary placidity, he had gone the hard way of rebellion. "Wasted" was the word my pen had almost tricked me into writing concerning the pile of religious ammunition directed against all such. But "is not My Word a Hammer?" said the Lord, and that holy hammer broke him. For what the Congo law could not do (by sjambok and chain), in that it was weak through Butugu's sinful flesh, God did in power. Ah, there is nothing breaks the rebel's back like the flash of memory—"My God hath remembered me."

Leading up to this "Year of Love," what was the raw native's line of defence, or had he any? Slaves, for instance, whose souls were ploughed with the ploughshare of anguish, why did they not troop under the Christ's banner? The curious answer is found in their deep-seated idea that this only was of God, this, the raw heathendom in which God had caused them to be born. Not once, but a hundred times, have I heard the native claim " God " as the Author of it all. " God's law " (*Mukanda wa Leza*) was the phrase for all their tribal customs, and the very variety of men and manners on the face of the earth was their argument against the unity that is in Christ. There are genuine phrases that have gone the round of the Garenganze for centuries, which, literally translated, look like the language of pious resignation : " Ah, God's time has not come yet." "Had it been God's gift to you, you would have got it." " God is great : whoever conquered Him? He killeth even the aristocrats." And so on, in dark fatalistic sing-song, the name of God bandied about on every subject, and blowing in on the soul like a cold Arctic blast. I have met serious students of theology who were embarrassed because the Africans have no idea of Satan and his sinister personality, whereas the real puzzle would be to find out how they could possibly know of the existence of a specific fallen angel named Diabolus, *alias* Satan. The master-stroke of the Devil is that he, in Africa, has not only lied most subtly all the centuries against God, but has hidden himself behind his own lie.

> " And so they've voted the Devil out
> And of course the Devil's gone,
> But simple people would like to know
> Who carries his business on."

Yet God was over all even then, and in some crude sense these poor wanderers from Him were under a schoolmaster leading them to Christ. Crudely, granted, yet even Paul dignifies that intuition of theirs by the exalted name of "law" when he insists that they, too, are a "law unto themselves." One of the strongest threads in the fabric of their national life is the austere creed of taboo, and here is a fresh "as we go to press" example. Just a minute ago I tried hard to get a tiny boy named Kasongo to eat a fish. Pinched with hunger, here was a little nipper with no "moral" backbone, yet he shut his milk teeth, and defied all my entreaty. No, he dare not break tribal taboo, dare not touch fish, wheedle him as you may. Poor superstition of course it all is, but at least the negro breed is thereby stronger in grit and tenacity of purpose, and in some sense this loyalty to law-keeping does not soften the fibre of his black mind. In fact, the day this type of negro weeps for sin will be the same glorious date when that very negro will welcome Christ into his life by the front door of fearlessness and not by the back door of cowardice. Nor will you need to spend long hours indoctrinating him with ideas as to the sanctity of law *per se*. He has got *that* in his bones, for in his own tribal taboo did he not "play the game"? Thus Christ subjugates all things unto Himself, and instead of casting away the old spear of taboo, he now converts it into a Gospel ploughshare. Is there no taboo in the Ecclesia? I trow there is. Are there no holy "thou shalt not's" in Christianity? And did the negro

29

not spend his life learning how sacred even a human "thou shalt not" can be?

Then, again, quite a bright streak of hope is seen in the conversion of chiefs of honourable status in the land. K——, one of these, tells his conversion in a manly, precise way. Chief on the Bukongolo Range, he says he often came down from the hills to attend the meetings, ay, even in the rain he made a try to be there. "Believe?" says he; "No, I wore out two gospel halls in Christ-rejection." Quaint idea to think of wearing out a hall as you wear out an old pair of boots. The first mud hall was eaten by white ants and had to be replaced by another, and as K—— saw even a third hall while yet a rebel at heart, this poignant fact was the straw that broke the camel's back: "I have actually worn out two meeting-houses in Christ-rejection." No beauty he, only one of the old cut-throats who did Mushidi's dirty work for a dirty reward. But the Gospel has even done something for his ugly face, for the old doggy and insinuating leer is gone and the gleam of the life eternal shoots out of the eyes. How true that a negro's black face is, after all, not the same thing as his countenance! God makes a man's face, but a man makes his own countenance. Certainly handsome is as handsome does in Africa, and old K—— has got one thing at any rate out of Christianity, for the dynamic of the Cross sends him to bed with a sweet mouth and a clean mind. At first, all alone in his own town, he had a hard battle, the saved chief and his wilful people being at daggers drawn. Christ seemingly, as of yore, had not come to send peace in their midst, but a sword, and the old tug-of-war between right and wrong began. No sugar-plum expressions here, for light fights darkness with a glittering blade, the gleam being all the brighter in the inky blackness. Like a living tree in a timber-yard, he grew nobly, and now, after six years, he has won a small nucleal band of Christians who daily meet in his town. Thus those stunted, stifled souls at long last get a chance. Like a toy town hall in the centre of his village you can descry a nice schoolhouse he has built for his people.

Too many Africans see Christ in a book as we see places in a map, but here is a genuine case of a young man converted by merely reading John's Gospel. Too big for our elementary school, he went his own way in sin, but still clung to his copy of John as a fetish. Then old Africa—the Africa of sin and sorrow—began to wind its tentacles round him, and he was speedily becoming the usual bleared-of-eye negro with whom Jesus Christ is the Great Unmentionable in his unhallowed hut. But he was reckoning without God and the Word of God, which is not bound—did he not still cling to his copy of John's Gospel? Well, watch the divine logic of events involved in the treasure of a truth that "where the word of a King is, there is power." One day the gun-cotton of John's Gospel came in contact with the tinder of his rebellion, and this K—— was literally exploded into the kingdom. For out from the pages of "John of the Bosom" came the assertive call, "Follow Me!" and that one word rugged off the terrible tentacles from his soul. K—— can only explain his conversion in the quaintly choice words: "I was startled to find that Christ could speak Chiluba. I heard Him speak out of the printed page, and what He said was, 'Follow Me!'" And then it was he entered the new era of reading the Old Book, for was it not a fact that now God was staring out at him from every page, and shouting in his ears? Those rays of light that darted out of Galilee long ago have lit up these poor dark glens with gladness. Simply and satisfyingly a soul settles for eternity on the living Word of God. An old negro chief from the South end has just sent in a message to his brethren here, and there is the same ring of assurance as to the Word of God. "Tell my brethren at Luanza," says he, "that Christ keeps me down here all alone by the Gospel according to Mark." The only portion of the Bible he has, to him "Mark" equates the whole revelation of God, and even "Romans" and "Ephesians" are only portions of the great "Marko," his first and faithful friend. Sterile though the soil be, the seed is the Word of God: you may count the apples on the tree, but who can count the trees in the apple? You may tell the acorns on the oak, but not the oaks in the acorn.

Yet such thick lips can drop pearls. It is delightful to see God taking up these Gentiles, and speaking with other lips and a stammering tongue, stiff old phrases going into the melting-pot of negro mouths and being poured out in fresh fluidity. "The Book of Acts," for instance, becomes "Words concerning Deeds"; "the

Lord's Table" becomes the "Feast of Memories," or the
"Table of Tears"; and as worship is in the spirit they
have cleverly coined the verb "to spirit" as the true
ideal of approach to God, for what but spirit can reach
"*The* Spirit"? Perceive the astute negro at this most
sensible word-coinage, for *pepa* is the verb "to spirit,"
just as, say, "a drink" is a noun with "to drink" as its
satellite verb. Sensible all this surely, for there you
have an otherwise materialistic negro ignoring the mere
sight of his eyeballs and talking away to nothing visible
with shut eyes—he is "spiriting," *i.e.* worshipping. Deep-
sea sounding some of their happy thoughts are. "Eternity," for example, is called "the lifetime of God
Almighty," and the gift of Life Eternal is merely a
pledge that they will live as long as God lives, eternal
death being "a dying as long as God is living." When
you, their white teacher, blunder along in your exposition
it is not uncommon to see a far-away look on your
hearers' faces, painfully suggestive of the fact that they
are all off on a scent of their own! For what to you
may be a mere commonplace of normal Christian thought
—"Book of Acts," for example—is to him full of sweet,
subtle suggestion—"Words about Deeds"—a full current
of new thought switched on. Sure, here it is we all learn
how much we have yet to learn, every truth in Africa
being like a bit of Labrador spar—it has no lustre as
you turn it in your hand until you come to a particular
angle, then it shows deep and beautiful colours. But
what if you miss the said angle precisely when your

negro spies it? This fact it is that sends your audience off on its own, the speaker losing the lustre at the precise moment when the black man has caught the accurate angle of flashing light. Thus, in Africa, what you do not say is often more eloquent than your long windy homily. Yes, black as coal every one of them; yet, after all, diamonds *are* made of soot, albeit the how, when, and where of the miracle we may not know. Moreover, it doth not yet appear what this black land of ours shall be, but we know that God with swift, silent steps can come and give the crystallising touch that makes the diamond flash out of the quondam soot. "Rags," the Arabs call our black parishioners, forgetful of the fact that rags make the whitest paper : so what man can do in the paper line surely God can surpass in souls.

Quite a serious theologian the negro becomes, and here it is, greatly daring, he taps all the unsuspected sources of language. In the things of God this young black Christian is in some sense a sort of negro Columbus setting out to discover a new world of wonder. His word for "heaven" is a good example of the Luban's finesse and regard for detail, coupled with a knowledge of sound philology. Shells we find on the beach, for pearls we must dive, and most appropriately has he dived for this great pearl-word "heaven"—is not each gate of The Glory a pearl? The plain philology of this word "*Mwiulu*," then, gives you the meaning of "heaven" as "the entering into all the highest times, and places, and manners, and methods of living life." This means that Christians, as "the heavenly people," are, literally and not exaggeratingly, "the folks who enter into all the highest places, *plus* the highest times, *plus* the very highest manners, *plus* the only first-class methods of service." Far from this long definition sucking all the juice out of such a luscious fruit as the word "heaven," a negro at my elbow claims that I have omitted two links in the chain of meaning : the link of cause, and the link of design. So that while the entering into all the highest times, highest places, highest manners, highest methods is ours, we must not omit this entering into life's highest causes and highest designs also! No chance example this, as dozens of instances prove. Take another. If you quote the Psalm to him, " Our times are in Thy hand," he will be forced to translate it in the gorgeous words—" All my life's why's and when's and where's and wherefore's are in God's hand !" The sane grammar of this is that particles of space are all necessarily units of time, place, manner, and degree (just as in English we say "the space between the table and the door," and " the space of half an hour ").

Simple in strength and strong in simplicity, the best sort of young black Christian delights to push out into the adjacent hamlets with the Gospel. Far from being professional preachers, they " talk " the Gospel—a straight talk in his own town being more tantalising to a raw negro than a hundred sermons. For in a sermon he knows where he is (or rather, you do, for he often nods), but these terribly personal talks jag him into contrition. After all, there is no need for shooting at sparrows with heavy artillery, and Africa's true evangelisation begins when the simple negroes start to *talk* about redeeming love among themselves. No English twang or mannerisms in that negro talk. With the converted African, Christ's mercy, like the water in a vase, takes the shape of the vessel that holds it. Your constant joy is to hear in a foreign lingo some simple old fact of faith taking a new meaning by one twist of the negro tongue. Here is a Chief who takes up the cudgels for his abandoned (?) race, and claims that if the Gospel is really for everybody then they have as much right as *we* to an offer of same. To meet his challenge, I read out the record of the impotent man at Bethesda, and venture to urge that here is one who has the same complaint as ignored Africa : " Sir, I have no man." So we get the opening, and advancing into the salvation of the subject I tell that tale of divine cure —the cure of the man that had no man to help while others got the good things. Then we come to the point. What I now want is an assurance from my petulant Chief that here at last he understands my drift. " Oh," he said, " that is very simple: the thirty-eight-years-sick man is like unto our abandoned Africa ; the man said, *I have no man,* but Christ said, *I'm your Man.*"

L'ENVOI

DOWN goes the sun like a ball of fire over dark Lubaland. The first sough of the cold night wind goes through like a dart. The distant dogs in the fishing hamlet howl. The frogs croak, croak, and the bitterns bump, bump. To climax weirdness, the fire has recently swept through the long yellow grass, covering the land with a dark pall. The sluggish stream by which we camp seems a mere trickle of liquid mud, the only hint of water being the deeper dye of green down its hollow. There you draw your drinking water the colour of bad tea; there, too, at sunset the reed-buck comes down to drink. And as the darkness deepens the sighing sounds of Africa's dark are heard saying—

"THE NIGHT COMETH WHEN NO MAN CAN WORK."

*　　　　　*　　　　　*

Afar the Golden-Crested Crane is calling!

INDEX

INDEX

2

INDEX

3

INDEX

INDEX

INDEX

6

INDEX

INDEX

INDEX

Kapara's, A lion at, 366.
Kapwasa, 394.
Kara ya Rova, The legend of, 269, 270.
Karema, 259.
Kasai, The source of the, 131.
Kasamina, 294.
Kasanga Valley, 348, 351.
Kasansu wrestles with lion, 369, 370.
Kasembe's capital, 359.
Kasenga, 132.
Kaseva, 197.
Kashobwe, 433.
Kasokota, 201.
Kasongo, 477.
Kasonkomona the ferryman, 35.
Katanga, 111, 299, 300, 302.
Katigile, 197.
Katondo, 338.
Katumwa, 43.
Kavalo, General, 296.
Kavamba, Lake, 319, 334.
Kavanga, Gates of the Morning, 344.
Kaveke, 12.
Kavoto, the Lion King, 266, 267.
Kavovo quoted, 26.
Kavungu, 163.
   Caravans bound for, 12.
   half-way point, 185.
   Revolt of carriers at, 67.
Kayumba's, 270.
Kazembe, 233, 422.
Kazombo, 138.
Keating's powder, 98.
Keve, Crossing the, 34, 35.
Khartoum, 195, 328.
Kidd, 405.
Kifumadzi desert, 28, 155 ff.
Killing the Best One, 216.
   the watches, 177.
Kilwa, 246, 398, 461.
King Fire, 157.
   -fishers, 399.
   The Great, 424.
   of Katanga, 240.
   of Mweru, 235.
   Water, 157.
Kings, Native, 116, 117.
Kinkondia, Killed at, 303.
Kinsman-advocate, 263.
Kishinga, 276.
Kissale, Lake, 303.
Kissing, 450.
Knives and forks taboo, 170.
Knowledge of God, The, 277, 423.
Kofwali case, 44.
Koni, 319, 473.
Koran, The, 174, 202.
Kundelungu Range, 112, 344, 350, 354, 358, 379.

Kunehe River, 42.
Kunje River, 51.
Kwanza River, 33, 75, 93, 94, 162.

Lak, The village of, 46.
Lake formed, A new, 396.
   an imaginary, 160, 161.
Lakes, The Great, 344.
   African—
      Bangweulu, 428, 467.
      Dilolo, 396.
      Great White Lake, 395.
      Kavamba, 319, 334.
      Kissale, 303.
      Mary, 395, 396.
      Musengeshi, 395.
      Mweru. *See* under name.
      Nyassa, or "Maravi," 204, 205, 411.
      Tanganyika. *See* under name.
Lamba at Mushidi's, 192.
Lambaite, A, 357.
Lamond, Mr. and Mrs., 467.
Lamp, No, 250, 251.
Lampstand in Tabernacle, 386.
Lane, Mr., 74, 75, 213, 320.
Language, Speaking the negro's, 347.
Largest crocodile, 435.
Last, Mr., 319.
Law unto themselves, A, 477.
Laws, Dr., 204, 411.
Lawsuits, 48, 132, 141-143, 245.
   about dog, 272-274.
   Final appeal in, 265.
Lecturing in England, 139.
Leeches, 435, 436.
Legat, 302.
Legend of Kara ya Rova, The, 269, 270.
Le Marinel, Paul, 302.
Leopard on floating island, 461.
   killed by woman, 106.
Leopold, King, 300, 460.
Leroy killed by cannibals, 330.
Letter, Mushidi's, to Sir A. Sharpe, 302, 303, 306.
   Mushidi's, to and from Stairs, 304, 305.
Lianas, 386.
Libyan Desert, The, 402.
Life like a sheet of paper, 356.
"Life-belt Island," 462.
Light is sown, 447.
Lightening the loads, 68, 69.
Lightning conductors, 349.
   kills herd, 269.
   shows snake, 251, 252.
   strikes house, 348, 349.
Likuku, 193.
Likurwe Hills, 291.
Lily-trotters, 399.
Lincoln's saying, 350.

9

INDEX

INDEX

INDEX

INDEX

INDEX

Paul, Testimony of, 423, 424.
Paying debts, 132, 134.
Pea-nuts, 36.
Peace instead of war, 126, 127.
  with God, 77.
Pecksniff, Mr., 474.
Peho, 116.
Pelicans, 399.
Perfume, Flowers without, 417.
Petroleum tin, Mushidi's head in, 309.
Pharisees, African, 95, 96.
Phillips Brooks, 472.
Philosopher, The African a, 280.
Phragmites, 461.
Pick-a-back, 136.
Pig, Killing the, 53, 54.
Pigmy forest, 402.
Pilgrim Town, 51.
Pilgrim's Progress, The, 36, 474.
Pilkington, 326.
Pimbwe, 259.
Pioneer, The, 18, 20, 21, 67, 415.
Pipes taboo, 243.
Pith trees, 458.
Plantations of God, The, 375, 379.
Pleading with condemned Arab, 201–203.
Plovers, Spur-winged, 399.
Plutarch, 277.
"Pneumatic tyres," 376, 382.
Pointing with the finger, 86, 87.
Points of the compass, 468.
Poison ordeal, 80.
Poisoned arrows, 268, 352, 353.
Poisoned fish, 88, 89.
Poisonous foods, 315.
Policeman's helmet, A, 120.
Polygamy, 201, 231, 287, 449.
Pomeroy, Mr., 415, 467.
Pope, The power of the, 325.
Popelin, 258.
Population, A mixed, 192.
Portuguese advance, 149.
  aliases, 22.
  in Bihe, 41.
  and Boers, 75.
  captives, 12.
  commandant, 44, 149.
  convict's boots, A, 214.
  Fort, The, 43, 44, 47, 150.
  lethargy, 5, 32.
  machila, 108.
  slavers, 27.
  wife, Mushidi's, 184, 185, 190, 191, 295.
Potato song, The, 412.
Poverty and riches, 419.
Powder and guns, Refusing to write for, 268.
Prætorian guard, 223.

Praise getting out at the toes, 55.
Praising God misunderstood, 215.
Preaching in forest glens, 354.
  to cannibals, 112.
  to chief, 75.
  to Mushidi, 240, 241.
  to soldiers, 327, 330.
Precedent, 8, 76, 231.
Prepared ways, 377–379.
Preserving man and beast, 437.
Priest murders brother, 80.
Prince of Wales, A local, 120.
Prisoner in his cell, 266.
Propertius, 140.
Protestant Popes, 324, 325.
Proverbs, 2, 30, 71, 122, 123, 175, 181, 198, 200, 231, 349.
Proxy, Medicine by, 179.
Prussia, Storks liberated in, 401.
Psalms (quoted), 16, 123, 228, 256, 437, 484.
Pumpkins, 380.
Punch, 410.
Purification after cannibal feast, 336.
Pyramids, 9.
Pyrenees, Africa begins at the, 149.
"Python," The, 49.

Quarantine, 209.
Queen Café au lait, 185.
  Matayu, 295.
  Maria de Fonseca. *See* Portuguese wife.
  Nyakatoro, 135.
  of Sheba, 450.
Questions, Asking, 140, 450, 454.
Quinine tabloids, 377.

Rabbit, The, 175.
"Rags," 482.
Railroads, 111, 163.
Rains, 98, 99, 118, 247.
Ratel kills African, 370.
Rats in flood, 324.
  as food, 312.
Reading and writing, 71.
Receipts, Records of, 177.
Red buck, A herd of, 87, 88, 269.
  sunsets, 285 ff.
Redeemed slaves, 219.
Redeeming slaves, 30.
Refusing to become cannibal, 333, 336.
Relief of Fort Lofoi, 330.
Returned Missionaries, 139.
Revolt, 330, 342.
Rhodes, Cecil, 300, 359.
Rhodesia, N.W., 150.
Rinderpest, 366.
River, Following the, 136.
  torrents, 347.

INDEX

15

INDEX

INDEX

INDEX

Voltaire, 180.
Vultures, 116, 162.

Wagogo tricks, 139, 185.
"Wake," 134, 135.
Walepa, 459.
Wales, Britons hiding in, 352.
Walk of life symbolised, 115.
Wangermée, Governor, 330, 338.
Wanyamwezi Hills, 198.
War averted, 125, 126.
   between Arabs and Africans, 361.
   brewing at Bihe, 74.
Wasenshi, 96.
Watches and clocks, 176.
Watching the corn, 311.
Water, bad, 157, 168, 439, 485.
   digging for, 156, 157.
   -bottle of human skin, 270.
   -fowl, 399.
   -rails, 399.
Waterloo flint-locks, 268.
Watershed, The, 112.
Waylaying caravans, 139.
Weather, The, 153.
Weeping at mother's grave, 452.
Well of Sychar, 263.
Wells, Digging, 156, 157.
Wesley, John, 383.
West Coast, The, 3, 95, 189.
   and East joining hands, 344, 364, 405.
Western road blocked, 213.
   opened, 126.
Wet, Getting, 71, 141.
Whistling up the hippos, 466, 467.
White ants, 312, 478.
   chalk acquittal, 132, 134.
   lady, The first, 415.
   Lake, The Great, 395.
   man, The first, 395.
     The only, 169.
     Parables of, 4.
   men and black, 79, 215, 395.
     killed by Mushidi, 257, 259.
     Names in Africa of, 21, 22.
   officers killed, 330.
   slaves, 215, 309.
   wife, The, 183. *See* Portuguese wife.

Whitefield, George (quoted), 110.
"Whites killed the Christ," 216.
"Wilson, John," party, 415.
Winds on the Lake, 420.
Winking with the eye, 27, 28, 408.
Winter and summer, 72.
Witch-doctors, 179.
Wives of fishermen, 427, 428.
"Wolda Gabriel," The, 242.
"Wolda Jesus," The, 242.
Woman and Commandant, 44.
   and leopard, 106.
   kills lion, 105.
   sacrificed, Old, 286, 287.
   Wild, 383–386.
Women, African, 348.
   and cannibalism, 336.
   evangelists, 355.
   Questions of, 450.
   Secret Society, 234.
Woodpecker reminds of home, 416.
Woodside, Mr., 33, 37.
Wounded monkeys, 85.
Writing, 71, 172, 173.
   Arabic, 201.
Written speech, No, 415.

Xenophon, 33, 178, 222.

Yeke band, The, 197.
Yellow flag of quarantine, The, 209.
   monkeys, 84.

Z., Senr., 42, 45.
Zambezi, The, 6, 112.
   The source of the, 112.
Zanzibar, 95, 303.
   road, The, 139.
   Sultan of, 199.
   A Western, 5, 32.
Zanzibaris, 259, 304.
Zebra Plains, The, 164.
Zebras, 164, 231.
Zebulun's portion, 156.
"Zenobia" class of women, 233.
Zentler, Mr., 319.
Zeruiah's sons, 295.

MORGAN & SCOTT LD., LONDON, ENGLAND.